Reforming Agricultural Markets in Africa

Other Books Published in Cooperation with the International Food Policy Research Institute

IFPRI

Intrahousehold Resource Allocation in Developing Countries: Models, Methods, and Policy
Edited by Lawrence Haddad, John Hoddinott, and Harold Alderman

Sustainability, Growth, and Poverty Alleviation: A Policy and Agroecological Perspective
Edited by Steven A. Vosti and Thomas Reardon

Famine in Africa: Causes, Responses, and Prevention
By Joachim von Braun, Tesfaye Teklu, and Patrick Webb

Paying for Agricultural Productivity
Edited by Julian M. Alston, Philip G. Pardey, and Vincent H. Smith

Out of the Shadow of Famine: Evolving Food Markets and Food Policy in Bangladesh
Edited by Raisuddin Ahmed, Steven Haggblade, and Tawfiq-e-Elahi Chowdhury

Agricultural Science Policy: Changing Global Agendas
Edited by Julian M. Alston, Philip G. Pardey, and Michael J. Taylor

The Politics of Precaution: Genetically Modified Crops in Developing Countries
By Robert L. Paarlberg

Land Tenure and Natural Resource Management: A Comparative Study of Agrarian Communities in Asia and Africa
Edited by Keijiro Otsuka and Frank Place

Seeds of Contention: World Hunger and the Global Controversy over GM Crops
By Per Pinstrup-Andersen and Ebbe Schiøler

Innovation in Natural Resource Management: The Role of Property Rights and Collective Action in Developing Countries
Edited by Ruth Meinzen-Dick, Anna Knox, Frank Place, and Brent Swallow

The Triangle of Microfinance: Financial Sustainability, Outreach, and Impact
Edited by Manfred Zeller and Richard L. Meyer

iii

Reforming Agricultural Markets in Africa

MYLÈNE KHERALLAH, CHRISTOPHER DELGADO,
ELENI GABRE-MADHIN, NICHOLAS MINOT,
AND MICHAEL JOHNSON

Published for the International Food Policy Research Institute

The Johns Hopkins University Press
Baltimore and London

The Johns Hopkins University Press
2715 North Charles Street
Baltimore, Maryland 21218-4363
www.press.jhu.edu

International Food Policy Research Institute
2033 K Street, N.W.
Washington, D.C. 20006
(202) 862-5600
www.ifpri.org

LIBRARY OF CONGRESS CATALOGING-IN-PUBLICATION DATA
Reforming agricultural markets in Africa : Mylène Kherallah . . . [et al.].
    p.   cm.
    International Food Policy Research Institute.
    Includes bibliographical references and index.
    ISBN 0-8018-7145-X (hardcover : alk. paper) — ISBN 0-8018-7198-0 (pbk. : alk. paper)
    1. Food industry and trade—Africa. 2. Agriculture—Economic aspects—Africa. I. Kherallah,
Mylène. II. International Food Policy Research Institute.
HD9017.A2 R43   2002
380.1'41'096—dc21

                                                                        2002005368

A catalog record for this book is available from the British Library.

Contents

Figures

Tables

Foreword

Sub-Saharan Africa is the only region in the world where hunger and poverty will get worse in the next two decades if present trends continue. Projections by the International Food Policy Research Institute show a disturbing future for the region: the number of malnourished children, for example, will increase from 32 million in 1997 to 39 million in 2020. Must coming generations of Africans succumb to such a fate? Not if governments in the region jumpstart their agricultural sectors. Market reform has been a central feature of efforts to do this since the early 1980s. This book discusses the successes, failures, and constraints African governments have experienced in this regard.

About 80 percent of all Africans depend on agriculture for their livelihood. The agriculture sector also accounts for 70 percent of full-time employment, one-third of total gross domestic product, and 40 percent of total export earnings. Alleviating hunger and poverty in Africa will require more investments in the agricultural sector, increased agricultural productivity, and more efficient and better functioning agricultural markets for both producers and consumers.

During the past two decades, most countries in Sub-Saharan Africa did undertake extensive economic reforms to reverse declining growth rates and reduce severe balance-of-payment deficits. Because of the importance of the agricultural sector in the region, agricultural market reforms occupied a central place in these efforts. The reforms in the agricultural sector were designed to reduce the bias against agriculture and promote growth. The expectation was that improving price incentives for farmers and reducing government intervention in the agricultural sector would be enough to generate a supply response and allow well-functioning markets to emerge quickly. Almost two decades later, however, the general consensus is that the reform programs in Sub-Saharan Africa have not met expectations. Analyzing the evidence suggests that the reform experience has varied widely across countries, with clear progress in some areas and mixed results in others.

This book reviews the extensive evidence on agricultural market reforms in Sub-Saharan Africa and summarizes the impact reforms have had on market performance, agricultural production, use of modern inputs, food security, and poverty. The contribution of this book lies in its attempt to distil the wisdom from many different studies in the context of a conceptual framework for market reform that goes beyond agriculture and beyond the events of the structural adjustment era. Specifically, reforms are set in the context of the history of market intervention, the aspirations of new governments, and the political economy of agricultural policy. A synthetic analysis such as this has not been done before and provides a good opportunity to put the market reforms in a more global context. The book also separately presents the experiences of reforms in fertilizer markets, food crop markets, and export crop markets, with substantial empirical evidence from several countries. This in-depth analysis adds to the richness of the book and will be a helpful reference for development practitioners. Finally, the book offers a new agenda for the development of agricultural markets in Sub-Saharan Africa, including the types of policy changes, investments, and partnerships needed to achieve this goal. The adoption of this agenda should contribute to agricultural growth and poverty reduction in Sub-Saharan Africa.

Per Pinstrup-Andersen
Director General
International Food Policy Research Institute

Preface

Beginning in the early 1980s, most countries in Sub-Saharan Africa initiated agricultural market reforms as part of the wider structural adjustment programs supported by donor organizations. In general, the reforms were designed to reduce or eliminate existing biases against the agricultural sector by aligning local prices with international ones, reducing overvalued exchange rates, minimizing government intervention, and promoting private sector participation in agricultural marketing activities. Since then, many researchers have analyzed the status and impact of these reforms in Africa. The International Food Policy Research Institute (IFPRI) itself has accumulated extensive knowledge on this issue through various surveys and case studies in the region. Until now, however, no efforts had been made to synthesize the findings from this research. Such a synthesis is important both to assess what we have learned so far about the status of agricultural market liberalization in Africa and to lay out the road ahead for the development of agricultural markets in the region.

This book provides such a synthesis. Using a common conceptual framework, it comprehensively reviews case studies on agricultural market liberalization in Sub-Saharan Africa. Based on that review, it analyzes the reforms in the fertilizer, food crop, and export crop markets in a number of African countries. The main questions the book addresses are: What has been the implementation experience of agricultural market reforms in Sub-Saharan Africa? Have agricultural market reforms led to an improvement in market performance? Has there been an aggregate agricultural supply response? How have reforms affected agricultural productivity and input use? Have they contributed to increasing the income of smallholder farmers and reducing rural poverty? Which countries and which subsectors have had a more successful reform program and why? What are the lessons from experience? What are the remaining constraints? What are the next steps for African agricultural markets?

The authors have benefited from discussions with Raisuddin Ahmed and Ousmane Badiane, as well as several researchers in the United Kingdom, including Andrew Dorward, Jonathan Kydd, and Colin Poulton at Wye College; Brendan Bayley, Alex Duncan, and Stephen Jones at Oxford Policy Management; Elizabeth Cromwell, Tony Killick, and Simon Maxwell at the Overseas Development Institute; Bob Baulch and Howard White at the Institute of Development Studies; Stefan Dercon at the Centre for the Study of African Economies; and William Masters from Purdue University. The authors thank Klaus von Grebmer and participants at the International Food Policy Research Institute Policy Seminar held on April 13, 2000, for their useful comments. Thanks are also due to Thomas Jayne and an anonymous reviewer for their helpful suggestions on an earlier draft. The usual disclaimer applies. The authors are also indebted to Heidi Fritschel and Uday Mohan for their substantial editorial contributions and to Diana Flores for administrative support.

Although this is a team-authored report, primary responsibility for the different chapters was as follows. The introductory and concluding chapters were prepared by Mylène Kherallah. Chapter 2 was written by Christopher Delgado, Eleni Gabre-Madhin, Michael Johnson, and Mylène Kherallah. Chapter 3 was written by Nicholas Minot, and Chapters 4 and 5 were prepared by Eleni Gabre-Madhin and Christopher Delgado, respectively. Michael Johnson also provided research assistance for the initial draft.

Reforming Agricultural Markets in Africa

1 Introduction

Objectives and Approach of the Study

Beginning in the early 1980s, most countries in Sub-Saharan Africa[1] embarked on structural adjustment and stabilization programs to reverse stagnating economic growth rates and severe macroeconomic imbalances. Because agriculture is so important in the region,[2] agricultural market reforms were at the forefront of these structural adjustment programs. Catalyzed by the so-called Berg report (World Bank 1981), the agricultural market reforms were generally designed to reduce or eliminate biases against agriculture by aligning local prices with international ones, reducing overvalued exchange rates, minimizing government intervention, and promoting private sector participation in agricultural marketing activities. State marketing institutions were to be restructured on a sound commercial basis and private traders would be permitted to operate as a way of increasing competition and encouraging efficiency (Dorward, Kydd, and Poulton 1998).

According to the proponents of agricultural market reforms: higher relative prices for agricultural commodities, coupled with more open and competitive markets, should have stimulated farmers to produce more, leading to higher agricultural and overall income. The evidence shows, however, that economic growth in Africa has stagnated or declined, especially in agriculture.

Since the reforms were initiated, numerous studies have been conducted to try to assess the impact of the reforms on the agricultural and overall economic performance of Sub-Saharan Africa. The objective of this book is to summarize the important research findings from this literature. It focuses on the

---

1. From this point forward, Sub-Saharan Africa refers to countries south of the Sahara excluding South Africa. For brevity, we will use "Africa" interchangeably with "Sub-Saharan Africa" to refer to this region.

2. Agriculture represents about 42 percent of gross domestic product (GDP) in the low-income countries and 27 percent in the middle-income countries of Sub-Saharan Africa, and it employs between 65 and 80 percent of the labor force. A large part of Sub-Saharan Africa's export earnings come from agriculture, accounting for as much as 60 percent of export income in more than half the countries (Abdulai and Delgado 1995).

three major agricultural markets in Africa—fertilizer, food crop, and export crop markets—and uses previous country case studies in each of these sub-sectors. Given the large amount of work on this topic, this synthesis is not an exhaustive account of all that has been written. Rather, it draws on examples from existing research to illustrate the main findings and bring out the policy implications that have emerged for Sub-Saharan Africa.

The questions that we address in this synthesis include the following: What has been the implementation experience of agricultural market reforms in Sub-Saharan Africa? Have agricultural market reforms led to an improvement in market performance? Has there been an aggregate agricultural supply response? What has been the impact on agricultural productivity and input use? Has it contributed to increasing the income of smallholder farmers and reducing rural poverty? Which countries and which sub-sectors have had a more successful reform program and why? What are the lessons from experience? What are the remaining constraints? What is the road ahead for African agricultural markets?

Review of Africa's Economic Performance

The general consensus is that, over the two decades following the start of the structural adjustment programs, the economic performance of Sub-Saharan Africa lagged behind other developing countries and the reform programs fell short of their expected outcomes (Commander 1989; Mosley and Weeks 1993; Cornia and Helleiner 1994; Spencer and Badiane 1995; Dorward, Kydd, and Poulton 1998; Eicher 1999; Mkandawire and Soludo 1999). Table 1.1 helps to demonstrate this fact by showing negative average annual growth rates of per capita GDP in Sub-Saharan Africa throughout the 1980s and 1990s, although there seems to be a slight improvement in the 1990–97 period compared with the previous decade. In contrast, Asian developing countries experienced significant per capita economic growth from the 1960s, although they had started at a lower level of development. An important distinction between the two regions that may accentuate the difference in their historical per capita performance is the higher population growth rates in Sub-Saharan Africa relative to Asia, although both seem to have declined in recent years.

Sub-Saharan Africa's dismal performance is even more pronounced in the agriculture sector. Table 1.1 shows a negative trend in per capita agricultural growth for every sub-period from 1968 to 1997. This is also clearly evident in Figure 1.1, which plots per capita agricultural production using 1989–91 as a base period. There was a persistent decline starting from the 1970s until the mid-1980s. From this latter period until the early 1990s, per capita agricultural production showed some signs of recovery. However, throughout the reform period of the 1990s, it has stagnated with no evidence of a significant turnaround. The poor performance of agriculture in Sub-Saharan Africa is espe-

TABLE 1.1 Average per capita growth rates in regions of the world, 1960–97 (percent)

Region[a]	1965–80	1980–90	1990–97	1965–97
Growth rates in per capita GDP				
Sub-Saharan Africa	1.4	−1.1	−0.6	−0.2
South Asia	1.1	3.3	3.7	2.3
Low-income countries	1.4	1.9	1.8	1.4
Growth in per capita agriculture value-added				
Sub-Saharan Africa[b]	−0.7	−0.5	−0.2	−0.9
South Asia	0.0	1.0	0.8	0.5
Low-income countries	−0.2	0.5	0.5	0.1

SOURCE: Based on authors' estimates from World Development Indicators time series data (World Bank 1999).

NOTES: Estimates are least-squares growth rates, estimated by fitting a linear regression trend-line to the logarithmic annual values of per capita GDP or agriculture valued-added in the relevant period.

[a]Grouped regions are based on World Bank definitions (South Africa is included in the Sub-Saharan Africa region).

[b]For Sub-Saharan Africa, data series on agriculture value-added begin in 1968. All series were valued at constant 1995 US$.

cially evident when contrasted with other developing countries, particularly Asian developing countries.

Another declining trend in Sub-Saharan Africa is its agricultural trade balance, which can be illustrated by its changing share of world agricultural trade. As Figure 1.2 demonstrates, since 1970 there has been a continuous decline in Africa's share of world agricultural exports, while its share of world agricultural imports has remained relatively constant. This has occurred in a world en-

FIGURE 1.1 Net per capita agricultural production, 1961–98

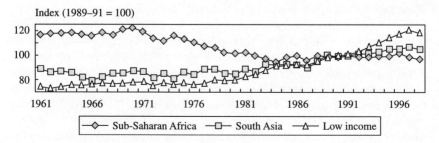

SOURCE: FAOStat database.

FIGURE 1.2 Sub-Saharan Africa's share of world agricultural trade, 1961–98

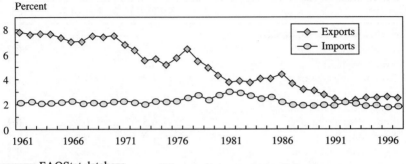

SOURCE: FAOStat database.

vironment of steadily declining real international prices for most of Africa's agricultural exports owing to technology and marketing improvements elsewhere in the world, especially in East Asia and the Americas (Donovan 1996). As shown in Table 1.2, the decline in the real world price of a few of the region's major export commodities ranges from 20 to 60 percent for the period 1980–98, with the sharpest decline occurring in the 1980s. Although there were some noticeable improvements during the 1990s, these gains did not return prices to their original 1980 levels.

The above trends raise the question of food security for the continent as a whole. Africa has been dealing with a negative food balance sheet since the 1970s, with food production growing at half the rate of population growth in the period 1970 to 1985 (Byerlee and Eicher 1997). In 1997 alone, Sub-Saharan Africa carried a food trade deficit of about US$1.5 billion and has not experienced a surplus since 1977. Overall, per capita food production has followed the same trend as agricultural production, with declining rates throughout the 1970s, a rising trend in the mid-1980s, and stagnation in the 1990s.

At the same time, according to Shapouri and Rosen (1999), about 50 percent of the population in Sub-Saharan Africa was undernourished in 1998. Their projections indicate that this share will increase to about 63 percent by 2008. These authors claim that Sub-Saharan Africa is the region of the world that is most susceptible to food insecurity; unless grain yields grow at a rate 60 percent higher than the growth achieved during 1980–97, then Sub-Saharan Africa's nutritional food requirements will not be met by 2008. The hardest-hit group is often the rural poor, who account for about 80 percent of the total number of poor people in most of Sub-Saharan Africa (Sahn, Dorosh, and Younger 1997). Consequently, the elimination of hunger, malnutrition, poverty, and resource degradation, in addition to reducing the spread of AIDS, is arguably the greatest challenge facing Sub-Saharan Africa today and for decades to come

TABLE 1.2 Percentage change in primary commodity world prices, 1970–98

	Period			
	1970–80	1980–90	1990–98	1980–98
Cotton	13	−36	−24	−51
Cocoa	35	−65	27	−55
Coffee[a]	5	−74	48	−61
Palm oil	−22	−64	123	−20

SOURCES: Calculations based on Delgado (1995:Table 3) for the period 1970–80, and World Bank (1999:Table 6.4) for the period 1980–98.

[a] Robusta coffee.

unless something is done to reverse these trends (McCalla 1999). Since the majority of the population in Sub-Saharan Africa derives its livelihood from agriculture and food markets are important for all consumers, including the poor, well-functioning and efficient agricultural markets are a necessary condition for an improvement in Sub-Saharan Africa's well-being.

The Scope of Agricultural Market Reforms in Africa

Most countries in Sub-Saharan Africa started implementing structural adjustment and stabilization programs in the early 1980s. The first structural adjustment programs, which were adopted between 1979 and 1984, were characterized by macro-demand management and stabilization policies with relatively few conditions (Delgado 1998). After 1984, however, structural adjustment programs became increasingly tied to conditionalities for broad-based policy reforms. Aid conditionalities or policy-based lending assumed two forms, a short-run macroeconomic stabilization program to reduce internal and external imbalances, and a long-run structural adjustment program to address resource allocation and efficiency problems inhibiting economic growth (Sahn, Dorosh, and Younger 1997). Stabilization programs almost always included exchange rate devaluation and reductions in public spending and were usually associated with the International Monetary Fund (IMF). Longer-run structural adjustment programs embodied a wide range of market liberalization and public sector reform programs and were associated with the World Bank (for further discussions on the definition and evolution of structural adjustment programs, see Kydd and Spooner 1990; Sahn, Dorosh, and Younger 1997; Delgado 1998).

Agricultural market reforms were at the forefront of a majority of the post-1984 structural adjustment programs in Sub-Saharan Africa, primarily because of the economic importance of agriculture in the region. They were designed to reduce or eliminate the bias against the agricultural sector and introduce market forces in the provision of agricultural services (World Bank 1981). The type of market reform measures undertaken were based on the observation that the agricultural sector has a higher share of tradables compared with other economic sectors (Guillaumont 1994). A large presence of tradables would support the notion that the improved terms of trade brought about by liberalization would lead to a vigorous agricultural supply response (Dorward, Kydd, and Poulton 1999). Additionally, it was hypothesized that state marketing boards were inefficient and costly, served mainly the interests of a select group composed of the urban elite, the industrial sector, and government bureaucrats, and provided a rich ground for corruption and rent-seeking activities. Therefore, it was believed that, by scaling back or entirely abolishing state control over agricultural marketing activities, a more efficient private sector would emerge to supply inputs and purchase and sell produce (Dorward, Kydd, and Poulton 1999).

More specifically, agricultural marketing reforms included three major types of measures:

1. liberalizing input and output prices by reducing or eliminating subsidies on agricultural inputs such as fertilizers and credit, realigning domestic crop prices with world prices, eliminating pan-seasonal and pan-territorial pricing, and reducing exchange rate overvaluation;
2. removing regulatory controls in input and output markets (for example, allowing the participation of the private sector in agricultural marketing), lifting restrictions on internal movement of food crops, and relaxing quantitative controls such as delivery quotas and licensing arrangements; and
3. restructuring public enterprises and withdrawing marketing boards from pricing and marketing activities and narrowing their role to more supportive activities (such as providing market information services and maintaining security stocks).

Issues in Evaluating the Impact of Agricultural Market Reforms

Before we move on to evaluate the impact of agricultural market reform in Africa in the coming chapters, it is important to highlight a few issues regarding impact evaluation. These include problems with the implementation of the reforms and methodological difficulties in assessing the appropriateness and effectiveness of the reforms. In this final section of Chapter 1 we also present an outline for the remainder of the book.

Although the implementation record of market reforms varies across African countries, in many cases reforms were only partially implemented and reversal was common. This is particularly true for fertilizer subsidies, which in many countries were eliminated only in the mid-1990s. In several crop sectors, parastatals remain active, especially in the cotton sector of West Africa and maize markets in Malawi, Kenya, and Zimbabwe. Slow and incomplete reform implementation is associated with several factors, including lack of political consensus with regard to reforms imposed by donor organizations, fear of disturbing patron–client relationships that are central to the existing political equilibrium between regions and ethnic groups, the desire by some to hold on to existing advantages, and aid conditionalities that were often poorly coordinated. Partial or incomplete reform implementation increases the difficulty of evaluating the impact of the reforms, and in extreme cases can render impact evaluation a moot exercise.

The problem of partial implementation is compounded by the fact that the debate over the appropriate sequence and timing of market reforms remains unresolved. Many economists have tied the lack of success of market reforms to their inadequate sequencing and timing. However, it has been harder to agree on the "optimal" path of reform (Kherallah and Govindan 1999). One school of thought argues for a "big bang" approach in which all sectors are liberalized at once (Sachs and Woo 1994). Proponents of this approach believe that rapid and complete reform packages are more likely to bring about larger benefits sooner and that an optimal path to reform does not really exist. A second school of thought advocates a gradual approach because it entails lower short-term adjustment costs and smaller political opposition (Choksi and Papageorgiou 1986; Michaely 1986; Edwards 1992; Rana 1995; Kherallah and Govindan 1999). Still other economists argue that sequencing does not matter as long as the government is committed to a set of credible and sustainable market reform measures (McPherson 1995).

A unique problem in assessing Sub-Saharan Africa's economic performance is the lack of adequate data, especially time series data. Even if data are available, their quality is often questionable. Production and market price data on food crops and other non-tradable agricultural products are especially difficult to find, and are complicated by the consumption of own production in smallholder agriculture. Where there are sufficient data, usually for export crops, the problem arises of accounting for the presence of parallel markets, especially in the pre-reform period (see, for example, studies on the illegal smuggling of cocoa from Ghana to neighboring countries—Azam and Besley 1989—and on the illegal trading of groundnut and fertilizer across the Gambia/Senegal border—Puetz and von Braun 1991).

A frequently cited difficulty when analyzing the impact of policy reforms is the absence of comparative scenarios with and without the policy in place. As a result, the tendency has been to use cross-sectional or cross-country data to compare different policy environments. In turn, many cross-country studies on Africa suffer from a tendency to treat the continent as a homogeneous entity (Bromley 1995). Africa is a vast continent with wide ecological, geographic, and climatic variations as well as a diverse set of colonial legacies, indigenous institutions, and farming systems (Maxwell 1998). The danger of generalizing about Africa is that it generates policy prescriptions that are far too broad to be useful for any one country. An acknowledgment of Africa's unique conditions adds to the problem of generalization (Bloom and Sachs 1998). Africa is characterized by an unusually difficult physical environment, inadequate infrastructure, and a large concentration of landlocked countries (Mkandawire and Soludo 1999). Based on these special circumstances, some development theorists go so far as to question the applicability of conventional economic development theory to much of Sub-Saharan Africa (Bromley 1995), while others seem to recommend that Africa recognize its agricultural limitations owing to its geography, demography, and health problems and commit itself to manufactured exports (Bloom and Sachs 1998).

Exacerbating these constraints is the susceptibility of Africa, and especially its agricultural sector, to exogenous factors independent of economic policy, including wars, civil unrest, droughts, and disease (Guillaumont 1994; Mkandawire and Soludo 1999). The pockets of civil unrest and conflicts include the Democratic Republic of Congo (formerly Zaire), Rwanda, Burundi, Angola, Sudan, Liberia, Sierra Leone, and Ethiopia. Many countries in Africa are prone to recurring and severe droughts and a high incidence of diseases such as HIV/AIDS, malaria, and tuberculosis. These can be very disruptive to the agricultural production of these countries and add to the excessive annual variability in yields and to the overall complexity in analyzing the status of agriculture in Africa.

A related problem is that the effects of agricultural market reforms are difficult to isolate from other ongoing reform policies or exogenous factors (Jayne and Jones 1997; Seppälä 1998). Barrett (1997) and Seppälä (1997) argue that, if the various reforms under structural adjustment programs are implemented simultaneously, they can have ambiguous effects on agricultural prices and performance. Furthermore, the indirect effects of a particular policy are often ignored, resulting in inaccurate conclusions. As Sahn, Dorosh, and Younger (1997) suggest, both direct and indirect effects need to be taken into consideration because in many cases the indirect impact can outweigh the direct one.

As a result of these methodological difficulties, as well as of varying analytical research tools, time periods, and criteria or measures of "success," different research studies may draw contradictory conclusions regarding the effect of reforms. In addition, even if the empirical findings are similar, there may be disagreement on the causes of the economic crisis, the prescriptions for improving economic performance, and the roles of the private sector, the donor community, and the state in helping reverse the crisis (see, for example, Killick 1993; Mosley and Weeks 1993; Cornia and Helleiner 1994; Stewart 1994; Mkandawire and Soludo 1999). These disagreements are often the result of different ideologies, experiences, and academic perspectives about how economies work.

Notwithstanding the above shortcomings, several studies have tried to assess the impact of reform policies on agricultural input and output markets, production, the use of modern inputs, food security, and poverty reduction. In the following chapters we summarize and discuss the results of these studies. More specifically, in Chapter 2 we explain the rationale for the market reforms in Africa and describe the general context in which they operated. In Chapters 3, 4, and 5 we synthesize the findings on the reforms in fertilizer markets, food markets, and export crop markets, respectively. The last chapter is devoted to conclusions, policy implications, and a new agenda for the development of agricultural markets in Africa.

2 The Context and Rationale for Market Reform

Agricultural market reforms have not occurred in isolation from other key events in Sub-Saharan economies, including macroeconomic adjustments, global shocks, and domestic political and economic factors. And just as the context of agricultural markets has shifted over time, so too has accepted policy thinking on the role of agriculture in economic growth and on how best to transform the agricultural sector through reform. Conventional thinking on reform itself has evolved substantially, from essentially a narrow focus on price alignment and balance of payments adjustment toward a broader vision encompassing the institutional and social dimensions of reform.

Before analyzing specific reforms in the fertilizer, food, and cash crop markets, therefore, it is useful to set the stage by tracing the evolution of government intervention in agricultural markets in Africa and clarifying the factors that led to agricultural market reforms in the 1980s and beyond. This chapter offers a chronological account of the development of agricultural markets while also weaving in the complex factors that influenced agricultural market outcomes. In the final section, we integrate the chronological and thematic discussions into a conceptual framework that links the process and impact of reforms to sectoral, macroeconomic, and global economic factors.

Colonial Intervention in Agricultural Markets

Before the economic reforms were initiated in the 1980s, many governments in Sub-Saharan Africa intervened in agricultural input markets such as fertilizer and seed, in markets for major traditional export crops (cocoa, cotton, coffee, and so on), and, in some countries, in markets for urban-consumed foodgrains (maize, rice, and wheat). The nature and extent of state intervention in these markets can be traced to both the colonial era that preceded it and the aspirations for rapid industrialization in post-independence Africa. The political economy of many contemporary African states remains deeply marked by the legacy of the colonial state, a state that was much more authoritarian in Africa than in the rest of the developing world (Young 1986). Ultimately, the colonial experience for much of Africa left behind an ideology about the role of the state in agricultural markets.

Colonial governments created a wide range of bureaucratic agencies and state organizations to monitor and control local indigenous institutions as part of an overall process of establishing state autonomy and security within the colonial territories. Driving this process was the overall key objective among the colonial "home" countries (Britain, France, and Portugal) to make the colonies self-sufficient and not dependent on fiscal outlays from the "home" budget (Killick 1994). The "revenue imperative," as Bates (1981) has termed it, induced states to promote export crops, tax their proceeds, and keep other costs of production low. From an administrative standpoint, taxing tradable agriculture was the easiest way to generate state revenues. Revenue collection from agriculture was accomplished through marketing boards, which proved quite effective at helping to capture a large portion of the profits generated in the smallholder agricultural sector (see, for instance, van der Laan and Haaren 1990; Sahn and Sarris 1992; Jones 1984.)

The structure and nature of intervention in the food and cash crop sectors during the colonial era varied from region to region in Africa. Whereas in West Africa the vast majority of export growers were indigenous smallholder farmers, in eastern and southern Africa most export crops were grown by white settlers on large estate farms. The general preference for supporting large-scale commercial estates (or plantations) under the control of European settlers gave rise to a dualistic or bimodal agrarian structure in eastern and southern Africa, consisting of both a large-scale commercial sector and a smallholder sector. The large-scale commercial estates normally produced a single export crop, including high-value foods such as coffee, tea, and cocoa, oilseeds, or industrial raw materials such as cotton, sisal, rubber, and tobacco. The smallholder subsector produced a variety of crops, both for subsistence and for commerce (including export crops). Cereals, such as white maize, also increased in importance as a staple, on both estates and smallholder fields—in the latter case to some extent displacing more traditional food crops such as millet, sorghum, and root crops.

In general, the settler colonies of eastern and southern Africa saw much more direct intervention in grain markets than any other part of Sub-Saharan Africa did (Jayne and Jones 1997). Besides the forced removal of smallholder peasants from high-potential farming areas, movements of maize (the primary grain in the region) from the smallholder subsector to urban centers and mining communities were generally restricted to a few licensed private traders. Furthermore, state buying stations were limited to European farming areas, and grain processing was designated to a handful of large-scale commercial millers. Finally, a two-tier pricing system administered by the grain marketing board for maize was commonly practiced. This pricing scheme guaranteed that European farmers received a price that was on average 30 to 60 percent higher than that paid to African farmers (Jayne and Jones 1997). This system often existed in the presence of pan-territorial pricing schemes limited to European farm lands, such as the surplus "maize belts" of Zimbabwe (Masters 1994). One important observation from the emergence of this dual pattern of agricultural development was that it was quite effective at achieving a European monopsony over grain trade. It also proved fiscally sustainable because it was financed in great part by consumers in the form of higher prices and by African farmers in the form of revenues collected from the two-tier pricing system (Jayne and Jones 1997).

Where settler agriculture was not prevalent, especially in West Africa, state intervention and marketing boards operated mostly in the export crop sector for the benefit of a few dominant European trading companies. Grain marketing boards and other forms of state intervention in grain markets were less influential in these countries, because it was difficult to control or regulate staple crop markets owing to the diverse and small-scale nature of food production and the large number of producers (Lele and Christiansen 1989; Sahn 1999). West African food staples range from root crops such as cassava and yam to coarse grains such as millet and sorghum. Cereals such as maize and rice were traditionally less frequently consumed in West Africa, although they have become increasingly important since 1960. Millet and sorghum are common in the semi-arid regions to the north.[1]

Smallholder farmers under the colonial state in West Africa were encouraged to participate actively in producing and marketing export crops (Berry 1993). In fact, prior to 1945, it was not uncommon to find African traders involved directly in export markets (Berry 1993). It was not until the postwar era that colonial governments brought West African trade under regulatory control through export marketing boards, in effect increasing their capacity to tax export crop markets while protecting European traders from African competition. Favorable commodity prices in world markets during this period allowed colonial governments to extract large economic rents from the trade in export crops (Berry 1993).

By independence, a large portion of the returns to smallholder African farming was being diverted to the colonial state. In contrast, large-scale agriculture—especially in eastern and southern Africa—benefited because it received a disproportionate claim to public and private service institutions and infrastructure. Consequently, the bimodal structure of agricultural development in eastern and southern Africa helped give the large-scale sector the appearance of efficiency relative to the smallholder sector, an appearance that would influence the post-independence preference for maintaining the bimodal pattern of agricultural development (Mellor, Delgado, and Blackie 1987).

---

1. Wheat also became important in the post-independence era.

Post-Independence Intervention in Agricultural Markets to 1972

Although intervention in agricultural markets was pervasive throughout the colonial era, it took on a much more active role in post-independence Africa. Fledgling governments were faced with an explosion of high expectations from newly independent populations, especially those in urban areas. Governments were also driven in part by the desire to embark on a development path of rapid industrialization, designed to promote catch-up with the developed countries and reverse the international inequities manifest under the colonial system (Eicher 1999). This was a period of great exhilaration in African political history; for the first time since European colonization, Africans had a right to self-determination. In accord with Western economic thought at the time, public intervention under the banner of state-led development plans was viewed as necessary to achieving rapid industrialization and overall economic growth. Direct involvement in agricultural marketing was the key implementation instrument in the largely agrarian economies of the continent.

African governments gave priority to industry and the provision of social services in part because of the dominant view that agriculture was backward and could not be relied on to stimulate overall economic growth (Eicher 1999). Hence, the general expectation among African governments was that rapid economic growth and development would be achieved by transforming the largely agrarian African state into an industrial economy. In order to finance such an enormous task, governments turned to the colonial model of extracting revenues from agriculture by taxing primary export commodities (Young 1986). This was seen as necessary, as it had been under colonial rule, owing to the administrative difficulties of other means of taxation (Killick 1994).

Taxation of agriculture was typically defended on the grounds that, during the early stages of development, agricultural surplus can be captured to help support industrialization and long-term growth (Sarris 1994).[2] Faced with a colonial inheritance of exporting a few primary products, a general goal was to design an industrialization policy that emphasized a diverse portfolio of industrial products using an import substitution framework similar to that adopted in Latin America decades earlier (Mkandawire and Soludo 1999). However, the success of such an approach relies on maintaining low wages and on imported capital goods and technology. Furthermore, trends in agricultural growth were often cited as promising, especially because per capita agricultural production was growing in the 1960s, as were international commodity prices and world commodity trade (Delgado 1996; Mkandawire and Soludo 1999). The main expansion of smallholder cash cropping in fact occurred during the 1960s and not during the colonial era.

---

2. This is often referred to as the structural transformation of an agrarian economy in the development literature. See Timmer (1988) for a complete exposition of this theory.

Adopting and extending the colonial practice of taxing export crops through marketing boards seemed a simple and logical thing to do during the 1960s. Marketing board intervention in agricultural markets became quite extensive throughout much of Sub-Saharan Africa, both to tax export crops and to subsidize food prices for the urban consumer. The boards were often given the authority to regulate and administer both producer and consumer prices in domestic markets, while at the same time restricting private trade to protect themselves from competition (Badiane 1994). They had obvious appeal for emerging African states, both as a useful instrument for implementing broad-based agricultural policies and as a means by which to mobilize public resources. Probably one of their most important roles, with far-reaching political consequences, was their mandate to assure cheap food for the urban population.

Cheap food policies served political ends for African leaders struggling to deal with politically sensitive urban populations and to meet civil service and military wage bills with limited revenue (Bates 1981). However, not all the nations in Africa had policies that were biased against the agricultural sector. The Côte d'Ivoire and Kenya, for example, saw considerable participation by elites in estate agriculture in the 1960s. Not surprisingly, agricultural support policies were quite good, ensuring a ready supply of the requisite inputs and timely procurement of output, construction of rural infrastructure, and organization of agricultural research. These policies were also of considerable benefit to small-holders in the same areas (Gbetibouo and Delgado 1984).

The type of food market intervention in the immediate post-independence period varied, depending on the type of staple commonly consumed in urban areas. The preferred staple in eastern and southern Africa is domestically produced white maize that has been industrially processed into meal. White maize was not readily available on world markets at the time (Jayne and Jones 1997), although South Africa later became a supplier to other African countries. Governments felt that it was appropriate to intervene in almost all aspects of production, marketing, and processing in the maize subsector in order to expand output and ensure a cheap supply to urban consumers. In West Africa, on the other hand, urban food price stability increasingly depended on parastatal imports of rice and wheat that were then resold at fixed prices (Delgado 1991).

An important characteristic of the expansion of marketing boards in eastern and southern Africa was that it carried with it several operational and political advantages (Masters 1994). A centralized policy system made it operationally easier to institute the extension of marketing activities over a larger geographical area and the common practice of administering pan-territorial pricing (fixing equal prices regardless of location). However, they had the effect that centrally located producers near major transport routes subsidized remote producers, with the opposite geographic impact applying to consumers. Remote producers and consumers in capital cities experienced greater political support than did close-in producers or consumers in remote areas, who typically were self-sufficient.

Governments in the 1960s also adapted colonial marketing boards to dismantle private trade previously in the hands of minority racial and ethnic groups who were perceived to have received preferential treatment during the colonial period, or who were otherwise not in political favor. Examples include South Asians in eastern and southern Africa (Jayne and Jones 1997), Lebanese in West Africa (van der Laan 1975), and the Ibo in Nigeria (Lele and Christiansen 1989). Such policies were politically attractive because they appeared to make good the promise of reversing the discriminatory practices of past colonial institutions (Masters 1994). State marketing boards were therefore also in effect entrusted with a broad mandate to act as an instrument of social policy (Seppälä 1998).

A common theme in this vein that emerged among all the countries in the post-independence period was a general distrust and lack of confidence in the ability of private traders to generate efficient markets and foster commercial agriculture (Sahn and Sarris 1992). Reusse (1987:299) notes that "the small independent operator in the post harvest system—be it as a trader, transporter or processor—was considered unable to play anything but a disturbing, wasteful and exploitative role." This helped justify direct interventions in all aspects of smallholder production and marketing as part of an overall rural development agenda. At the same time, post-independence agricultural policy in much of Africa continued to favor large-scale estate or plantation agriculture, preferring to maintain a dualistic pattern of agricultural development in which the smallholder subsector played a minor role. This view is exemplified in Malawi, which heavily taxed the smallholder export subsector—more than at any time in its colonial history—in order to expand large-scale tobacco production (Kydd and Christiansen 1982; Lele 1990).

Intervention in Agricultural Markets after 1973

Although export cropping expanded throughout the 1960s, gradual changes were beginning to occur in both the internal and the external policy environment that affected the direction of agricultural market intervention.

Internally, urbanization in most African countries continued to occur at a rapid pace, as did substantial import substitution for basic consumer goods. Elites previously in close contact with rural areas began to invest more in urban areas and non-agricultural enterprises, even in those countries where estate export agriculture had been important. Although "urban bias" in agricultural marketing policy had not yet become recognized as an issue, the underlying conditions for its emergence were beginning to be felt. Import substitution strategies for basic consumer goods began to extend to import substitution for intermediate goods, a much trickier task in small and poor African agrarian societies, motivating increased calls for industrial protection in Africa. In Côte d'Ivoire, for example, the effective protection coefficient for industry went from 1.23 in 1971 to 1.76 in 1978, where a value of 1.0 would be consistent with free trade (Zartman and Delgado 1984). By raising the costs of industrial inputs and consumer goods relative to the profits and prices of agricultural products, the impact of increasing protection of industry was to impose a de facto tax on agricultural producers.

At the same time, major external changes were occurring. Most significant among these was the oil price shock of 1973–74, which in a short period doubled the oil import bill of African countries, doubled the price of fertilizer in dollar terms, and cut the rate of growth of world agricultural commodity trade in half, leading to real price declines for Africa's agricultural exports (Lewis 1980). The latter changes led to the imposition of fertilizer subsidies, even in countries where fertilizer had been unsubsidized in the 1960s. Because governments were unable to trim fiscal expenditures sufficiently to adjust to their reduced circumstances, foreign exchange rates—which were mostly market rates in 1970—became rapidly overvalued after the oil shock. This further taxed the producers of agricultural exportables relative to the rest of the population (Krueger, Schiff, and Valdes 1991). Input subsidies to export crop producers were in part a countervailing policy to provide some incentive for export cropping.

For most producers, heavy input subsidies did not make up for the loss from low producer prices. The overt political objectives of government and rent-seeking activities among government and marketing board officials meant that the benefits from subsidized inputs usually accrued to a small number of farmers with political clout (Killick 1994). Furthermore, inefficiencies in input delivery systems and in crop payments by the marketing boards were quite widespread in most countries, contributing to a weak response to input subsidy incentives (Jayne and Jones 1997). Declines in overall agricultural production followed as the majority of smallholder farmers invested less in purchased inputs (pesticides, fertilizer, and fungicides), labor for crop maintenance, and other inputs (Sahn, Dorosh, and Younger 1997).

In terms of industrial performance, frequent shortages in essential inputs meant that much of the industrial sector in Sub-Saharan Africa had to operate below capacity. A large number of companies in the industrial sector were state-owned enterprises or parastatals that operated as monopolies in domestic markets in the 1970s. The overall result was an inefficient and overprotected domestic industry that could not compete effectively in international markets, and eventually failed to contribute much to overall economic growth—as evidenced in the high rate of industrial failures in much of Sub-Saharan Africa in the 1970s (Killick 1993). For the agricultural sector, overvalued exchange rates contributed further to the lowering of the real prices received by producers of export crops; in Sub-Saharan Africa these were in many instances less than half their world market prices (World Bank 1981; Lele 1990; Jaeger 1992; Oyejide 1993; Schiff and Valdes 1995). This implicit taxation only exacerbated the already explicit taxation of export crops.

Drought contributed to the disasters facing African agriculture in the 1970s, and there was also a sharp price spike on world markets for rice and wheat in 1975. Domestic African food prices were kept low through imports and outright subsidies in some cases. Per unit costs of essential imported goods, including food, were also indirectly subsidized through overvaluation of the exchange rate. This resulted in frequent shortages of foreign exchange and declining performance of the export sector (Killick 1993). On the macroeconomic front, shortages in the exchange rate market often forced governments to impose quantity restrictions or high import tariffs on imported inputs, further exacerbating the structure of disincentives to export production.

It is doubtful that the scale of growth of parastatal marketing boards in the 1970s would have been possible without the sustained support of donors (Coulter 1994; Jones 1995). The advent of food aid in response to drought during this period breathed new life into marketing boards. Donors recognized that concessional food aid distribution to targeted groups required an institutional infrastructure that could not be built in a day; parastatal grain marketing boards could provide a permanent presence ready to intervene in years when it was needed. According to Lele (1991), between 1970 and 1987, the value of total donor assistance to some African countries varied between 35 percent and 75 percent of total government expenditures, with Tanzania, Burkina Faso, and Senegal receiving the highest proportional amounts. These countries also experienced the greatest growth in parastatals. From a donor perspective, it was easier to support marketing boards because they were often the sole marketing institution supported and approved by government. Through project investments in vehicles, equipment, or technical assistance personnel, donors such as the World Bank and others were indirectly supporting and financing parastatals.

Several additional problems arose as a result of the nature and scale of state intervention in agricultural markets across much of Sub-Saharan Africa in the 1970s. One example was the extension of pan-territorial pricing, instituted in the 1960s, to larger numbers of people and remoter areas. Marketing boards during this period began to develop unsustainable budget deficits and were increasingly plagued by bureaucratic inefficiencies (Jones 1998). The high operating costs of marketing boards in the 1970s can be attributed to several factors. The most important was the desire to reach a broader segment of society under pan-territorial pricing, regardless of geographical location. This was a common practice in eastern and southern Africa. In order to equalize prices at different locations, marketing boards had to absorb most of the transport burden between surplus and deficit areas (Masters 1994).

Adding to the costs of transporting agricultural produce between producers and consumers were the storage costs arising from pan-seasonal pricing.[3] Furthermore, restrictions on private trade prevented farmers and consumers from using potentially lower-cost marketing channels. The results were unsustainable draw-downs on public budgets and wide margins between producer and consumer prices. The large-scale subsector, which was often located in the areas better served by infrastructure and thus was disadvantaged by pan-territorial pricing (which favored producers in remote areas), responded to the disincentive by switching to uncontrolled crops, in effect reducing its contribution to grain output (Masters 1994). This contributed to the instability in marketing board purchases as the share of smallholder grain production increased (Jayne and Jones 1997). Large-farm grain deliveries to parastatals are typically less subject to fluctuations in volume than are smallholder deliveries because of greater control over inputs and a more commercial orientation.

Increasing problems with the agricultural market intervention system in the 1970s led to the emergence of parallel markets and cross-border smuggling (Bates 1981, 1989; Morris 1988; Roemer and Jones 1991). A decreasing proportion of agricultural sales in the 1970s went through official channels; the rest went through parallel markets (Bates 1981). This reduced the state's ability to generate revenue from smallholder agriculture by limiting its tax base (Sahn and Sarris 1992). Evidence of parallel markets in this period is well documented (Agbodan 1989 for Togo; Berthelemy, Azam, and Faucher 1988 for Madagascar and Mozambique; Bevan, Collier, and Gunning 1989 for Kenya and Tanzania; Roemer and Jones 1991 for Africa in general). The emergence of parallel markets was costly to the economy as a whole and to the efficiency of marketing boards in particular, because the profitable side of official marketing activities continued to decline while subsidizing state intervention continued unabated, effectively draining limited government resources (Seppälä 1998).

The Crisis Leading to Market Reforms

The rapid industrialization strategy of the 1960s and early 1970s depended on extracting resources from a predominantly underdeveloped agricultural sector. Thus, throughout the 1970s, incentives to producers of foreign exchange earnings from agriculture were declining, while foreign exchange consumption was being stimulated. Furthermore, the dangers of this situation were masked by two phenomena. First, bad weather in Brazil in the second half of the 1970s led to very high prices for coffee, cocoa, and tea; these greatly inflated foreign exchange inflows to many African countries. Second, the oil price shock of

---

3. Further evidence of the ramifications of both pan-territorial and pan-seasonal pricing schemes is discussed in Rugambisa (1994) for Tanzania and in Masters and Nuppenau (1993) for Zimbabwe.

1973–74 led to the reinvestment of billions of "petrodollars" in African countries, further expanding foreign exchange reserves and motivating special industrial tariff creation to protect the new factories that were built. Once tropical beverage prices returned to normal in the late 1970s and foreign investment in these items slackened off, sudden macroeconomic collapse would follow.

The second oil shock in 1979 further increased demands on foreign exchange, depressed world trade, and abruptly reduced demand for African export commodities. Furthermore, Brazilian production of tropical exports resumed at high levels, joined by emerging exports of palm oil, coffee, cotton, and cocoa from Asia that had been encouraged by the high prices of the late 1970s. Moreover, many African countries in the semi-arid belt experienced drought in the early 1980s. Figures for Côte d'Ivoire help demonstrate the problem: the net barter terms of trade (what a unit of Ivorian exports would buy in terms of Ivorian imports) declined 40 percent from 1978 to 1982 (Zartman and Delgado 1984). In addition, imprudent industrial investments made with easy petrodollar credit in the 1970s had to be repaid with increasing amounts of agricultural exports.

By the early 1980s, the degree of real exchange overvaluation was extreme in Zambia, Uganda, and Tanzania. In contrast, the countries within the Communauté Financière Africaine (CFA) zone of West Africa had relatively lower inflation rates, thus the degree of overvaluation was more modest during the 1970s and first half of the 1980s. Declining world prices in primary exports during the 1970s meant that fewer resources were available for subsidizing imports of rice and wheat for the urban consumer in West Africa. In many instances governments borrowed to finance food imports, especially as population growth rates continued to exceed agricultural growth rates in the 1970s, shifting the food balance sheet of many countries in Sub-Saharan Africa (Byerlee and Eicher 1997). While the terms of trade continued to deteriorate, the scale of public expenditures remained unchanged.

By the end of the 1970s, faced with little potential for growth because of a failing industrial sector, a stagnating agricultural sector, rapidly deteriorating international terms of trade, and unsustainable fiscal deficits, many African countries were experiencing serious fiscal and balance-of-payments crises. Although mismanaged policies may have contributed to the parlous state of many African economies at the time, it has been argued that many of these policies were strategies for political survival in the context of international economic upheaval and rising demands by vocal urban interest groups (Bates 1981; Killick 1993). It had become clear to the donor community that lending in this difficult structural (and frequently distorted) policy environment was unsustainable and contributed less to agricultural growth (Knudsen and Nash 1991). By the 1980s, under the guidance of the International Monetary Fund (IMF) and the World Bank, many African countries were forced to accept structural adjustment and stabilization programs to reverse their declining economic performance.

Agricultural Market Reforms in the Context
of Structural Adjustment

Following a general global trend toward market liberalization, donors and international agencies strongly advocated the reduction of direct state intervention in agricultural marketing and pricing. The objectives were to redress the bias against producers and enhance economic development in Sub-Saharan Africa (World Bank 1981). The conventional logic underlying the pursuit of agricultural market reforms was that, as governments remove price controls and restrictions on private trade, lower levels of price taxation and greater private sector marketing efficiency result in higher producer prices and decreased marketing costs. Higher producer prices stimulate higher production (through a positive price elasticity of supply) and higher demand for inputs and hired labor, leading to economic growth (Barrett and Carter 1994).

The early structural adjustment programs—in the period 1979 to roughly 1984—were qualitatively very different from the later structural adjustment programs (Husain 1994). The early phase was a reaction to the unsustainable budget deficits and foreign exchange shortages that resulted from events of the 1970s. The strategy underlying the structural adjustment programs was based on the premise that the emerging agricultural and overall development problems were the result of artificially distorted price incentives, particularly for export crops that were still controlled by governments. Economic adjustment required incentives to be shifted from the net consumers of tradables—civil servants, workers in protected manufacturing industries, service providers, and so forth—to the net producers of tradables—the tens of millions of export crop producers (Delgado 1998).

The early structural adjustment strategy thus had four parts: (1) free up nominal exchange rates to permit them to react to supply and demand pressures on foreign exchange reserves; (2) unify tariffs to equalize effective exchange rates faced by different sectors; (3) undertake fiscal austerity to prevent wage inflation from causing a surge of demand for imports; and (4) liberalize export crop markets to ensure that increased foreign exchange earnings from export crops make their way back to farmers rather than go to reimburse the debts of parastatals (World Bank 1981). These prescriptions provided a clear, internally consistent, theoretically justified, simple strategy for promoting agricultural exports. The early structural adjustment strategy relied on policy reforms rather than investment and institution building. However, the policy content of the reforms primarily concerned events outside the agricultural sector per se, and only peripherally addressed non-price policy issues within agriculture.

The conditionalities imposed in the first structural adjustment loans to African countries by the World Bank from 1979 through 1983 were phrased in general terms, particularly with respect to agricultural market interventions (Hussain 1994). As with bail-out loans made by the Bretton Woods institutions to other countries in preceding decades, it was expected that African governments would devise specific strategies to meet the general conditions of the loans (Delgado 1998). By the mid-1980s it became apparent that this was not going to happen in Sub-Saharan Africa. In part this was the result of the political impasse in many countries in coping with such sweeping changes, especially when there had not in fact been much political change over time. In part it was due to the lack of institutions and trusted skilled advisors that could devise such strategies and feed them up through the political process. Coupled with a deepening economic crisis caused by high energy prices, by rapid declines in world agricultural prices owing to recession and agricultural policy in developed countries, and by a series of devastating droughts in the early 1980s, it became clear on all sides that something had to be done.

Thus, from the mid-1980s, structural adjustment loans extended by the World Bank and bilateral donors imposed a detailed set of policy conditions that had to be met before funds would be available. Because agriculture was often still the main source of export revenue and the predominant source of fiscal receipts, and agricultural parastatals accounted for a large share of unsustainable budget deficits, the detailed conditions dealt heavily with reforming agricultural markets (Delgado 1998). The conditionalities included far-reaching institutional changes as well as changes to specific pricing policies. The institutional changes involved scaling down government marketing agencies, providing enabling environments for traders, and maintaining food security stocks (World Bank 1995; Seppälä 1997). Regarding the objective of an enabling environment, there was wide agreement that governments must foster the emerging private sector through measures to simplify licensing and lower fees and taxes. Other problems facing traders were a lack of credit and poor infrastructure, yet few resources existed for this type of institutional support (Platteau 1996). As a consequence, in the late 1980s and early 1990s, many African governments adopted more market-oriented policies. Although this shift in policy is often attributed to pressure from the World Bank, the International Monetary Fund, and other international organizations, a more fundamental cause was severe macroeconomic imbalance, mainly balance-of-payments pressures.

Because of the adverse effects of structural adjustment on sectors of the population, a sea-change occurred in policy thinking about the conditionalities outlined in the reform process. Thus, the concept of "adjustment with a human face" was popularized (Cornia, Jolly, and Stewart 1987). The implications of this change in thinking were threefold. First, the principle was accepted that trickle-down effects would not take care of the basic needs of the poor; thus a role might, under some conditions, be retained for targeted assistance. Second, the principle was accepted that many market interventions in fact taxed the poor more than the rich, thus giving further support to the liberalization of markets for export crops. Third, the concept was introduced that trade-offs between growth and equity should be quantified, and certain improvements in overall efficiency sacrificed if the welfare cost to the most vulnerable was too great (Delgado 1998); this could help slow down the rate of dismantling of institutions designed to integrate people living in remote areas into the national economy.

The key element of the concept of adjustment with a human face was the reaffirmation of the need to build the right sorts of institutions to support the participation of the poor in economic growth, while discarding institutions that hindered their participation. This added a new twist to the evolving awareness, since the Berg report (World Bank 1981), of the interdependence between the sustainability of agricultural market reforms in Africa, events in world commodities markets, and the macroeconomic and trade policy environment chosen by governments. Essentially, by the time of the main reform era in the late 1980s and early 1990s, agricultural market reform debates had graduated from technical discussions among sector and trade experts into political debates concerning fundamental institutional change backed by major economic and political reforms.

In the following three chapters, specific reforms related to the fertilizer, food, and cash crop markets are outlined in more detail. In the next section of this chapter, a common conceptual framework is developed to visualize the linkages among elements of the reform process and to assess the impact of the reforms on different economic outcomes.

A Conceptual Framework for Assessing Agricultural Market Reforms

It follows from the above discussion that agricultural market reforms occurred not in a vacuum, but rather within the context of domestic and external political economy interests, global economic trends, and macroeconomic adjustments. Moreover, policy thinking, both globally and domestically, on agricultural market reforms evolved substantially over the period of reforms. Therefore, the analysis of the process and impact of agricultural market reform cannot be viewed in isolation from these important linkages. As shown in Figure 2.1, a complex set of factors influenced and was influenced by agricultural market reform. In this section, we explore these linkages in order to develop a conceptual framework for viewing the outcomes of specific market reforms.

Market reform can be seen in terms of actors, influences, and outcomes. Over the process of reform, national actors such as governments, civil society, and interest groups, in congruence or in conflict with external actors, such as bilateral donors, international lending institutions, and nongovernmental agencies, had a fundamental influence on the market reform process. The process itself is defined by the pace and scope of reforms, the timing and sequencing of different reform measures, and the commitment given to reform by the various actors. Process matters to market reform outcomes. Countries in which reforms were implemented quickly and decisively had different outcomes than coun-

FIGURE 2.1 Agricultural market reform linkages

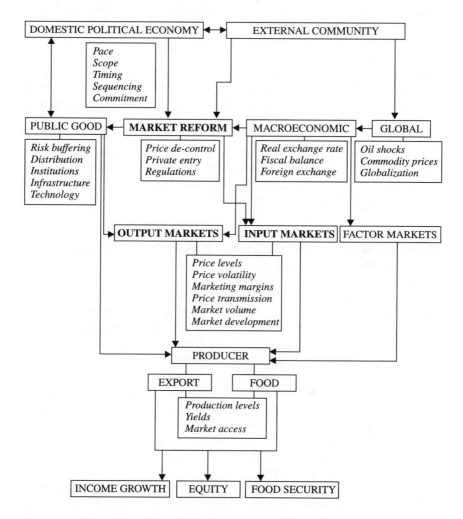

tries characterized by policy reversals and incomplete reforms. Questions that arise concern the extent to which reform follows a blueprint and whether or not patterns can be discerned in successful reforms.

Political economic considerations nationally were shaped by the perceived role of the state in the provision of public goods. These public goods concern the management of export earnings risk, the social contract with urban consumers and rural producers and its redistributive role, the provision of institutions and services such as those concerned with quality control and market organization, and the provision of infrastructure, such as transport and storage, and of technology. Internationally, the interests of the external community in pushing for reforms were rooted in global economic trends as well as its perceived role in promoting economic growth in Sub-Saharan Africa. Finally, another key actor in agricultural market reform, whose voice has not been articulated in a direct manner, is the smallholder producer. Important issues are the extent to which national political economy interests and the interests of the external community were linked; how these interests defined the market reform process; and, fundamentally, whether reform, in the context of these interests, occurred at all.

In addition to the influence exerted by local and external interest groups, the previous discussion highlighted how macroeconomic and global economic trends had a key impact on agricultural market reform. Domestic macroeconomic balances are themselves closely tied to world market trends, in terms of both commodity output prices and imports. Foreign exchange availability and real exchange rate movements have a direct impact on the profitability of both export and food production, because inputs such as fertilizer and seed are mainly imported. The simultaneous impact of oil shocks, falling commodity prices, the move toward greater openness of world markets, and overvalued exchange rates created unsustainable fiscal deficits for state-owned marketing enterprises. Other factors internally led to the rationale for reform: high marketing costs by parastatal enterprises, thin and volatile markets, low producer prices that implicitly taxed producers, and weak price transmission.

Internal and external, national and international, these influences ultimately led to the undertaking of agricultural market reforms across Sub-Saharan Africa. These reforms consisted mainly of the abandoning of price controls, allowing private sector entry into agricultural trading activities, eliminating or easing trade restrictions, and removing or reducing the state role in marketing. The pertinent question is what were the economic outcomes or impacts of market reforms. The outcomes can be distinguished at three principal levels: the market itself, production, and growth and equity.

At the first level, the liberalization and privatization of agricultural marketing affect the nature and efficiency of the market itself. Thus, the impact of reform can be observed directly on agricultural price levels, the extent of price transmission between markets, or market integration, the stabilization or volatility of market prices, changes in the size of marketing margins, and investments by private traders and other efforts to improve the functioning of markets.

Second, the outcome of market reform can be viewed in terms of its broader impact on agricultural production. This can be evaluated by changes in supply levels and in productivity in response to price changes, as well as in terms of the access and extent of farmers' use of private markets.

At the third level, market reform has an impact on equity, food security, and income growth. The impact of reform on welfare can be assessed by evaluating the gains and losses from resulting changes in producer and consumer prices, for both urban and rural populations. The impact of reform on food security can be measured through the changes in the marketed surplus of food and access to domestic and imported food supplies. Finally, the impact of market reforms on income growth can be assessed from the changes in producer incomes resulting from changes in producer prices and the potential effects on the incomes of urban and rural consumer households.

Alongside the above three levels of outcomes, market reform also has an impact on the provision of public goods, defined as goods and services whose benefits cannot be captured privately owing to significant fixed costs and prohibitively high exclusion costs. For example, establishing a national market information service is very costly, while at the same time it is very difficult to exclude beneficiaries. In turn, the provision of public goods, either privately or through the state, has implications for the effective functioning of the liberalized market. The withdrawal of the public sector in the wake of market reform has included in many instances the exit of the state from some of the positive functions provided most appropriately by the public sector, such as information, law enforcement, product standardization, grading and inspection, as well as investments in infrastructure. This raises important questions regarding the extent to which market reform has enabled the internalization of public externalities in agriculture. In what areas does the private sector fall short of effectively providing public goods? What is the appropriate role of the public sector where private incentives do not exist? Examples of market reform reducing the provision of public goods are the loss of quality control and grading mechanisms, which were dismantled along with the removal of export marketing boards, the loss of marketing services in remote areas, and the increased transaction and price risks faced by producers with the abandoning of public buffer stock schemes.

In the following chapters, the themes outlined in this conceptual framework are taken up systematically and viewed in light of the empirical literature on market reforms in Sub-Saharan Africa. The conceptual framework developed here highlighted the three dimensions of market reforms: actors, influences, and outcomes. Actors and influences can be both domestic and international, and influences on reform are both internal and external to the agricultural sector. The conceptual framework further distinguishes three layers of direct outcomes—agricultural marketing, production response, and economic growth—and the indirect impact on the provision of public goods (institutions and infrastructure) essential to the functioning of markets.

3   Input Market Reform: The Case of Fertilizer

We found three reasons for focusing on fertilizer rather than seed, pesticides, or other farm inputs as an example of input market reform. First, fertilizer is arguably the most important purchased input in African agriculture, whether importance is measured in terms of average farm expenditure or the proportion of farmers purchasing it. Second, policy interventions in fertilizer markets were more widespread than for other inputs, and the fiscal and administrative burdens of subsidized fertilizer distribution in the 1970s and 1980s far exceeded those associated with other inputs. Finally, economic reforms have probably affected fertilizer use more than they have the use of seed and other inputs. This is partly because of the greater degree of intervention in fertilizer markets before the reforms. In addition, unlike seed, fertilizer is almost always imported, so fertilizer markets were affected by reforms in trade and exchange rate policy as well as by changes in input policy.

Farmers in Sub-Saharan Africa use less fertilizer than farmers in any other region of the world. On average, they apply 9 kilograms of nutrient per hectare of arable land, compared with an average of 107 kilograms per hectare for all developing countries (see Table 3.1). Since 1980, fertilizer use in Africa has grown at just 0.7 percent annually, far less than the 4.0 percent growth in developing countries as a whole. Furthermore, fertilizer use in Africa actually declined in the mid-1990s.

These patterns are particularly worrisome given the slow growth in agricultural output in Africa. Since fertilizer use is credited with about one-third of the increase in world grain production in recent decades, improving the performance of fertilizer markets is a critical component of efforts to increase agricultural productivity and reduce rural poverty in Africa.

Fertilizer markets in Sub-Saharan Africa have undergone fundamental change over the past 20 years. In the 1970s, most countries tightly controlled the importation and distribution of fertilizer, making it available to farmers at heavily subsidized prices. During the 1980s and early 1990s, many African countries reduced or eliminated controls on fertilizer markets and phased out the subsidies. The policy changes were induced by various factors, including

TABLE 3.1 Fertilizer application rates by region, 1980–81 to 1996–97

Region	Application rate (kilograms of nutrients per hectare of arable land)			Annual growth, 1980–81 to 1996–97 (percent)
	1980–81	1990–91	1996–97	
World	88	100	98	0.7
Developed countries	120	112	86	−2.1
Economies in transition	104	104	33	−6.9
Developing countries	57	89	107	4.0
Latin America and the Caribbean	64	63	71	0.7
Near East and North Africa	45	67	65	2.3
Sub-Saharan Africa	8	10	9	0.7
East Asia and Southeast Asia	121	179	238	4.3
South Asia	37	80	93	5.9

SOURCE: FAO (1998a).

the fiscal burden of the subsidies, greater recognition of the limitations of central planning, and pressure from international organizations. Also affecting fertilizer markets were changes in macroeconomic and trade policy, most notably import liberalization and the adoption of market-determined exchange rates.

These reforms have been controversial. In a number of countries, fertilizer demand has fallen substantially as a result of higher fertilizer prices. The impression is widespread that, perhaps more than other reforms, liberalization of the fertilizer market has had adverse effects on agricultural productivity and rural income.

To examine the impact of economic reforms on fertilizer markets in Africa, this chapter addresses the following issues:

- What policy reforms have been implemented that affect fertilizer use in Africa?
- How have these reforms in×uenced the patterns of fertilizer use?
- How have changes in fertilizer use affected agricultural production, food security, and poverty?
- What policy and institutional changes would promote the efµcient use of fertilizer in Africa?

Factors Influencing Fertilizer Use

Fertilizer use varies substantially from one country to another and, within each country, from one farmer to another. This variation provides information on the factors that influence fertilizer use, thus helping to explain the constraints on fertilizer use in Africa. We begin with a discussion of some factors that help to explain the low use of fertilizer in Africa relative to other regions. Then we review the variation in fertilizer application rates across African countries and the factors associated with these differences. Finally, we examine the determinants of farm-level fertilizer use, summarizing studies based on survey data.

Fertilizer Use in Africa Compared with Other Regions

Why are fertilizer application rates in Sub-Saharan Africa much lower than those in Latin America and Asia?

One important factor is the higher cost of fertilizers in Sub-Saharan Africa. Nitrogen-to-maize price ratios in Africa are typically in the range of 5 to 10, whereas the median value for seven Asian and Latin American countries is 2.9 (see Pinstrup-Andersen 1993; Heisey and Mwangi 1997). One reason for this difference is that there are economies of scale in fertilizer procurement and most African countries are small importers by international standards. For example, Shepherd and Coster (1987) found that the median c.i.f. cost of fertilizer for seven African countries was US$240 per ton, compared with c.i.f. costs of US$115–178 per ton in four Asian countries. Townsend (1999) examines the determinants of the ratio of domestic to world fertilizer prices using data from 31 African countries. He finds that the ratio is increased by distance from major fertilizer markets and fertilizer import tariffs, and is reduced by the proportion of paved roads and the volume of fertilizer used in the country.

Another reason for the high price of fertilizer in Africa is the high cost of domestic marketing. Shepherd and Coster (1987) found that the cost of fertilizer marketing and distribution for a sample of 11 African countries ranged from US$57 to US$268 per ton, compared with US$18 to US$73 per ton in 9 Asian countries. Malawi is often cited as a country facing high distribution costs. Donovan (1996) presents data showing that, over the period 1984–90, the cost of transporting fertilizer from the port ranged from US$134 to US$183 per ton, representing 89 to 135 percent of the c.i.f. value of the fertilizer. The high distribution costs in Africa are related to poor roads, sparse fertilizer demand, lack of competition, and policy restrictions. In addition, because fertilizer demand depends partly on rainfall, which is known only at the time of planting, traders face uncertainty in fertilizer demand and the risk of having to hold stocks until the following season. This risk is built into traders' marketing margins.

In addition to the higher costs of fertilizer in Africa, several other factors have been suggested as reasons for the low application rates compared with other regions:

- Irrigation is much less widespread in Sub-Saharan Africa. According to one estimate, 30 percent of the arable land in Asia is irrigated compared with less than 5 percent in Africa.
- Many of the crops grown in Africa, including cassava, yams, sweet potatoes, sorghum, and millet, are less responsive to fertilizer. By comparison, wheat and rice, which represent a much larger share of crop area in Asia, have modern varieties that are responsive to fertilizer.
- The low population density in Sub-Saharan Africa reduces the incentive to invest in land-saving technology such as fertilizer. When expansion of the cropped area is relatively inexpensive, there is less motivation for intensifying the use of existing farmland (Hayami and Ruttan 1971).

We are not aware of any studies that attempt to measure the contribution of each of these factors in explaining differences in application rates between African and Asian countries.

Patterns in Fertilizer Use across African Countries

In this section, we highlight the diversity of patterns in fertilizer use across countries in Sub-Saharan Africa, as well as shedding some light on the factors that influence fertilizer use.

In Reunion and Mauritius, application rates are over 300 kilograms of nutrient per hectare of arable land. Excluding these small sugar-producing nations, the highest application rates are found in Zimbabwe (57 kg/ha), followed by Swaziland, Kenya, and Malawi (see Figure 3.1). At the other extreme, fertilizer application rates are less than 3 kg/ha in five countries: Gabon, Democratic Republic of the Congo, Rwanda, Uganda, and Central African Republic.

Although economic theory suggests that rising population density should stimulate agricultural intensification and land-saving technology such as fertilizer, the pattern is not consistent across African countries. Certainly, the sparsely populated Gabon, Democratic Republic of the Congo, and Central African Republic fit this pattern, but Rwanda, Uganda, and Nigeria, with high population densities and low application rates, do not. It is notable, however, that the four mainland countries with the highest fertilizer application rates all have significant large-scale farming sectors. Kenya and Zimbabwe have large-scale commercial farm sectors growing maize, wheat, and export crops; Malawi and Swaziland have estate sectors specializing in tobacco and sugar, respectively.

Four countries—Zimbabwe, Ethiopia, Nigeria, and Kenya—account for three-fifths of the fertilizer use in Africa (see Figure 3.2). Each of these countries uses over 100,000 tons of nutrients per year. Other important fertilizer users are the Sudan, Côte d'Ivoire, Malawi, and Zambia, using 40,000–90,000 tons annually. Desai and Ghandi (1990) examine the correlation between national average

FIGURE 3.1 Fertilizer application rates by country, 1996

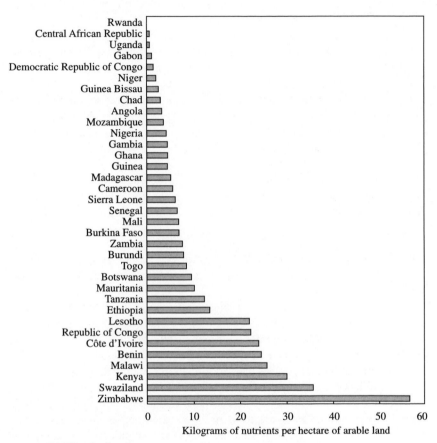

SOURCE: FAOStat database.

fertilizer application rates and various country characteristics using data from the period 1979–83. They found that fertilizer application rates were higher

- In southern Africa and in Anglophone countries;
- In countries with a high proportion of land in maize and a low proportion of land in roots and tubers;
- In countries with greater spending on agriculture, more agronomists per hectare, a larger share of mechanized farming, and a denser road network; and
- In countries with fertilizer subsidy programs.

Contrary to expectations, fertilizer application rates were not correlated with population density, income per capita, export crop area, irrigated area, or hav-

FIGURE 3.2 Share of fertilizer use by country, 1996

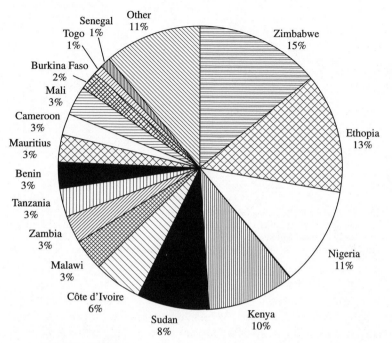

SOURCE: FAOStat database.

ing a coastline. These results should be interpreted with caution because the analysis was based on simple bivariate correlations without controlling for other variables. Thus, Anglophone countries may have higher application rates because they grow more maize and/or have a larger share of mechanized farm land.

Naseem and Kelly (1999) update this analysis using FAO data from 1970 to 1994. They find that most of the correlations identified by Desai and Ghandi still hold, although there are some exceptions. For example, in their analysis, the fertilizer application rates are correlated with cotton area in three of the five subperiods, but are not correlated with maize area.

Patterns in Farm-Level Fertilizer Use

In most African countries, less than one-third of the farm households use fertilizer, as shown in Table 3.2. Of the nine countries listed, only two have fertilizer adoption rates of 50 percent or more (Kenya and Benin). Furthermore, because the countries in the table are among the main fertilizer users in Africa, the rates for the countries excluded from the list are likely to be lower.

What factors determine which households use fertilizer and which do not? This section examines farm-level studies of the determinants of fertilizer use in

TABLE 3.2 Percentage of farmers using fertilizer by country

Country	Year	Percentage of farmers using fertilizer
Benin	1998	50
Cameroon	1990	22
Ethiopia	1995	33
Ghana	1987	14
Kenya	1996	61
Malawi	1998	35
Tanzania	1991	27
Tanzania	1994	15
Zambia	1986	31
Zimbabwe	1989	19

SOURCES: Benin and Malawi (excluding large-scale farms)—Minot, Kherallah, and Berry (2000); Cameroon (excluding the three northern provinces)—Minot (1991); Ethiopia—Demeke, Said, and Jayne (1996); Ghana—Jebuni and Seini (1992); Kenya—Mose (1998); Tanzania, 1991—Ferreira (1994), 1994—MAC (1997); Zimbabwe (excluding large-scale commercial farmers)—Kinsey (1991).

Sub-Saharan Africa (see Reardon et al. 1999 for a more in-depth survey). First, there is ample evidence that relative prices are an important factor in farmers' decisions to use fertilizer in Africa. Farmers tend to apply more fertilizer to crops that have high value-to-cost ratios (as discussed later in this section). In addition, after fertilizer subsidies were removed and real exchange rates depreciated, aggregate fertilizer demand fell in a number of countries, including Senegal, Malawi, Ghana, and Tanzania (see below). The few econometric studies of fertilizer demand in Africa confirm the significance of price incentives (see Chembezi 1990; Croppenstedt and Demeke 1996; Minot, Kherallah, and Berry 2000; Govindan and Babu 2001).

Second, household characteristics affect fertilizer use. For example, family labor has been found to be positively correlated with fertilizer use, presumably owing to the labor required for applying fertilizer and for extra weeding (see Green and Ng'ong'ola 1993; Croppenstedt and Demeke 1996; Mbata 1997; Minot, Kherallah, and Berry 2000). On the other hand, in five out of six countries where this issue has been examined, female-headed households are no less likely to use fertilizer than are male-headed households (see Green and Ng'ong'ola 1993; Jha and Hojjati 1993; Croppenstedt and Demeke 1996; Adugna 1997; Minot, Kherallah, and Berry 2000). Somewhat surprisingly, few studies find that fertilizer use is associated with education or extension contact.

Third, the characteristics of the farm also play a role. Fertilizer use tends to be greater in the high-potential zones where rainfall is higher and the soils are richer. This is the case in Zimbabwe, Zambia, Kenya, and Ethiopia. On the other hand, fertilizer use in Benin and Ghana is greater in the semi-arid north because of cash crop production there. Land tenure is probably not a major factor. Most farmers have usufruct rights under customary land tenure systems. Atwood (1990) argues that investments in land (particularly annual investments such as fertilization) are not necessarily reduced by customary land tenure systems. The relationship between farm size and fertilization is complex. On the one hand, large-scale commercial farmers in Zimbabwe, Malawi, Zambia, and Kenya are more likely to use fertilizer than are small-scale farmers (Kinsey 1991; Howard and Mungoma 1997). This is attributed to the fact that larger farmers have better access to credit and extension and they are located on high-potential land. On the other hand, farm surveys in a number of countries find that small farms are more likely to use fertilizer, perhaps because they are cultivated more intensively (Adugna 1997; Nkonya, Schroeder, and Norman 1997; Minot, Kherallah, and Berry 2000; Croppenstedt and Demeke 1996).

A fourth factor is the price and availability of other inputs, particularly water and improved seed. Fertilizer use among small farmers also grew in parallel with the adoption of hybrid maize seed in Zimbabwe, Zambia, Malawi, and Kenya (see Eicher and Kupfuma 1997; Hassan and Karanja 1997; Howard and Mungoma 1997; Smale and Heisey 1997). In a study of Tanzania, Nkonya, Schroeder, and Norman (1997) show that fertilizer use spurs the adoption of improved seed, and vice versa. Water is also a complementary input in that it increases the productivity of fertilizer. As discussed earlier, the adoption of fertilizer is greater in areas with high rainfall and it even varies by year, because farmers wait to see how good the rain will be before applying fertilizer. Irrigated plots are much more likely to be fertilized than others, partly owing to the complementarity between fertilizer and water and partly because irrigated plots are generally used to grow high-value crops such as vegetables or rice.

Fifth, fertilizer use is positively associated with income and/or animal ownership in a number of studies (Jha and Hojjati 1993; Croppenstedt and Demeke 1996; Adugna 1997; Mbata 1997; Minot, Kherallah, and Berry 2000). Income and assets ownership may be an indicator of the ability to bear the risk associated with purchased inputs and/or the ability to overcome cash constraints in the absence of well-functioning credit markets.

Finally, one of the strongest predictors of whether or not a farmer will use fertilizer is the combination of crops grown. A number of crops are rarely fertilized because their market value is low or they do not respond well to fertilizer, for example cassava, yams, sweet potatoes, sorghum, and millet. Maize is in an intermediate position: it is more often fertilized than other staple food crops, but less than 40 percent of the maize area receives any fertilizer.[1] At the

---

1. Heisey and Mwangi (1997) estimate that 37 percent of the maize area in 11 Sub-Saharan countries is fertilized. These countries include all the main maize-growing countries of the continent.

other extreme, tobacco, cotton, coffee, tea, sugarcane, and irrigated rice are often fertilized. For example, 99 percent of cotton growers in Benin fertilize this crop, whereas only 33 percent of non-cotton growers use fertilizer on any crop. Similarly in Malawi, about three-quarters of the small-scale tobacco growers fertilize the crop, but just one-quarter of other farmers use fertilizer on any crop (Minot, Kherallah, and Berry 2000). In Cameroon, fertilizer use is strongly associated with cotton production in the north and with arabica coffee production in the south. Furthermore, fertilization of one crop may depend on what other crops are grown. Dioné (1989) noted that cash crop farmers in Senegal are more likely to use fertilizer and other inputs on food crops. Similarly, holding other factors constant, cotton farmers in Benin and tobacco farmers in Malawi are more likely to fertilize their maize than are their neighbors who do not grow these crops (Minot, Kherallah, and Berry 2000). This may reflect the effect of the cash crop income, the effect of experience with fertilizer, or the fact that, in Benin, cotton growers can obtain inputs on credit.

Two clarifications should be made here. First, although export crops are often fertilized, this is not a universal pattern. Cocoa and cashew nut trees are not widely fertilized. Although cotton is heavily fertilized in West Africa, very little fertilizer is used by Tanzanian cotton growers. Similarly, coffee is often fertilized in Kenya, but rarely in Uganda and Rwanda. Second, although export crops are much more likely to be fertilized than food crops, this does not imply that most fertilizer is applied to export crops. Maize probably receives more fertilizer than any other crop in Africa, partly because it is widely grown (Heisey and Mwangi 1997). As shown in Table 3.3, maize receives more fertilizer than any other crop in three of the four largest consumers of fertilizer in Sub-Saharan Africa: Zimbabwe, Kenya, and Nigeria. It is also the main fertilized crop in Malawi, Tanzania, Zambia, Ghana, Lesotho, and Angola.

Thus, the evidence suggests that African farmers respond in predictable ways to changes in the economic environment. Almost all the factors found to influence fertilizer demand do so in a way consistent with expectations. However, the fact that indicators of household resources, such as income and asset ownership, are positively associated with fertilizer use suggests that this rationality is subject to cash and credit constraints and risk aversion.

Fertilizer Policy in Sub-Saharan Africa

We begin with a brief description of the regulations, institutions, and policies governing fertilizer markets in the 1970s and early 1980s. Then we examine the changes that have been implemented in fertilizer markets since the early 1980s.

Fertilizer Policy before Reform

Until the 1980s, fertilizer markets in most countries in Sub-Saharan Africa were characterized by five types of policy interventions.

TABLE 3.3 Fertilizer use by crop by country

Country	Year	Crop	Share of total fertilizer use (percent)
Angola	1991	Maize	66
		Banana	21
		Vegetables	14
Benin	1998	Cotton	61
		Maize	23
		Vegetables	7
Burkina Faso	1991	Cereals	54
		Cotton	46
		Groundnuts	1
Côte d'Ivoire	1994	Rice	35
		Cotton	24
		Maize	22
Ethiopia	1995	*Teff*	45
		Wheat	20
		Maize	15
Ghana	1991	Maize	64
		Vegetables	11
		Rice	10
Kenya	1996	Maize	28
		Sugarcane	22
		Coffee	14
Lesotho	1989	Maize	77
		Sorghum	12
		Wheat	8
Madagascar	1990	Sugarcane	35
		Rice	28
		Potato	18
Malawi	1998	Maize	64
		Groundnuts	9
		Tobacco	7
Mauritius	1993	Sugarcane	89
		Tea	5
		Potato	2
Nigeria	1996	Maize	24
		Yam	12
		Rice	11
Tanzania	1992	Maize	52
		Tobacco	30
		Rice	9
Togo	1990	Cotton	58
		Maize	24
		Sorghum	9

(continued)

TABLE 3.3 *Continued*

Country	Year	Crop	Share of total fertilizer use (percent)
Zambia	1996	Maize	95
		Millet	3
		Soybeans	2
Zimbabwe	1995	Maize	42
		Tobacco	19
		Cotton	7

SOURCES: Benin and Malawi—Minot, Kherallah, and Berry (2000); Ghana—Bumb et al. (1994); others from FAO (1999).

First, fertilizer imports and distribution were controlled, either directly or indirectly, by the government. Many of the state enterprises used to manage fertilizer import and distribution were colonial institutions retained by the new independent governments or were created soon after independence. The Food and Agriculture Organization of the United Nations (FAO 1986:53) reports that input distribution was controlled by a state monopoly in 30 of 39 African countries surveyed.[2] In some cases, a state enterprise was dedicated to fertilizer importation and distribution. In others, the Ministry of Agriculture distributed fertilizer through extension agents or farmer cooperatives. And sometimes a parastatal marketing authority managed both crop marketing and input delivery. In any case, the allocation of fertilizer among regions was an administrative decision, often based on extension recommendations or usage in previous years.

The second element of fertilizer policy was the imposition of price controls and subsidies on the retail price of fertilizer. In many countries, fertilizer subsidies were introduced in the mid-1970s in response to the first oil price shock, which drove up the price of nitrogenous fertilizers. According to the World Bank (1994:88), before market reforms were introduced, 22 of 26 African countries surveyed had fertilizer subsidies and two more sold "some" fertilizer at subsidized prices. Explicit subsidies ranged from 10 to 80 percent of the full cost of the fertilizer (see Table 3.4). In addition, the prices set by the government were often pan-territorial and pan-seasonal, implicitly providing a higher level of subsidy to farmers in remote areas compared with those close to the source of the fertilizer.

Third, the government often followed a policy of channeling credit to farmers for the purchase of agricultural inputs. In some cases, commercial

2. The exceptions were Kenya, Zimbabwe, Swaziland, and Mauritius, which had competitive distribution channels, and Cameroon, Côte d'Ivoire, Central African Republic, Malawi, and Liberia, which were classified as having both competitive systems and government controls (FAO 1986). Even in some of these countries (such as Malawi), the degree of effective competition in fertilizer markets was low.

TABLE 3.4 Fertilizer subsidy rate, 1975–98 (percent of full cost)

Year	Benin	Cameroon	Ghana	Kenya	Madagascar	Malawi	Nigeria	Senegal	Tanzania	Togo	Zambia
1975			86		45			70	75	82	74
1976			82		38		85	57	66	79	46
1977		61	62		38		85	53		84	34
1978		48			38		85	50	50	76	36
1979	75	54	80		38		85	54		78	17
1980	75	53	65				85	61			48
1981	75	58	45				85	70	60	83	45
1982		48	45				85	77	60	48/60	18
1983	47		45			29	83	50	60	50/62	−11
1984	45				16	25	50		60	43/62	15
1985	35		60		16	21	34	16		8/54	
1986	29		56			18	82	27		18/59	
1987	10	66	42			24	82	20		24/50	
1988		37	30			24				0/35	
1989		30	15		26		80	9			
1990		19							78		
1991		15							55		
1992		10						40			
1993		7				16			25		
1994						11					
1995											
1996											
1997											
1998											

SOURCES: Benin—Soulé (1999); Cameroon—Lele, Christiansen, and Kadiresan (1989); Walker (1994), referring to southern seven provinces only; Ghana—Sijm (1997); Kenya—Lele, Christiansen, and Kadiresan (1989); Madagascar—IFPRI (1998:9); Malawi—USAID (1990); Gisselquist (1998), referring to fertilizer for smallholders only; Nigeria—Lele, Christiansen, and Kadiresan (1989); Idachaba (2000); Senegal—Lele, Christiansen, and Kadiresan (1989); Tanzania—Lele, Christiansen, and Kadiresan (1989); MAC (1997); Togo—Atchou (1990), where the two figures refer to the subsidy on fertilizer used on cotton and other crops, respectively; Zambia—Kinsey (1991).

NOTE: Blank cells indicate no information is available.

banks were required to allocate a certain percentage of their loans to agriculture, and in many countries specialized banks for agriculture were established. Interest rates were negative in real terms, and loan repayment was facilitated by the legal monopsony of state marketing boards. For example, the newly independent government in Zimbabwe increased the number of loans to smallholders fourfold between 1980 and 1985 (Eicher and Kupfuma 1997). In Malawi, the Smallholder Agricultural Credit Administration provided credit through credit clubs, with the number of recipients rising from 150,000 to 300,000 over the 1980s (Kinsey 1991). In Tanzania and Zambia, credit was channeled through the state-supported cooperative system (Kinsey 1991; Howard and Mungoma 1997). In Senegal, the Programme Agricole provided groundnut seeds and fertilizer on credit to all growers in the 1960s and 1970s (Kelly et al. 1996). In many of the Francophone West African countries, the cotton parastatals have long provided inputs on credit to cotton farmers. In spite of the efforts to target loans to smallholders, much of the credit tended to go to estates, large farmers, and commercial cash crop growers; only a minority of small farmers obtained credit.[3]

Fourth, a large portion of fertilizer imports was in the form of aid-in-kind provided by donor agencies. According to Bumb (1990), in more than 20 African countries all fertilizer imports were in the form of aid-in-kind in the 1980s. The problems associated with fertilizer aid are (1) annual fluctuations depending on donor funding and priorities, (2) limited selection of fertilizer types, and (3) disruption of private fertilizer markets from occasional inflows of concessionary fertilizer (see Bumb 1990; Townsend 1999).

Fifth, the incentives for fertilizer use were strongly affected by exchange rate policy and trade restrictions. In the 1970s, the oil price shock and deficit spending caused the fixed exchange rates to diverge from market rates. By the early 1980s, the degree of overvaluation was extreme in a number of countries. According to one review, the parallel exchange rate premium[4] in 1981–86 was over 40 percent in 14 of the 17 countries examined. Furthermore, the premium was over 100 percent in seven countries: Mozambique, Ghana, Guinea, Tanzania, Nigeria, Uganda, and Mauritania (World Bank 1994:228). Overvalued exchange rates provided an implicit subsidy to imports, leading to excess demand and the need to ration foreign exchange. In the process of allocating foreign exchange among competing needs, priority was generally given to machinery, fertilizer, fuel, and raw materials.

---

3. For example, at its peak, Zimbabwe's Agricultural Finance Corporation made loans to 77,000 smallholders in 1985—86, or fewer than 10 percent of small farmers in the country (Eicher and Kupfuma 1997). Similarly, even the relatively successful Smallholder Agricultural Credit Administration in Malawi reached fewer than a quarter of small farmers (Kinsey 1991).

4. The parallel exchange rate premium is the percentage gap between the parallel market exchange rate and the official exchange rate. A higher premium indicates a greater degree of overvaluation.

Although these five characteristics describe the general tendencies in African fertilizer policy, there was considerable diversity across countries. Fertilizer subsidies and state intervention were modest in Kenya and Zimbabwe (although they restricted imports and imposed price controls), but quite heavy in Tanzania, Zambia, and Nigeria. Exchange rate distortions were minor in Francophone West Africa owing to the low inflation maintained under the Communauté Financière Africaine (CFA), but extreme in Ghana, Uganda, and Tanzania. Furthermore, most countries went through a series of policy regimes, giving responsibility for fertilizer distribution to different state enterprises and changing the subsidy rate on an annual basis (see Table 3.5).

The motives for these policies also varied. The preference for administrative allocation of fertilizer (and other commodities) reflected a general suspicion of markets and traders, combined with what, in retrospect, seems to have been excessive optimism about the ability of the state to manage commercial activities efficiently. It was often assumed that efficiency could be assured only with large-scale "modern" transport, processing, and storage operations, and that only the state could mobilize resources for such operations. In large measure, these beliefs reflected prevailing currents of thought in the industrialized countries. Second, the distribution of fertilizer by a crop marketing parastatal with monopsony power facilitated the recovery of input credit (Poulton et al. 1998). Third, the availability of donor funding for activities organized by the state or by state enterprises contributed to the expansion of public sector commercial activities. Fourth, the establishment of state enterprises created opportunities for patronage, in which government officials could offer employment to friends, family, and supporters.

Similarly, various explanations for fertilizer subsidies have been advanced (see Fontaine 1991). In many cases, the subsidies were introduced as a way to protect farmers (and indirectly urban consumers) from the fertilizer price increases associated with the oil price shock of 1973–74. In addition, these subsidies were seen as a way to offset the impact of high rates of taxation of agricultural (particularly export crop) production. Economic arguments for subsidies focused on the observation that farmers might apply less than the optimal amounts if they were (1) uninformed about the returns to fertilizer use, (2) risk averse, or (3) cash constrained owing to imperfect credit markets. From a political economy perspective, Bates (1981) argues that the rationing of subsidized inputs allowed government officials to reward political loyalty and/or gain financially from the distribution of scarce resources.

Fertilizer Market Reform

In the 1980s and early 1990s, many African governments adopted more market-oriented policies. Although this shift in policy is often attributed to pressure from the World Bank, the International Monetary Fund, and other international organizations, a more fundamental cause was severe macroeconomic

TABLE 3.5 Summary of policy changes affecting fertilizer markets

Benin	Cameroon	Ethiopia	Ghana	Kenya	Malawi
1960s: Compagnie Française pour le Développement du Textile (CFDT) organizes cotton channel, including input delivery, credit, and marketing; another state enterprise serves other farmers	1960s: fertilizer distribution managed by cotton parastatal in the north, by Ministry of Agriculture and coffee cooperatives in the south	1974: revolution introduces socialist central planning	1960s: Ministry of Agriculture (MoA) organizes importation of fertilizer, distribution by regional MoA offices and state-owned Farmer Services Companies	1961–63: fertilizer subsidies first introduced	1970s: Agricultural Development and Marketing Corporation (ADMARC) distributes fertilizer at subsidized pan-territorial prices and purchases grain at fixed prices
1971: two operations unified under the state-owned Société Nationale de Coton	Late 1970s and early 1980s: fertilizer subsidies of 40–65 percent	1976: Agricultural Marketing Corporation (AMC) created; agricultural price controls; AMC imposes production quotas on farmers; private grain movement illegal	1970s: fertilizer subsidies range from 50 to 86 percent	Mid-1970s: fertilizer subsidies phased out, but price controls continue to hold price below market levels	1981: first structural adjustment program
1970s: fertilizer subsidies reach 75 percent	1987: fertilizer reform program initiated to phase out subsidies and liberalize market in seven southern provinces; cotton parastatal continues to control fertilizer distribution in north	1983–85 drought and policy contribute to famine	1981–82: macroeconomic instability including inflation over 100 percent and extreme overvaluation	1983: fertilizer market reform program to liberalize fertilizer imports and set realistic margins	1983: responsibility for fertilizer distribution given to Smallholder Fertilizer Revolving Fund
1982: Société Nationale pour la Promotion Agricole (SONAPRA) formed, has		1988: partial liberalization of grain movement	1983: first structural adjustment pro-	1990: fertilizer prices decontrolled	1985: start of three-year donor-supported program to phase out fertilizer subsidies
		1990: restrictions on grain movement		1993: import restrictions and foreign exchange rationing eliminated	

monopoly on cotton marketing, ginning, and export	1994: fertilizer subsidy eliminated in seven southern provinces	and AMC crop quotas eliminated	gram; depreciation of the real exchange rate over rest of decade	1994–98: growth in number of importers and distributors; greater availability of fertilizer	1986: deteriorating economic situation; government abandons subsidy reform; subsidies stay at 25–30 percent
1983: fertilizer subsidies at 47 percent	1994: 50 percent devaluation of the CFA franc	1992: end of parastatal monopoly on fertilizer distribution	1984: subsidy eliminated for one year		1991 Norsk-Hydro starts to distribute fertilizer
1988: fertilizer subsidies eliminated		1993: Sasakawa Global 2000 (SG 2000) project begins input/credit scheme	1985: subsidy reintroduced through failure to adjust nominal price		1993–95: new program to reform fertilizer markets; subsidies phased out
1992–97: liberalization of fertilizer imports, though market still dominated and regulated by SONAPRA		1994: New Agricultural Extension Program extends SG 2000 concept nationally, the National Extension Program is major buyer and distributor of fertilizer	1989: legalization of private retail trade in fertilizer		1995: fertilizer distribution deregulated; Drought Recovery Inputs Program
1994: 50 percent devaluation of the CFA franc			1990: legalization of private wholesale trade in fertilizer		1998: Starter Pack Initiative provides small quantities of seed and fertilizer to all farmers; ADMARC still main supplier
			1991: legalization of private fertilizer imports and elimination of fertilizer subsidy		

(continued)

TABLE 3.5 *Continued*

Mali	Nigeria	Tanzania	Zambia	Zimbabwe
1970s: fertilizer subsidies of 50 percent; fertilizer distributed through parastatal crop authorities: Compagnie Malienne pour le Développement du Textile (CMDT) for cotton and Office du Niger (ON) for rice	Early 1970s: each state has separate fertilizer subsidy and distribution system	1967: Arusha Declaration adopts socialist principles; Tanzania Fertilizer Company (TFC) created and given monopoly on fertilizer imports; TFC and Tanganyika Farmers' Association control fertilizer distribution; pan-territorial prices fixed	1970s: all fertilizer procured by National Maize Board (NAMBOARD); distributed directly to large farmers and through cooperatives to small farmers; pan-territorial prices; fertilizer subsidy 50–85 percent	1927: factory for phosphate fertilizer starts operations
Early 1980s: fertilizer subsidies reduced to 15–25 percent	1976: government creates department to centralize fertilizer procurement; plans uniform subsidy of 75 percent; actual subsidy 80–85 percent; fiscal cost over US$150 million	1970s: fertilizer subsidy 60–75 percent; cost is US$5–15 million per year	1980s: consumer subsidies on maize meal increase demand for maize; cost over US$20 million per year	1969: factory for nitrogenous fertilizer starts operations
1987: fertilizer subsidy eliminated	1982: fall in oil prices starts cumulative macroeconomic instability	Early 1980s: economic crisis with inflation, shortages, and macroeconomic imbalances	1986–90: attempts to reduce maize subsidy result in riots and reversals	1970s: fertilizer produced by two state enterprises; imports highly restricted, fertilizer distributed by a cooperative and a state enterprise; most fertilizer goes to large-scale commercial farmers
1994: 50 percent devaluation of the CFA franc	1982–86: under pressure from donors and fall in oil prices, fertilizer subsidy reduced from 85 to 28 percent; even so, cost of subsidy reaches US$240 million	1986: first donor-assisted economic reform program initiated	1989: NAMBOARD disbanded; private traders enter fertilizer marketing	1975: direct fertilizer subsidies discontinued
				1980–86: government policy to assist black smallholders increases credit, extension, and input delivery to this

1986: structural adjustment program launched; factory for nitrogenous fertilizer begins production

1986–89: nominal price fixed in spite of inflation; subsidy rises to 80 percent

1990: structural adjustment program abandoned

1994: economic reforms reinitiated; fertilizer subsidies reduced; devaluation

1997: fertilizer subsidy removed; distribution liberalized

1999: 25 percent subsidy reintroduced

1986–89: food markets liberalized and movement controls eliminated

1990–94: fertilizer subsidy reduced from 70 percent to zero

1993–94: private importers allowed access to subsidy; massive over-imports

1996: fertilizer markets stabilize

1991–92: reforms delayed by drought

1993–95: pan-territorial prices and subsidies on maize and fertilizer eliminated

1995: Food Reserve Agency (FRA) created to manage strategic reserves of maize

1998: FRA gets involved in distribution of fertilizer

group; maize output doubles

1991: Economic Structural Adjustment Programme launched

1993: maize meal subsidy removed; foreign exchange market eases imports

1993–95: fertilizer price controls lifted

1998: 10 private distributors, but distribution market dominated by Zimbabwe Fertilizer Company and Windmill (a cooperative)

imbalance, mainly balance-of-payments pressures. This imbalance was in turn due to the policies of fixed exchange rates combined with rising inflation, itself a consequence of monetized fiscal deficits. Declining terms of trade exacerbated these trends in some countries, Zambia and Cameroon being notable examples.

In the case of fertilizer, market reform was also catalyzed by a number of sector-specific problems.

1. The fiscal cost of the subsidy was often in the range of tens of millions of dollars. In Nigeria, the cost rose to US$240 million in 1985, representing almost 32 percent of agricultural spending and 4 percent of the federal budget (Lele, Christiansen, and Kadiresan 1989). Although tolerable during the commodity boom of the 1970s, these costs became increasingly difficult to support in the 1980s.
2. Problems of late and insufficient delivery of fertilizer were chronic. The process of estimating demand, applying for foreign exchange allocations, procuring the fertilizer, and distributing it to farmers involved a long series of bureaucratic steps, delays in any one of which would result in late delivery of fertilizer. The combination of exaggerated demand owing to the subsidized price and of fiscal constraints meant that fertilizer delivery was often less than farmers wanted.
3. The argument that fertilizer subsidies assisted the poor was contradicted by studies showing that fertilizer use was concentrated among larger and better-endowed farmers. Although adoption and application rates are not consistently higher on large farms, large farms tend to use a disproportionate share of fertilizer and thus capture a disproportionate share of the subsidy.
4. Finally, the argument that fertilizer subsidies were useful in compensating farmers for the heavy taxation of export crops and for price controls on food lost its relevance as export and food markets were liberalized.

During this period, four types of policy change affected fertilizer markets in Africa. First, the subsidies on fertilizer were phased out, often over a period of three to five years. This was accompanied by removal of price controls on fertilizer. By 1992, subsidies had been removed in 17 of 27 countries surveyed (World Bank 1994), and three more countries (Malawi, Tanzania, and Cameroon) were in the process of phasing out fertilizer subsidies.

Second, the importation and distribution of fertilizer, previously monopolized by the state, were opened up to private companies. Generally, domestic distribution of fertilizer was liberalized before fertilizer imports. In 1992, 23 of 27 African countries surveyed had liberalized fertilizer marketing to some degree (World Bank 1994).

Third, many countries restructured their financial system to restore viability and give it greater market orientation. Faced with high costs and mounting debts, governments tightened the terms of agricultural credit, relaxed the regulations regarding sectoral allocation of credit, raised interest rates to make them positive in real terms, and reduced or eliminated financial support to unviable cooperatives and financial institutions. In Zimbabwe, the terms for agricultural credit were tightened in the late 1980s in the face of declining repayment rates (Eicher and Kupfuma 1997). In Senegal, the problem of loan repayment grew during the 1970s as a result of poor harvests, politicization of cooperative management, and disputes over the size of debts, which led to the closure of the parastatal in charge of credit, input delivery, and groundnut marketing in 1980 (Kelly et al. 1996). In Tanzania, the Cooperative Rural Development Bank (CRDB) saw repayment rates fall from 70–80 percent in the early 1970s to just 10 percent in the late 1980s, leading to severe financial problems for the CRDB and the cooperatives (Sijm 1997). In Malawi, the Smallholder Agricultural Credit Administration collapsed owing to financial problems linked to low repayment rates in the 1990s. And in Benin the Caisse Nationale de Crédit Agricole (CNCA) collapsed in 1988, following the politicization of lending practices and falling repayment rates. The system of agricultural credit was then restructured and there was rapid growth in depositors and lending in the 1990s (Soulé 1999). In most cases, the collapse of the credit system predated market reform, but, by introducing competition in crop purchasing, the reforms made it more difficult for crop buyers to recover input credit, thus preventing the re-establishment of a credit system on the same scale as before.

Fourth, the incentives to use fertilizer were strongly affected by the real depreciation of the exchange rate, a key component of most reform programs. During the initial phases of adjustment, this usually involved a series of devaluations to stimulate the production of exports and import substitutes. As the fixed exchange rate approached the market rate, many African countries allowed the exchange rate to float, subject to some restrictions. Over the 1980s, 21 of 26 African countries surveyed depreciated their real exchange rate. In some countries—Uganda, Nigeria, Ghana, Zambia, Tanzania, and Madagascar (World Bank 1994:229)—the real exchange rate[5] increased over 100 percent. In January 1994, the CFA franc was devalued by 50 percent, increasing the real exchange rate in 11 Francophone countries of West and Central Africa. As a result of these policy changes, by 1996–97 the parallel exchange rate premium was below 10 percent in all but a handful of African countries (Townsend 1999:175). By raising the cost of foreign exchange to its market value, these policies removed the implicit subsidy on imported goods, including fertilizer. At the same time, they eliminated the need for the government to ration foreign exchange and reduced the need for it to restrict imports.

---

5. The real exchange rate is defined here as the ratio of the price of tradable goods to the price of nontradable goods. Thus, an increase represents a depreciation of the real exchange rate.

Tables 3.4 and 3.5 summarize the reforms affecting the fertilizer sector in selected African countries. They illustrate wide variation in the timing and extent of these reforms. In the area of subsidies, for example, Kenya and Zimbabwe never had significant fertilizer subsidies, although they had price controls and import restrictions until the early 1990s.[6] Several Francophone West African countries phased out their subsidies in the 1980s, whereas in Tanzania, Malawi, and Nigeria subsidies continued into the 1990s.

Nor has market reform always been a continuous process. In some countries, early attempts to remove fertilizer subsidies were abandoned, only to be restarted and completed later. Nigeria, Malawi, and Ghana all had announced programs to phase out fertilizer subsidies in the mid-1980s. In Ghana, the subsidy was eliminated in 1984–85 but, in order to sell government stocks, the nominal price was fixed for 1986, thus reintroducing the subsidy. It was phased out again in the late 1980s (Jebuni and Seini 1992). In Malawi, the government launched a program to phase out subsidies over 1985–88, but abandoned the effort in the second year owing to poor rains, disruption of the transport routes through Mozambique, and a large devaluation (USAID 1990). Fertilizer subsidies were removed in 1995–96, but the new Starter Pack Initiative involves free distribution of small amounts of fertilizer and seed to smallholders. In Nigeria, the government reduced fertilizer subsidies from over 80 percent to about 30 percent in 1985, but, by failing to adjust the nominal price following a large devaluation, dramatically increased the subsidy the following year. The subsidy was removed in the mid-1990s, but reintroduced by the new government in 1999 (Idachaba 2000).

State enterprises have been marginalized in fertilizer distribution in a number of countries, such as Kenya, Tanzania, Ghana, and Uganda. However, state-owned enterprises continue to dominate fertilizer distribution in Francophone West Africa. In Mali, for example, two state enterprises account for 95 percent of fertilizer distribution (Egg 1999). In Benin, the cotton parastatal distributes 85 percent of the fertilizer. Although it contracts private companies to import and deliver fertilizer, it fixes pan-territorial prices based on the average bid (Soulé 1999). West African governments have been reluctant to liberalize cotton marketing, in part because of concerns about the ability of competitive cotton buyers to provide credit and ensure repayment. Experience in Ghana and Zimbabwe suggests that it is possible to provide input credit in a liberalized market, but it requires institutional mechanisms that allow buyers to share information on debts and repayment (Poulton 1998; Goodland and Gordon 1999).

State enterprises are involved in fertilizer distribution outside West Africa as well. In Malawi, the Agricultural Development and Marketing Corporation

---

6. Zimbabwe discontinued direct fertilizer subsidies in 1975, though locally produced fertilizer was cross-subsidized by taxes on imported fertilizer (Sakala 1990). In addition, subsidized credit to small farmers in the 1980s facilitated the growth in fertilizer use (Eicher and Kupfuma 1997).

(ADMARC) competes with private distributors, but a recent survey indicates that 61 percent of the fertilizer used by small farmers is purchased from ADMARC (Minot, Kherallah, and Berry 2000). Similarly, two state enterprises in Zimbabwe produce fertilizer and a third dominates fertilizer distribution, although private firms now compete in importing and distributing fertilizer (Gisselquist and Rusike 1998). In Zambia, private firms are involved in fertilizer distribution, but over half the fertilizer is supplied by the Food Reserve Agency at pan-territorial prices (Jayne et al. forthcoming).

In Ethiopia, although official fertilizer subsidies have been phased out and distribution has been liberalized, the regional governments still play a dominant role. First, the National Extension Program (NEP) provides inputs on credit at low interest rates to millions of small farmers, making NEP the largest buyer and distributor of fertilizer in the country. Second, a number of "private" companies with close affiliations with regional authorities tend to dominate distribution, sometimes on the basis of noncompetitive contract allocation (Stepanek, Jayne, and Kelly 1999a; Stepanek, Kelly, and Howard 1999b).

In summary, most African countries have eliminated universal fertilizer subsidies, liberalized fertilizer importation, and opened up fertilizer marketing to private firms. Nonetheless, the state continues to be involved in fertilizer markets in many countries. In some cases, particularly in Francophone West Africa, marketing parastatals are still the main suppliers of fertilizer. In others, fertilizer subsidies have been reintroduced through starter pack programs or subsidized credit programs. And in some cases, private firms operate under contract to state agencies under conditions that limit competition and create opportunities for rent-seeking. Thus, in spite of much progress, fertilizer markets are not fully competitive in many African countries.

The Impact of Reforms on Fertilizer Markets

In this section, we review the impact of fertilizer sector reforms on several aspects of fertilizer markets. In particular, we examine the emergence of private firms in the fertilizer market, evidence of cost reduction, and the impact of reform on prices.

Fertilizer Market Structure

Proponents of market liberalization argued that private firms would quickly enter the market and carry out more efficiently the distribution functions previously carried out by the government. Skeptics argued that the private sector in Africa was not sufficiently developed to undertake these functions or that oligopolistic behavior would emerge, preventing any benefits from accruing to farmers. The experience has been somewhat in between: private firms have emerged to take over these functions and there is evidence of cost savings in a number of countries. At the same time, private importers made costly mistakes, particularly in the first few years, and oligopolistic behavior has been an issue, partly owing to noncompetitive practices of the government.

In Benin, the cotton parastatal—Société Nationale pour la Promotion Agricole (SONAPRA)—began to withdraw from input delivery in 1992–93 by contracting private firms to import and distribute fertilizer and insecticide. By 1997–98, nine private firms imported and distributed all of the fertilizer and insecticides for cotton farmers.[7] In spite of this apparent liberalization, SONAPRA maintains control over the entire process by virtue of its position as the dominant buyer. Bidaux, Raymond, and Soulé (1997) criticize the lack of price competition, the insecure position of the distributors, and the lack of responsiveness to farmer demand.

In Tanzania, private companies were initially reluctant to import and distribute fertilizer because they had to compete with the Tanzania Fertilizer Company, whose operations were subsidized. In 1993–94, private importers were made eligible for the subsidy, resulting in the entry of eight companies, some with little or no experience in the market and few facilities. They imported two years' worth of fertilizer, resulting in large unsold stocks and several bankruptcies. The elimination of the subsidy by 1995 and the unsold stocks depressed activity for several years, but since then the market has stabilized and the number of importers has risen to 10 (MAC 1997).

The fertilizer reforms in Cameroon involved introducing competition among fertilizer importers and allowing private distributors. In the first few years of liberalization, there were just three or four importers but they competed with a dozen firms for contracts. Furthermore, they were a completely different set of companies from those that imported under the old administered system. The number of distributors increased from 4 to over 20 in the first five years of the program. Walker (1994) notes that they sought various ways of reducing costs, including local bagging of bulk fertilizer, shipping in larger lots, and seeking new lower-cost suppliers. A farm survey found that small farmers and farmers in the highlands (where most of the fertilizer is sold) were generally more satisfied with the new system, whereas larger farmers and those in the lowlands (where demand is lower) were less satisfied (Minot 1991).

Ethiopia liberalized fertilizer importation and distribution in the early 1990s. However, three-quarters of the fertilizer in Ethiopia is distributed through the New Extension Program, which provides millions of farmers with inputs on credit. Thus, regional governments are the main buyers. In some regions, contracts are allocated competitively, while in others the government appoints a single distributor, often a "private" company closely affiliated with government officials. Stepanek, Jayne, and Kelly (1999a) and Stepanek, Kelly, and Howard (1999b) report that in all regions there were examples of barriers

---

7. SONAPRA continues to import some inputs for research and to maintain a buffer stock in case of emergency.

to entry and changes in the rules of participation after firms had incurred major expenses.

In 1990, the Kenyan government decontrolled prices and deregulated fertilizer imports and distribution. Mose (1998) describes the vigorous response of the private sector, citing estimates that, as of 1996, there were 10–12 private importers, 500 distributors/wholesalers, and roughly 5,000 fertilizer retailers. Omamo and Mose (1998) argue that the emergence of specialized large-scale importer-distributors in urban areas as well as numerous small-scale retailers in rural centers has increased competition and reduced costs, with the cost savings being transmitted to farmers in the form of lower prices. At the same time, they find that commercial credit remains a constraint and that high-potential areas are much better served than the low-potential areas.

In Zimbabwe, price controls on fertilizer were eliminated between 1993 and 1995. Ten private firms have entered the fertilizer market, compared with just two in the 1980s. A large South African company began selling high-analysis composite fertilizer, prompting local companies to offer similar products. Many of the new firms sell specialized fertilizer products not previously available. The number of registered fertilizer products has increased from 18 in 1990 to over 275. Gisselquist (1998) reports that there is not yet evidence of greater competition or declining prices and that some regulations continue to hamper the market, including protectionist tariffs, import permits, and registration of fertilizer products.

Fertilizer Marketing Costs

Given that market liberalization often induces the entry of private importers and distributors, the next question is whether this is translated into lower marketing costs. Indeed, one of the main arguments against the state monopoly in fertilizer distribution was that it was costly and inefficient. Surprisingly, only a few studies have looked at this issue.

In Cameroon, the fertilizer subsidy was cut from 66 percent in 1987–88 to 10 percent in 1992–93. If costs had remained unchanged, the retail price of fertilizer would have increased 165 percent.[8] In fact, the retail price of fertilizer increased just 42 percent over this period. In the first two years of the program, the c.i.f. cost of fertilizer fell 40 percent, while the cost of distribution fell 31 percent. The fall in the c.i.f. cost was attributed to the identification of lower-cost suppliers, economies of scale from larger shipments, and reduced profit margins (Walker 1994:52, 54, 68).

In Benin, the cotton parastatal now contracts private firms to import and distribute fertilizer rather than carrying out these functions itself. Although the private firms do not compete on the basis of price, even this limited liberalization has reduced fertilizer marketing margins: fertilizer prices are now about 25

---

8. This is calculated as $(1.0–0.10)/(1.0–0.66) = 2.65$, or a 165 percent increase.

percent above the c.i.f. price compared with 40–50 percent above before the reforms (Bidaux, Raymond, and Soulé 1997:20).

Fertilizer markets in Ethiopia vary in the level of competition across regions. Stepanek, Jayne, and Kelly (1999a) and Stepanek, Kelly, and Howard (1999b) find that fertilizer prices are higher in regions with a government-appointed supplier than in regions that use a competitive tender system to buy fertilizer for the National Extension Program.

In addition, it is worth noting that fertilizer market liberalization has often led to a dramatically reduced market share for the state enterprise(s) that previously controlled the fertilizer market. The Kenya Farmers Association, a state-supported enterprise that dominated fertilizer marketing in the 1980s, was displaced by private importers and distributors in most parts of the country after liberalization in 1990 (Omamo and Mose 2001). Similarly, the Tanzania Fertilizer Company (TFC) had a virtual monopoly on fertilizer imports until the 1992–93 season when competition was first introduced. Within four years, the entry of private importers and distributors reduced the TFC market share to just 14 percent (MAC 1997). Although the evidence is circumstantial, it strongly suggests that the private firms that entered the fertilizer market had lower costs than the state enterprise(s) they were displacing.

Fertilizer Prices

How did the economic reforms of the 1980s and 1990s affect the incentives to use fertilizer? We focus on the ratio of the price of fertilizer to the price of the crops being fertilized. This ratio has the advantage of adjusting for inflation and taking into account the impact of economic reforms on crop prices. In addition, simple models of farmer behavior indicate that the optimal rate of fertilizer application depends on this price ratio.

We have argued that fertilizer market liberalization tends to reduce costs, but this is offset by the removal of fertilizer subsidies and exchange rate reforms. In the simplest case, removing a 50 percent subsidy should cause the retail price to double. In practice, the price may rise by less than this amount for two reasons:

1. The pre-reform policies often resulted in fertilizer shortages, which gave rise to parallel markets in which fertilizer sold at a price above the official price (see Smith et al. 1997). If the data reflect these parallel market prices, then eliminating the subsidy and liberalizing the market will cause the price to rise by less than the expected amount.
2. Opening fertilizer importation and distribution to private companies (or to a wider range of private companies) may increase competition and efficiency, thus reducing the cost of fertilizer delivery. The extent of cost savings depends on the degree of inefficiency in the state-managed distribution system that existed before the reforms and on the degree of competition achieved after the reforms.

The effect of real exchange rate depreciation on the fertilizer-to-crop price ratio depends largely on whether the crop is tradable[9] or not. Real depreciation causes an increase in the price of imported fertilizer, but it causes a similar increase in the price of tradable crops. Thus, the fertilizer-to-crop price ratio (at the border) should remain roughly unchanged for export crops such as coffee, tea, cotton, and cocoa, as well as for import substitutes such as rice and wheat. If the price ratio remains the same, the optimal rate of fertilizer application for tradable crops is unaffected. However, to the extent that depreciation increases the real price of the tradable crops and results in more land being allocated to them, the total volume of fertilizer used on tradable crops would increase even without a change in application rates.

The above analysis ignores the effect of marketing margins, which often represent 50–90 percent of the c.i.f. value of fertilizer and sometimes exceed the c.i.f. value (see FAO 1986:39; Lele, Christiansen, and Kadiresan 1989). If marketing costs are fixed and tradable, which is plausible given that vehicles and fuel are tradable goods, then the conclusion remains unchanged: depreciation will have no effect on the fertilizer-to-crop price ratios for tradable crops. But if part of the marketing costs (such as wages) are nontradable, then the ratio may increase or decrease. As a rule, if marketing costs are significant and at least partly nontradable, devaluation will cause the fertilizer-to-crop price ratio for export crops to *fall* somewhat.[10] In the case of import substitutes, assuming that fertilizer is more expensive than the crop and that the marketing margins are the same for both, devaluation will cause the fertilizer-to-crop price ratio to *rise* somewhat.[11]

With regard to nontradable crops, we expect the fertilizer-to-crop price ratio to rise following real depreciation since, by definition, depreciation increases the price of tradables (including fertilizer) relative to nontradables. Nontradable crops such as sorghum, millet, cassava, yams, and sweet potatoes are not likely to be affected by this shift in relative fertilizer prices because they are generally not fertilized. Maize, on the other hand, receives more fertilizer

---

9. Tradable goods are goods whose prices are determined largely by world prices because they are imported or exported or they are close substitutes for traded goods. Export crops, manufactured goods, and fuel are generally considered tradables. Nontradable goods are those whose prices are determined by domestic supply and demand because there is no international trade. Services, building materials, and staple food crops are often nontradable.

10. For example, assume that the f.o.b. price of an export crop is US$300, the c.i.f. price of urea is US$150, and the marketing costs for both are nontradable at 1,000 local currency units (LCUs) per dollar, and the exchange rate is 10 LCU/US dollar. Then a devaluation that raises the exchange rate to 20 LCU/dollar reduces the urea crop farm-gate price ratio from $(1,500 + 1,000) / (3,000 - 1,000) = 1.25$ to $(3,000 + 1,000) / (6,000 - 1,000) = 0.80$.

11. For example, assume the c.i.f. price of an importable is US$90, the c.i.f. value of urea is US$150, and the marketing costs for both are nontradable at 1,000 local currency units (LCUs). Then a devaluation that raises the exchange rate to 20 LCU/dollar increases the urea crop farm-gate price ratio from $(1,500 + 1,000) / (900 + 1,000) = 1.32$ to $(3,000 + 1,000) / (1,800 + 1,000) = 1.43$.

than any other crop in Africa (Heisey and Mwangi 1997). Thus, we expect the real depreciation of exchange rates in Africa to have the greatest effect on the fertilization of maize.

Table 3.6 summarizes the changes in fertilizer-to-crop price ratios in 10 African countries since the early 1980s.[12] Whenever possible, we use the period 1981–84 to represent "before" the reforms and 1994–96 to represent "after." It should be recognized, however, that the nature and extent of reforms varied across countries, as described above. The price ratio has more than doubled in 4 of the 10 countries (Benin, Ghana, Nigeria, and Tanzania) and increased by at least 50 percent in three more (Zambia, Malawi, and Senegal). On the other hand, the price ratio fell in Ethiopia, Kenya, and Zimbabwe.

The Impact of Reforms on Fertilizer Use

Background

Fertilizer use in Sub-Saharan Africa rose significantly from 432,000 tons of nutrients in 1970 to 1.34 million tons in 1993 (see Figure 3.3). This represents an annual growth rate of 5.0 percent, indicating that fertilizer use increased in per capita terms. Fertilizer use continued to grow through the 1970s, in spite of the fourfold spike in world fertilizer prices associated with the oil price shock of 1974 and smaller price increases resulting from the 1979–80 oil price shock. This is an indication of the degree to which farm-level fertilizer prices were insulated from world prices by subsidies and price controls. The slow growth in fertilizer use stopped in 1993, and fertilizer use dropped 20 percent between 1993 and 1995 before rebounding to 1.30 million tons in 1996. The data for 1996–99 seem to indicate a resumption of slow growth. Fertilizer application rates, expressed as kilograms of nutrients per hectare of arable land, follow a similar trend (see Figure 3.3). These rates have risen from an average of 5.3 kilograms/hectare in the 1970s to 8.7 kilograms/hectare in the 1980s and 9.2 kilograms/hectare in the 1990s.

If we look at the country composition of African fertilizer demand, it becomes apparent that the drop in Nigeria fertilizer use alone is sufficient to explain the decline in fertilizer consumption in 1994 and 1995 (see Figure 3.4).[13] In 1992 and 1993, Nigeria used roughly 450,000 tons of nutrient, accounting for over one-third of the total for Sub-Saharan Africa. By 1995, Nigeria's fertilizer demand had fallen to 183,000 tons. The reasons for this decline are discussed below.

---

12. We tried to use the crop that is most fertilized in each country, but this was not possible owing to data limitations. In Ethiopia, for example, *teff* is the most widely fertilized crop but price data are scarce. Similarly, cotton receives most of the fertilizer in Mali.

13. Fertilizer use declined in some countries other than Nigeria, but these decreases were offset by increases in other countries.

TABLE 3.6 Changes in fertilizer prices from the early 1980s to the mid-1990s

| Country | Type of price | Relative price of fertilizer | | |
		Early 1980s	Mid-1990s	Percentage change
Benin	NPKSB/cotton	0.6	1.2	102
	NPKSB/maize	0.9	1.8	113
Ethiopia	Nitrogen/maize	6.4	1.9	−70
Ghana	Nitrogen/maize	2.2	10.2	364
	AS/maize	0.1	0.7	689
Kenya	Urea/maize	6.6	4.8	−27
Malawi	Nitrogen/maize	10.7	7.7	−28
	AS/maize	2.1	3.5	63
	Urea/maize	2.3	2.9	27
Mali	Urea/paddy	1.8	2.1	18
Nigeria	Nitrogen/maize	2.0	7.0	250
Senegal	Nutrient/groundnuts	0.6	1.0	80
Tanzania	Nitrogen/maize	1.6	3.6	125
	Nitrogen/maize	2.6	7.0	169
Zambia	Nitrogen/maize	3.3	5.4	64
Zimbabwe	Urea/maize	5.5	4.8	−13

SOURCES: Benin—NPKSB/cotton prices (1981–85 and 1994–96) from Bidaux, Raymond, and Soulé (1997), NPKSB/maize 1984–85 prices from World Bank (1999), 1994–96 prices from Office National d'Appui à la Sécurité Alimentaire (Benin), fertilizer prices from Bidaux, Raymond, and Soulé (1997); Ethiopia—prices (1983 and 1992) from Heisey and Mwangi (1997); Ghana—price ratios (1982–87 and 1991–94) from Heisey and Mwangi (1997), prices (1981–85 and 1990) from Sijm (1997:628); Kenya—prices (1980 and 1993) from Yanggen et al. (1998); Malawi—nitrogen/maize ratios (1977–87 and 1988–94) from Heisey and Mwangi (1997), AS price ratios (1981–85 and 1991–92) from Sijm (1997:629), urea prices (1988–89 and 1994–96) from Government of Malawi (1997); Mali—price ratios (1981–85 and 1989) from Sijm (1997:630); Nigeria—1985–92 and "post-subsidy" figures from Townsend (1999); Senegal—price ratios (1980–83 and 1993–94) from Kelly et al. (1996); Tanzania—price ratios (1980–85 and 1995) from Heisey and Mwangi (1997), 1981–85 prices from Turuka (1995), 1995–96 prices from MAC (1997); Zambia—price ratios (1971–89 and 1990–94) from Heisey and Mwangi (1997); Zimbabwe—prices (1980 and 1993) from Yanggen et al. (1998).

NOTE: In some countries, the price ratio does not correspond to the most widely used type of fertilizer, but lack of data prevents the use of a more appropriate price ratio.

Changes in Fertilizer Use since the Early 1980s

We can study the impact of fertilizer market reform in a crude way by examining country-level patterns in fertilizer use before and after the reforms. The period 1981–85 is used to describe the situation "before" reform. Although several countries launched structural adjustment programs in the early 1980s, few had begun to substantially liberalize fertilizer markets during that period. The

FIGURE 3.3 Trends in fertilizer use and application rates, 1970–99

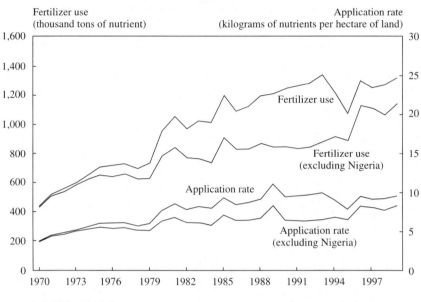

SOURCE: FAOStat database.

FIGURE 3.4 Trends in fertilizer use by country, 1970–99

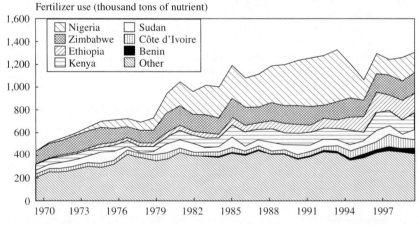

SOURCE: FAOStat database.

period 1994–96 is considered "after" the reforms.[14] Table 3.7 shows the average annual use of fertilizer in the two periods and the growth rates, presented in order of the volume used in the latter period. Several points can be made about these data.

First, it is clear that the impact of reforms has varied widely from country to country. Fertilizer use has increased 22 percent annually in Uganda, which restored peace and carried out a successful reform program between the two periods. Fertilizer use has fallen at a similar rate in Rwanda and Somalia, which suffered from war and political chaos in the mid-1990s.[15] These three countries are very minor users of fertilizer, however, using less than 3,000 tons of nutrient each in both periods.

If we focus on countries that currently use more than 10,000 tons of nutrient per year, fertilizer use increased in 14 of the 21. The annual growth rate was at least 3 percent in Benin, Ethiopia, Togo, Burkina Faso, Côte d'Ivoire, and Mali. Fertilizer use grew 2–3 percent per year in Kenya and the Democratic Republic of the Congo, and 1–2 percent per year in Mauritius, Madagascar, and Tanzania. Growth was positive but small (0–1 percent per year) in Zimbabwe, the Sudan, and Réunion.

In the case of Ethiopia, the base period (1981–85) was a time when the government forced farmers to supply an annual quota at below-market prices to the Agricultural Marketing Corporation and tightly restricted grain movement. These repressive and extractive policies, combined with bad weather, led to a major famine in 1983–85. Furthermore, current policy involves the provision of inputs on credit to millions of farmers. Thus, it is not surprising that the reforms, most of which have been implemented since 1990, have stimulated fertilizer demand.

The other five countries with growth rates of at least 3 percent per year have some common features:

1. A significant share of the fertilizer is used on cotton production. Cotton is by far the most important crop being fertilized in Benin, Togo, Mali, and Burkina Faso. In Benin, for example, 62 percent of the fertilizer is used in cotton production (Minot, Kherallah, and Berry 2000). In Côte d'Ivoire, coffee and cocoa are more important in terms of export revenue, but as of the late 1980s the cotton parastatal accounted for 80 percent of the demand for domestic fertilizer (Koffi 1990:29).

---

14. One advantage of using the same periods for all countries is that this controls for variation in international fertilizer prices. We use three-year averages to reduce the influence of "exceptional" years, such as drought years.

15. Table 3.7 does not include four countries that used no fertilizer in the latter period (Liberia, the Seychelles, Djibouti, and Cape Verde). Liberia used 2,300 tons in the earlier period, and the other three countries used less than 500 tons.

TABLE 3.7 Changes in fertilizer use between 1981–85 and 1994–96

Country	Annual fertilizer use (thousand tons of nutrient)		Percentage change	Annual percentage change
	1981–85	1994–96		
Nigeria	250	205	−18	−1.6
Zimbabwe	159	164	3	0.2
Ethiopia (including Eritrea)	46	142	209	9.9
Kenya	85	111	30	2.2
Sudan	66	67	2	0.2
Côte d'Ivoire	41	66	63	4.2
Zambia	75	50	−32	−3.2
Tanzania	30	35	16	1.2
Malawi	38	34	−10	−0.8
Mauritius	26	32	22	1.7
Cameroon	45	31	−30	−2.9
Benin	6	31	407	14.5
Mali	20	29	42	3.0
Burkina Faso	11	24	107	6.3
Senegal	22	17	−21	−2.0
Togo	5	15	204	9.7
Réunion	14	15	7	0.6
Ghana	20	12	−37	−3.8
Madagascar	11	12	17	1.3
Democratic Republic of Congo	9	11	27	2.0
Angola	11	10	−6	-0.5
Níger	3	9	181	9.0
Mozambique	21	9	−57	−6.7
Chad	6	9	45	3.2
Swaziland	13	8	−36	−3.6
Lesotho	4	7	54	3.7
Burundi	2	5	152	8.0
Mauritania	1	4	601	17.6
Sierra Leone	2	3	54	3.6
Uganda	0	3	1,015	22.3
Guinea	0	3	515	16.3
Republic of Congo	2	2	0	0.0
Botswana	1	2	80	5.0
Guinea-Bissau	1	1	124	7.0
Central African Republic	1	1	−8	−0.7
Gambia	2	1	−65	−8.4

(continued)

TABLE 3.7 *Continued*

Country	Annual fertilizer use (thousand tons of nutrient)		Percentage change	Annual percentage change
	1981–85	1994–96		
Gabon	2	0	−79	−12.4
Somalia	2	0	−93	−20.1
Comoros	0	0	. . .	. . .
Rwanda	1	0	−97	−24.7
Total	1,055	1,180	12	0.9
Total excluding Nigeria	805	975	21	1.6
CFA countries	123	168	36	2.6

SOURCE: FAOStat database.

2. All five countries are in the CFA franc zone, so all were affected by the 1994 devaluation of the CFA franc. As discussed above, the devaluation roughly doubled the prices of both fertilizer and cotton, so the "optimal" application rate was little affected. But the higher cotton prices have stimulated production, thus increasing fertilizer demand.
3. The cotton sector in these countries is managed by state-owned enterprises (SOEs). These SOEs pay pan-territorial, pan-seasonal prices that are announced before planting and they maintain a monopsony on cotton marketing. More importantly from the point of view of fertilizer use, the monopsony allows them to provide inputs on credit and to be assured of loan recovery at harvest.

In the case of Benin, the growth in fertilizer use may well be overestimated because of the 1994–95 elimination of fertilizer subsidies in neighboring Nigeria. By reducing informal (and unrecorded) imports from Nigeria, Benin was forced to expand formal (and recorded) imports. According to FAO statistics, fertilizer use in Benin almost doubled between 1993 and 1995, whereas cotton production expanded 25 percent over the same period. Similarly, fertilizer use in Niger jumped from less than 2,000 tons to 10,000 tons between 1993 and 1995. Since the main staples in Niger are millet and sorghum, which are rarely fertilized, and the main agricultural export is livestock, there is no obvious reason for the dramatic increase in fertilizer use.

Among the 21 largest fertilizer users in Africa, seven saw fertilizer use fall between 1981–85 and 1994–96. Ghana and Zambia experienced the greatest percentage reduction in fertilizer demand (3–4 percent per year). The fertilizer markets in these countries have two features in common. First, the majority of fertilizer is applied to maize. In Ghana, maize receives 64 percent of fertilizer use (Bumb et al. 1994), while in Zambia the figure is close to 90 percent (Muleya 1990:98). Second, both had highly overvalued exchange rates in the early 1980s, providing a large implicit subsidy on imported goods, such as fertilizer, that could count on foreign exchange allocations. As part of the reform process, between 1980 and 1990/91 the real exchange rate rose 471 percent in Ghana and 132 percent in Zambia (World Bank 1994).

There are some differences, however. In Zambia, there were several policy reversals in the 1980s, and most of the significant reforms in maize and fertilizer marketing occurred after 1990. The reduction in fertilizer use occurred in 1994–96. In Ghana, the reforms were applied more consistently and earlier, including elimination of fertilizer subsidies by 1990. Fertilizer demand fell from 20,000–30,000 tons of nutrient in the early 1980s to less than 10,000 tons in the mid and late 1980s. In the 1990s, fertilizer use rose, reaching 21,000 tons in 1997.

Although the proportional reduction in demand was greatest in Ghana and Zambia, the *absolute* reduction in fertilizer demand was greatest in Nigeria. Several policy changes and events contributed to this decline. In 1994–95, Nigeria eliminated the fertilizer subsidy system in response to repeated financial scandals in the system (Idachaba 2000).[16] In addition, after allowing the gradual liberalization of the exchange rate in the early 1990s, this policy was reversed in 1994. The exchange rate was revalued and pegged, causing the parallel exchange rate premium to rise to 100 percent by the end of 1994 (Moser, Rogers, and van Til 1997). Furthermore, a ban on rice imports was lifted in 1992, leading to over 1 million tons of rice imports in 1993, which depressed grain prices (FAOStat; Olayemi 1999). Finally, a banking crisis reached a point of "virtual collapse" in 1994, compounded by political disturbances following the annulment of the 1993 presidential elections and the return to military rule (Lewis and Stein 1997).

The other countries in which fertilizer demand was lower in the mid-1990s than in the first half of the 1980s are Cameroon, Senegal, Malawi, and Angola. In Cameroon, fertilizer demand fell from 50,000 tons in 1987 to 17,000 tons in 1990, the period over which most of the fertilizer subsidy was phased out. Exacerbating the effects of subsidy removal were adverse trends in producer prices for coffee (Walker 1994). Since 1990, fertilizer use has climbed back to 34,000 tons. The biggest jump occurred in 1994, when the devaluation of the CFA franc made cotton and coffee exports more profitable, stimulating fertilizer demand.

In Senegal, groundnuts were for many years the main crop being fertilized. Fertilizer demand peaked in the mid-1970s, but began to decline owing to the fiscal unsustainability of the system of taxing groundnut producers in order to subsidize inputs on credit and rice consumers. Input credit was discontinued in 1980, and subsidies were phased out over the 1980s. Fertilizer demand has

---

16. In 1999, the Obasanjo regime reintroduced a 25 percent fertilizer subsidy, reportedly to fulfill a campaign promise to farmers in the northern states (Idachaba 2000).

fluctuated significantly, though without a trend. The share of fertilizer used on groundnuts has fallen relative to that used on cotton (Kelly et al. 1996).

An important factor in how much fertilizer demand changed with the reforms is the proportion of fertilizer applied to tradable crops. As discussed earlier, both subsidy reduction and real depreciation reduce the demand for fertilizer for nontradable crops, but only the subsidy reduction will have an unambiguously negative impact on fertilization of cash crops. Figure 3.5 shows that, in countries devoting a larger share of fertilizer to cash crops, fertilizer use grew more rapidly through the reform period. This relationship is statistically significant, although the exclusion of numerous other variables that could intervene means that the results should be interpreted cautiously. There are, however, a number of outliers in this pattern. Ethiopia allocates a large share of fertilizer to food crops, primarily *teff,* wheat, and maize, yet it has seen fertilizer use rise significantly since the early 1980s. The reasons for this growth were discussed earlier. On the other hand, Cameroon allocates a relatively large share of fertilizer to cash crops (primarily cotton, coffee, and cocoa), yet fertilizer use has declined since the early 1980s.

FIGURE 3.5 Growth in fertilizer use as a function of share allocated to cash crops, 1981–85 to 1994–96

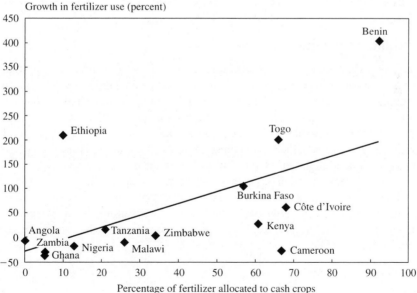

SOURCES: Tables 3.3 and 3.7.
NOTE: $p = .03$; $R^2 = .33$.

Changes in Fertilizer Use since the Early 1990s

It is worth asking whether the trends in fertilizer use over past decades are maintained when we look at the more recent past. We are interested for two reasons. First, the 50 percent devaluation of the CFA franc in 1994 provides an opportunity to study the impact of devaluation on fertilizer demand. Second, it is plausible that fertilizer market reform has an initial negative effect, but that the growth in fertilizer use resumes as the private sector enters the market and the new system stabilizes.

Table 3.8 examines the changes in fertilizer use between 1992–93 and 1995–96. The table reveals that overall fertilizer use in the CFA countries grew almost 35 percent over this three-year span, implying annual growth of over 10 percent. Senegal is the only country in which fertilizer use declined over this period. Thus, it appears that, in the CFA countries, the effect of higher fertilizer prices on fertilizer demand was more than offset by the incentives to expand production of exports—cotton in most cases. It should be noted, however, that the elimination of fertilizer subsidies in Nigeria probably affected formal (recorded) fertilizer demand by reducing (unrecorded) smuggling of fertilizer from Nigeria to neighboring countries, including Benin, Niger, and Cameroon.

For Sub-Saharan Africa as a whole, fertilizer use fell almost 19 percent over the three-year period. As discussed earlier, the drop in Nigerian fertilizer use is sufficient to explain the overall decline. Excluding Nigeria and the CFA countries, growth in fertilizer use has been quite modest: 2.2 percent over three years.

The Impact on Agricultural Production

The task of identifying the impact of fertilizer reforms on agricultural production is complicated by a number of intervening factors, particularly changes in weather, international prices, and other aspects of agricultural policy. In cases where fertilizer use and crop production move together, it is not always clear which is the causal factor. Fertilizer subsidy removal may have caused fertilizer use to fall, thus reducing output, or declining international prices may have caused a reduction in output and hence a fall in fertilizer use.

In this section, we draw on evidence from two approaches. The first is to estimate econometrically the impact of fertilizer prices or fertilizer use on crop production using time series data. The second is to examine the historical relationship between national fertilizer use and production of the crop receiving most of the fertilizer.

Econometric Studies

Econometric studies have been used to examine the impact of prices on input demand and output supply. When fertilizer prices are used in the estimation of output supply, the results can be used to simulate the impact of removing fer-

TABLE 3.8 Changes in fertilizer use in the countries of the Communauté Financière Africaine following the 1994 devaluation

Country	Annual fertilizer use (thousand tons of nutrient)		Percentage change	Annual growth (percent)
	1992–93	1995–96		
Côte d'Ivoire	55	67	22.4	7.0
Benin	16	36	118.0	29.7
Cameroon	21	32	53.7	15.4
Mali	24	30	26.8	8.2
Burkina Faso	21	24	14.3	4.6
Togo	11	17	54.1	15.5
Senegal	21	16	−26.2	−9.6
Níger	1	10	623.4	93.4
Chad	8	10	24.3	7.5
Republic of Congo	2	3	25.0	7.7
Central African Republic	1	1	4.3	1.4
CFA countries	189	255	34.9	10.5
Nigeria	502	159	−68.3	−31.8
Other countries	711	727	2.2	0.7
Sub-Saharan Africa	1,402	1,141	−18.6	−6.6

SOURCE: FAOStat database.

tilizer subsidies on agricultural output. The advantage of this approach is that it evaluates the effect of fertilizer prices on output, holding constant other factors such as crop prices and weather.

An early simulation study addressing the issue of fertilizer subsidies is Braverman and Hammer (1986). They construct a model of the Senegalese agricultural sector incorporating markets for five crops and fertilizer. The model was calibrated to represent the late 1970s when fertilizer subsidies were about 75 percent. According to simulations carried out with this model, removing fertilizer subsidies (increasing prices 300 percent) would cause groundnut and rice production to fall 4–5 percent and cotton production to fall 30 percent; millet output would fall 1 percent, and maize output would rise 1 percent. If fertilizer subsidy removal were combined with a doubling of cotton prices (to reach export parity), grain production falls 15–29 percent, cotton production rises 150 percent, and groundnut production is unchanged.

Chembezi (1990) estimates the supply of maize and tobacco and the demand for nitrogen using 22 years of data from Malawi. He concludes that a 10 percent increase in fertilizer price would in the long run reduce maize output by 5 percent and tobacco output by 3 percent.

Govindan and Babu (2001) use a similar approach and more recent data from Malawi to estimate the output supply for five crops and demand for fertilizer and labor. They conclude that removing the 25 percent fertilizer subsidy would reduce fertilizer demand by 7 percent and maize output by just 1 percent.

Delgado and Minot (2000) use panel data from 12 years and 20 regions in Tanzania to examine the determinants of maize supply. The explanatory variables included lagged real domestic crop prices, rainfall, and the real price of fertilizer. The effect of fertilizer price on maize supply was statistically insignificant. One possible explanation is that official fertilizer prices were not a good indicator of the true cost of obtaining fertilizer under the pre-reform system. Alternatively, fertilizer use may have been so low initially that lower use had a negligible impact on production.

Studies of the relationship between fertilizer prices and output have two limitations when used to assess the impact of reforms. First, in using the results it is necessary to assume that eliminating a 50 percent subsidy, for example, will double the retail price. This assumes away any cost savings associated with a more competitive fertilizer import and distribution system. Second, these studies generally do not attempt to capture the impact of reform on fertilizer availability, the timing of delivery, credit, and other factors that affect fertilizer demand and hence output.

Other econometric studies adopt a production function approach, in which agricultural output is estimated as a function of the quantities of various factors of production including labor, land, rainfall, and fertilizer. One such study used data on 150 farm households in the southern highlands of Tanzania over five years (Hawassi et al. 1998). The southern highlands are the main maize surplus zone, but incentives to use fertilizer on maize have been adversely affected by the elimination of the fertilizer subsidy and pan-territorial pricing, which had favored this remote region. During the study period, the fertilizer subsidy was reduced from 78 percent to zero. Based on an estimated production function, Hawassi et al. conclude that the elasticity of maize output with respect to fertilizer use is 0.21 in the intermediate zone and 0.38 in the wet highland zone. They also find that application rates on maize fell 20 percent over the five-year period. These results imply that the removal of the 78 percent fertilizer subsidy reduced maize output by 4–8 percent.[17]

Jayne et al. (1997b) estimate the value of agricultural output as a function of various factors of production using time series data from seven countries. In Kenya and Zambia, fertilizer use was a significant determinant of the value of agricultural output, although only in Kenya was it a significant determinant of

---

17. The authors argue that subsidy removal reduced maize output by roughly 15 percent based on the coefficient on a dummy representing the latter two years of the period. This is problematic, however, because (1) the coefficient is positive in both equations and (2) fertilizer application rates are already controlled.

the per hectare value of agricultural output. No significant relationship between fertilizer use and the value of output was found in the other five countries (Burkina Faso, Ethiopia, Mali, Senegal, and Zimbabwe).

Frisvold and Ingram (1995) examine the determinants of the value of output per hectare using panel data for 28 African countries. They find that the elasticity of output with respect to fertilizer use is just 0.02. Similar results are found by Thirtle, Hadley, and Townsend (1995). The point is not that fertilizers have no effect on production, but rather that the aggregate effect is rather small because application rates are so low, and other less quantifiable factors may have as much effect as the quantity of fertilizer used.

Historical Trends

In this section, we focus on the relationship between trends in the use of fertilizer in selected countries and the output of the main crop fertilized in that country. The advantage of this approach is that it captures the less quantifiable elements of fertilizer market reform such as cost reduction, improvement in timing, availability, and selection of fertilizer. The disadvantage, of course, is that it also "captures" a host of other unrelated influences such as population growth, weather, international prices, and agricultural reforms affecting commodity markets.

Table 3.9 shows the change in fertilizer use in 17 African countries between 1981–85 and 1994–96, as well as changes in the output of the crops accounting for the most fertilizer use.[18] As mentioned earlier, these two periods correspond roughly to before and after the reforms in fertilizer markets, although the nature and extent of the reforms vary widely across countries.

Of the 17 countries listed, fertilizer use grew in 11. In Benin and Burkina Faso, dramatic growth in fertilizer use (407 and 107 percent) was matched by equally dramatic expansion in the main fertilized crop, cotton. Production of the second crop (maize in Benin and rice in Burkina Faso) also grew substantially. Mali presents a similar story, with large increases in cotton and rice output. Ethiopia, Kenya, Madagascar, and Tanzania also show positive growth in fertilizer use and crop output, although the second crop in Kenya (coffee) declined.

In six countries, fertilizer use declined between the early 1980s and the mid-1990s. The drop was greatest in Ghana (37 percent), followed by Zambia, Cameroon, Senegal, Nigeria, and Malawi. Since about 64 percent of the fertilizer in Ghana is applied to maize, it is surprising to see that maize output rose 128 percent over the period and rice production 204 percent. Clearly, the negative effect of lower fertilizer use on crop production was overwhelmed by

---

18. The 17 countries are among the top 20 consumers of fertilizer in Sub-Saharan Africa. The other three countries were excluded for lack of information on fertilizer reforms (the Sudan and Réunion) or lack of information on the main crops being fertilized (the Democratic Republic of Congo).

TABLE 3.9 Changes in output of fertilized crops between 1981–85 and 1994–96

Country	Change in fertilizer use, 1981–85 to 1994–96 (percent)	Main crops fertilized	Annual crop production (thousand tons)		Percentage change
			Early 1980s	Mid-1990s	
Benin	407	Cotton	53	344	544
		Maize	331	541	63
Burkina Faso	107	Cotton	83	188	126
		Rice	44	80	82
Cameroon	−30	Cotton	87	193	122
		Coffee	108	58	−47
		Maize	422	610	45
Côte d'Ivoire	63	Rice	451	956	112
		Cotton	157	231	47
		Maize	448	546	22
Ethiopia[a]	209	Wheat	716	1,026	43
		Maize	1,274	2,194	72
Ghana	−37	Maize	435	994	128
		Rice	64	193	204
Kenya	30	Maize	2,084	2,640	27
		Sugarcane	4,010	4,333	8
		Coffee	97	91	−6
Madagascar	17	Sugarcane	1,571	2,139	36
		Rice	2,087	2,436	17
Malawi	−10	Maize	1,357	1,498	10
		Tobacco	66	123	88
Mali	42	Cotton	130	315	143
		Rice	144	453	214
Mauritius	22	Sugarcane	5,546	5,078	−8
Nigeria	−18	Maize	1,107	6,539	491
		Yam	4,987	23,057	362
		Rice	1,300	2,823	117
Senegal	−21	Cotton	39	35	−11
		Groundnuts	706	705	0
Tanzania	16	Maize	1,835	2,463	34
		Tobacco	14	29	112
Togo	204	Cotton	30	117	286
		Maize	170	342	101
Zambia	−32	Maize	937	1,056	13
		Tobacco	2.85	3.45	21
Zimbabwe	3	Maize	1,902	1,925	1
		Tobacco	99	197	99

SOURCE: FAOStat database.

[a] In Ethiopia, *teff* receives the most fertilizer, but production data are not available.

other factors, including macroeconomic stability, liberalized grain markets, and greater availability of fertilizer.

In Zambia, where 90 percent of the fertilizer was applied to maize, fertilizer use fell 32 percent from the early 1980s but maize output grew by 13 percent and tobacco production by 21 percent. Nonetheless, per capita maize output has fallen. Howard and Mungoma (1997) report that the elimination of pan-territorial pricing, fertilizer subsidy removal, and real depreciation of the Zambian kwacha have encouraged farmers near transportation routes to diversify into higher-value cash crops (including tobacco), while those in more remote locations have reverted to subsistence crops that do well without fertilizer.

Malawi shows a similar pattern. In spite of a reduction in fertilizer use, maize production has increased about 10 percent, although again this is less than population growth over the period. There is substantial growth (88 percent) in the main fertilized export crop, tobacco, partly owing to liberalization of smallholder production.

In Cameroon, fertilizer use fell 30 percent from the early 1980s, but cotton production grew 122 percent. On the other hand, coffee production fell by almost half. Much of this decline is related to the fact that world coffee prices reached a historic peak in 1985 and 1986, but fell to one-half that level by the mid-1990s. Walker (1994) attributes the falling fertilizer orders by the coffee cooperatives in the late 1980s to both higher fertilizer prices and falling world coffee prices. The production of maize, the third major crop in terms of fertilizer use, increased 45 percent over this period.

Senegal is the only country examined in which a reduction in fertilizer use is associated with stagnation or reductions in the output of the two most fertilized crops. Kelly et al. (1996) describe the events contributing to the near collapse of fertilizer use on groundnuts: the collapse of the credit system in 1980, declining world groundnut prices, fertilizer subsidy removal in the late 1980s, and farmer preferences to use scarce cash resources to buy seed rather than fertilizer. The fall in cotton production is harder to explain, given its rapid growth in other West African countries such as Benin, Mali, and Burkina Faso.

Fertilizer use in Nigeria fell 18 percent between the early 1980s and the mid-1990s, but maize production grew almost sixfold. The periods chosen for "before" and "after" are not very appropriate in the case of Nigeria, which, as described earlier, maintained large fertilizer subsidies until the mid-1990s. Fertilizer use continued to grow until 1992–93, after which it fell precipitously. The growth in maize production is the result of Nigerian policy to use oil revenue to support farmers in the north with fertilizer subsidies, credit, and improved seed. Farmers there have shifted from sorghum and millet to maize. The 1989 policy of banning wheat and rice imports to protect domestic producers further increased the incentives to grow grains. Given this sequence of events, it is more appropriate to compare the period 1992–93 with 1996–97. Between these two periods, fertilizer use dropped 69 percent and maize output fell about

10 percent. Production of other crops (cotton, sorghum, soybeans, cowpeas, and rice) either was stable or increased during this period. Yields were stable, except for rice whose yield declined. It is difficult to escape the conclusion that much of the fertilizer used under the subsidy system was wasteful in that it did little to boost agricultural output or yields.

It is sometimes argued that agricultural production is maintained, in the face of falling fertilizer use, by extensification, that is by expanding area to compensate for declining yields. This could have negative environmental consequences, particularly if farmers expand into fragile, marginal land. Thus, we are interested not only in production trends but in whether fertilizer reform might have adversely affected yields. We focus on maize because most of the countries in which fertilizer use has declined are important maize producers, and the negative impact of extensification would be greatest for a crop that occupies a large area, as maize does in most of these countries. Table 3.10 shows the change in maize yields for countries in which an important share of fertilizer is applied to maize. The table reveals that between 1981–85 and 1994–96 maize yields fell in 3 of the 12 countries: Zambia, Zimbabwe, and Côte d'Ivoire. Of these three, only Zambia also experienced a reduction in overall fertilizer use (although fertilizer may have been diverted from maize to other crops in Zimbabwe and Côte d'Ivoire). Furthermore, maize area expansion in these three countries was similar to that experienced by the nine countries with rising maize yields.[19] Thus, at least in the case of maize, there is little evidence that reduced fertilizer use has led to lower yields and extensification of production. The aggregate relationship between fertilizer use and maize yields appears to be weak.

In interpreting these numbers, it is important to recall that the low application rates in Africa mean that a given percentage change in fertilizer use will have a relatively small percentage impact on agricultural production. In other words, low application rates imply that fertilizer does not contribute much to output in many countries, and, where it does not contribute much, changes in fertilize use will not have much effect.

The Impact on Poverty and Rural Incomes

One of the original motivations for implementing fertilizer subsidies was that this would assist the poor to gain access to modern technology and expand agricultural output, and thus reduce rural poverty. In this section, we examine the impact of fertilizer policy reform on rural incomes and poverty. Surprisingly few studies have addressed this issue, so we must make use of indirect evidence.

---

19. According to FAO data, the maize area expansion was 7 percent in Zimbabwe, 21 percent in Zambia, and 27 percent in Côte d'Ivoire. The median growth in maize area for the 12 countries was 21 percent.

TABLE 3.10 Change in maize yields before and after reforms

Country	Yield (tons per hectare) 1981–85	1994–96	Percentage change
Benin	0.73	1.09	50.4
Cameroon	1.32	1.49	12.9
Côte d'Ivoire	0.83	0.80	−4.1
Ghana	0.87	1.51	73.3
Kenya	1.72	1.89	9.8
Malawi	1.17	1.24	5.7
Mozambique	0.45	0.71	57.8
Nigeria	1.26	1.30	2.7
Tanzania	1.35	1.50	11.0
Uganda	1.26	1.47	16.7
Zambia	1.81	1.67	−7.8
Zimbabwe	1.41	1.32	−6.3

SOURCE: FAOStat database.

The first question is how many people benefited from fertilizer subsidies? Since fertilizer subsidies were generally not targeted, almost all fertilizer users were beneficiaries. In a few countries (Benin and Kenya), at least half the farmers use fertilizer (see Table 3.2). In most countries of Sub-Saharan Africa, however, only a small minority of farmers used fertilizer even during the 1980s. In most of the main fertilizer-using African countries, 15–35 percent of farmers used fertilizer. Thus, in these countries, at least two-thirds of the farm households never benefited from fertilizer subsidies.

Because the benefits of a fertilizer subsidy are roughly proportional to the amount of fertilizer used, the next question is how does fertilizer use vary across income groups? If fertilizer subsidies benefited the poorest households disproportionately, it would be easier to justify them on equity grounds. As mentioned earlier, cash and credit constraints mean that, in some countries, the adoption and use of fertilizer are greater among those farmers with higher incomes, or at least higher cash incomes. This pattern has been found in studies of Kenya, Zambia, Benin, Malawi, and Ethiopia (Jha and Hojjati 1993; Croppenstedt and Demeke 1996; Mbata 1997; Minot, Kherallah, and Berry 2000). A different study of Malawi and one of Tanzania found no relationship between fertilizer use and off-farm income (Green and Ng'ong'ola 1993; Nkonya, Schroeder, and Norman 1997).

Another pattern discussed earlier is that fertilizer use tends to be concentrated in the high-potential zones with greater rainfall and better soils. This is particularly true in the southern and eastern African countries that apply fertilizer primarily to maize: Zimbabwe, Zambia, Malawi, Tanzania, and Kenya. To the extent that the poor live disproportionately in the low-potential areas, poor rural households were less likely to benefit from fertilizer subsidies than were rich rural households. Conversely, the costs of subsidy removal were more heavily born by the latter group. These two patterns suggest that the burden of subsidy removal will be more likely to fall on higher-income rural households.

This conclusion does not apply to all countries, however. In Ghana, for example, fertilizer use is concentrated in the drier northern half of the country. According to results from the 1987 Ghana Living Standards Survey, poverty is also greater in the north than in the south. Jebuni and Seini (1992) interpret this to mean that poor rural households were more adversely affected by subsidy removal than were rich rural households. Similarly, fertilizer use in Benin is more common in the cotton-growing northern departments and poverty is greater in the north (Minot, Kherallah, and Berry 2000). On the other hand, it should be recalled that cotton farmers in Benin and maize farmers in Ghana have probably benefited overall from agricultural reforms, if strong growth in output of the main crops is an indication.

How important were fertilizer subsidies relative to household income? The value of the subsidy to a household is roughly equal to the per unit subsidy multiplied by the quantity of fertilizer used. Among the 38 African countries for which FAO data are available, the median level of fertilizer use in 1985 was 4 kilograms of nutrient per rural inhabitant and most of the main fertilizer users were in the range of 4–8 kilograms per person (FAOStat). Given a 50 percent subsidy (and assuming that the full subsidy was passed on to the farmer), the benefit would be US\$1.30–2.60 per rural inhabitant.[20] For many rural households, this would represent about 1–2 percent of income. Thus, fertilizer subsidies cannot be considered a major contribution to household income.

A few studies have attempted to evaluate the impact of subsidy removal on rural incomes. In the model of the Senegalese agricultural sector described in the previous section, the authors simulate the elimination of the fertilizer subsidy, leading to a 300 percent increase in fertilizer prices. Taking into account the impact on crop production and the contribution of crop income to total income, the model suggests that rural incomes would fall by 1.7 percent in the Groundnut Basin and in the South and by 0.6 percent in the Fleuve region.

Tower and Christiansen (1988) develop a model of the agricultural sector in Malawi that includes a smallholder sector, an estate sector, and an industrial sector. The agricultural sector uses fertilizer, labor, and a fixed stock of land. In this model, removing a 10 percent subsidy reduces smallholder agricultural output by 1.5 percent. Since farmers have non-farm income, the impact on rural incomes would presumably be somewhat less.

In summary, two-thirds to three-quarters of the farmers in Africa were probably unaffected by fertilizer subsidy removal because they did not apply fer-

---

20. This assumes a delivered cost of US\$300 per ton of urea, which is 46 percent nitrogen.

tilizers. The burden of fertilizer subsidy removal probably fell disproportionately on larger, higher-income farmers in the high-potential zones. Furthermore, even relatively large subsidies probably contributed less than 2 percent of household income. On the other hand, the positive impacts of fertilizer market reforms, such as better availability, timing, and product choice, have not been evaluated.

Conclusions and Policy Implications

In response to the fiscal burden of fertilizer subsidies and growing evidence of the inefficiencies of state-managed marketing systems, most African countries have eliminated universal subsidies and price controls, while opening fertilizer importation and distribution to the private sector. At the same time, state enterprises continue to be a dominant supplier of fertilizer in a number of countries, particularly in West Africa. In addition, the development of a competitive fertilizer market is constrained by starter pack programs, subsidized credit schemes, and sporadic donor-funded fertilizer programs. And, in some cases, the private firms operate under contract to state agencies under conditions that limit competition and create opportunities for rent-seeking. Thus, although fertilizer markets in almost every African country are more competitive now than they were in the early 1980s, many are still affected by some degree of government intervention that reduces market competition.

The results of fertilizer marketing reform have been less positive than was originally expected by proponents of liberalization, but the impact has been less negative than is generally perceived today. The reforms have not met expectations in several respects:

- The cost savings associated with privatized markets were not sufficient to prevent fertilizer prices from rising in response to subsidy removal and devaluation.
- The greater availability and better timing of fertilizer delivery have not often been enough to offset the demand-reducing effect of higher fertilizer prices.
- Partly as a result of these two factors, the growth in fertilizer use has been slow in the post-reform period, and fertilizer use has fallen in some countries.
- It is difficult to restore or expand systems for providing input credit in the context of liberalized output markets because repayment is more difficult to enforce. This is particularly true in the case of staple food crops because the large number of buyers and the complexity of the marketing channels make it difficult to monitor crop sales.

On the other hand, fertilizer market reform has fulfilled the expectations of proponents in some respects:

- Private importers, distributors, and retailers have emerged to fulfill the functions formerly carried out by state enterprises and government ministries, contrary to the fears of those who argued that the private sector was not sufficiently developed.
- The elimination of the fiscal burden associated with fertilizer subsidies has contributed to smaller fiscal deficits and, indirectly, to macroeconomic stabilization in many countries.
- There is good evidence that the private sector can import and distribute fertilizers at significant cost savings compared with the state-administered systems.
- Comparing the early 1980s and the mid-1990s, fertilizer use has fallen in 7 of the main fertilizer-using countries but increased in 14. Almost all of the overall decline in 1994–95 is attributable to a sharp drop in fertilizer use in Nigeria. Overall, fertilizer use and application rates are higher today than in the 1970s and 1980s.
- It is difficult to find evidence of any adverse impact of fertilizer market liberalization on agricultural production. Agricultural production appears to be more sensitive to weather, agricultural policy, and shifts in exchange rates than to fertilizer policy.
- Institutions are slowly evolving to provide input credit to farmers, particularly those growing cash crops. Repayment is easier to enforce, and thus more likely to be offered, when the number of buyers is small and crop sales are easy to monitor.

Furthermore, it is important to recognize that fertilizer use has been adversely affected by some factors unrelated to fertilizer market liberalization:

- Real depreciation of local currencies during the 1980s and 1990s reduced the incentives to fertilize nontradable crops such as maize.
- Many of the countries in Africa with the largest fertilizer use apply it mainly to maize, demand for which is limited by its nontradability and the low income elasticity of demand.
- Maize producer prices have declined in Ghana and in most countries of southern Africa, thus reducing the profitability of applying fertilizer to maize.
- The deterioration or collapse of the credit systems in a number of African countries affected fertilizer demand. In most cases, this collapse predated market reform and was caused, not by market reform, but by the financial unsustainability of those systems. On the other hand, as mentioned above, it is more difficult to re-establish sustainable broad-based systems for providing input credit when output markets are liberalized.

In addition, it should be recalled that for a number of large fertilizer users (Nigeria, Kenya, Zimbabwe, Tanzania, and Malawi), fertilizer liberalization and/or subsidy removal were implemented only in the mid-1990s, so that it is still early to evaluate the results.

The emphasis in fertilizer market reform has, until now, been on the withdrawal of the state from direct commercial activities such as the production, importation, and distribution of fertilizer. More progress can be made in this area, as discussed below, but there are also areas where the government needs to do more, not less. In particular, the government must play a more active role in facilitating the development of a competitive fertilizer sector and improving smallholders' access to modern inputs including fertilizer. Below, we present a number of strategies for promoting the development of the fertilizer sector in Sub-Saharan Africa:

STRENGTHEN COMPETITION IN FERTILIZER MARKETS. The evidence suggests that competitive unsubsidized fertilizer markets are better able to deliver adequate supplies of fertilizer to farmers at the right time for a lower cost relative to state-managed distribution systems. In principle, a competitive market could include commercially oriented state enterprises, but in practice these enterprises are almost invariably given subsidies, low-cost credit, or special access to scarce resources. Of course, minimizing costs is not the only objective of government, and state involvement in fertilizer distribution could be justified in some circumstances to assist poor farmers, to respond to drought and other natural disasters, or to overcome market failures in the provision of credit. In practice, however, such programs have not been very effective in achieving their goals and have created temptations for misuse of state funds. Thus, the burden of proof should be on the proponents of such interventions to demonstrate (1) that the social objectives are being met and (2) that intervention in fertilizer markets is the most effective way to achieve that objective.

Even in cases where the government dominates fertilizer marketing, it is often possible to do so in a way that maintains some degree of competition. For example, in a number of Francophone West African countries, the government maintains a monopoly (or near monopoly) on fertilizer distribution in order to preserve the system of providing input credit (among other reasons). Benin has introduced some competition by contracting private importers and distributors to supply fertilizer. Furthermore, the government is launching an experiment to liberalize cotton marketing, using a farmer-owned organization to act as a clearing house to ensure farmer repayment of input credit. This would also allow farmer organizations to select suppliers and negotiate prices, thus stimulating more competition in fertilizer marketing. The lessons learned from this experiment will be useful to other West African cotton-growing countries.

In other African countries, private enterprises are able to operate and compete but the fertilizer market is subject to uncertainty owing to intervention by the state. This is the case in Zambia, which distributes fertilizer through the Food Reserve Agency, and in Malawi, which distributes, free of charge, small packets of fertilizer as part of the Starter Pack Initiative. The Malawi case is representative of a broader pattern in which donor agencies are responsible for sporadic injections of fertilizer as a form of in-kind foreign assistance. Given the arguably suboptimal levels of fertilizer use by African farmers, such programs may increase the value of output by more than the cost of the program. Thus, careful analysis is needed to see whether or not the objectives are being met and at what cost. Who are the beneficiaries and are they poor? How much additional crop output is generated relative to the cost of the program? Assessment of the counterfactual—what would happen in the absence of these programs—must take into account the fact that policy-related uncertainty in the fertilizer market discourages investment by private firms in the distribution network.

REDUCE TRANSPORTATION COSTS.   The evidence suggests that transportation costs represent a large share (over half in some cases) of the farm-gate cost of fertilizer. Improved transport infrastructure would facilitate the adoption of fertilizer and other inputs in two ways. First, it would reduce the farm-gate cost of the inputs. Second, it would increase the farm-gate price of crops sold by surplus-producing farmers, thus improving the profitability of input use. Another, less costly, approach to reducing transportation costs would be to improve efficiency and competition in port facilities, railroads, and trucking.

PROMOTE REGIONAL FERTILIZER MARKETS.   As mentioned earlier, one reason for the high cost of fertilizer is the low volume of demand in each country. In ocean freight, for example, large shipments are significantly less expensive than smaller ones. Thus, another strategy for reducing costs is to promote the development of regional fertilizer markets that would allow importers and manufacturers to achieve economies of scale. Even countries that have relatively liberalized fertilizer markets often maintain regulations that restrict regional fertilizer trade, including

- Regulations requiring approval to sell new types of fertilizer,
- Unnecessary labeling requirements,
- Restrictive licensing of fertilizer importers and distributors,
- Requirements that fertilizer traders obtain import permits, and
- Preferential treatment to local manufacturers or locally based distributors in terms of credit, contracts, and import permits.

Further deregulation in these areas would increase the regional trade, allow economies of scale in manufacturing and transportation, and lower costs to farmers.

RESTORE MARKETS FOR INPUT CREDIT.   The revitalization of the markets for seasonal agricultural credit is a key ingredient in facilitating the use of fertilizer and other modern inputs. In many countries, the credit system has collapsed as a result of low repayment rates, so the emphasis must be on financial viability. The main problem in agricultural credit markets is that lenders cannot easily determine the trustworthiness of borrowers. One approach to ensuring repayment is to use the crop as collateral. This is easiest when one company has a legal (and enforceable) monopoly on buying the crop, but it is also feasible in the context of a competitive output market. In the latter case, institutions must be devised for monitoring the sale of the crop and imposing sanctions on farmers who avoid repayment. Monitoring is easier when the marketing channels are few and the number of buyers is small, as is typically the case with export crops. The state can play a role in mediating between farmers, buyers, and financial institutions over the rules and institutions needed to ensure credit repayment and in enforcing those rules.

In the case of food crops, it is more difficult to use the harvest as collateral. Crop sales are difficult to monitor because of the large number of buyers and the complexity of marketing channels. In this situation, other strategies may be more effective in overcoming the problem of enforcing repayment. One alternative is group lending schemes, in which a group of lenders is held responsible for the unpaid debts of its members. Another is graduated lending, in which loan amounts are progressively increased, provided that past loans are repaid.

LIBERALIZE REGIONAL MARKETS IN MAIZE. Most of the fertilizer in Africa is applied to maize, yet various policies restrict regional trade in maize for food security reasons. For example, Tanzania allows maize exports from its maize-surplus southern highlands region only when food security has been assured in other parts of Tanzania, a condition rarely met. Similarly, Malawi attempts to achieve self-sufficiency in maize rather than import from northern Mozambique. In the absence of international trade in maize, any expansion in maize output will face an inelastic demand and declining prices. The incentives for applying fertilizer to maize are limited in this situation. If restrictions on regional maize trade were relaxed, the use of fertilizer on maize would be more profitable.

PROVIDE BETTER INFORMATION TO FARMERS. Market liberalization has changed the economics of fertilizer use both by raising fertilizer-to-crop price ratios and by allowing regional variation in prices. As a result, fertilizer recommendations need to be revised in two ways. First, they need to be updated based on recent crop and fertilizer price data. Second, they need to be regionally disaggregated to take into account spatial variation in prices. Agronomic studies of the economics of fertilizer use should also attempt to incorporate transaction costs, labor costs, capital costs, and risk. In the past, recommendations were often based on idealized conditions of good soils, adequate water, and guaranteed prices.

QUESTION FERTILIZER SUBSIDIES. In principle, fertilizer subsidies could be justified on efficiency grounds if fertilizer is underutilized owing to lack of information or to risk aversion on the part of farmers. Or they could be justified on equity grounds if they assisted poor farmers in a cost-effective way. However, conventional fertilizer subsidy programs cannot be justified on efficiency grounds because of the high cost and poor performance of state-controlled distribution networks. Nor can universal fertilizer subsidies be justified on equity grounds, because the benefits are proportional to fertilizer use and are thus not well targeted to poor households. If a fertilizer subsidy program is to be economically justifiable, it should be designed (1) to preserve a competitive fertilizer marketing system, and/or (2) to provide benefits to poor farmers in a cost-effective way.

It is not clear that either goal is feasible. The New Extension Program in Ethiopia is designed to combine competitive markets with subsidized input credit, but is plagued with unrecoverable debts and favoritism in procurement. The Starter Pack Initiative in Malawi provides small quantities of free inputs to small farmers, although it is currently dependent on donor funding. Further experimentation is perhaps warranted, but the results so far are not promising. In general, poor rural households would benefit more from spending on basic social services, targeted safety-net programs, and investment in infrastructure and agricultural research than they would from fertilizer subsidies.

4 Food Markets in Sub-Saharan Africa: Reform and Beyond

Over the past two decades, most countries in Sub-Saharan Africa have witnessed fundamental transformations of their food economies. Since the early 1980s, donors and multilateral agencies have advocated food market reforms as a central component of overall structural adjustment programs. In this period, reforms enacted by African countries, though uneven and often slow, have gone beyond the relatively limited reform agenda set forth by the World Bank's Berg Report in 1981 (Jayne and Jones 1997; Seppälä 1997). A large empirical literature attests to the significant achievements of these food market reforms, which have included both the withdrawal of state agencies from pricing and marketing activities and the relaxation of regulatory restrictions on private trade. These achievements are, notably, increased entry by private traders into food trade, reduced marketing margins, increased producer prices, and the improved transmission of price signals in the economy (Beynon, Jones, and Yao 1992; Barrett 1994; Jones 1996). In spite of these achievements, however, the question lingers whether the liberalization of food markets has effectively addressed the key reasons for African governments initially intervening in food markets through the creation of agricultural parastatal enterprises or marketing boards (Dorward, Kydd, and Poulton 1999). That is, has food market reform succeeded in increasing production, stimulating farm productivity growth, and stabilizing food prices?

The Food Policy Dilemma and the Social Contract

Because food plays a dual role, serving both as a source of producer income and as an urban and rural wage good, the conflict between these two roles defines the food policy dilemma that confronts food market liberalization efforts (Sahn, Dorosh, and Younger 1997). The current food policy dilemmas in much of Sub-Saharan Africa are rooted in the historical context, in which the controlled marketing systems inherited by post-independence African governments became the vehicle for promoting the objectives of redressing the neglect of smallholder agriculture. Particularly in eastern and southern Africa, an implicit "social contract" between governments and the African majority incorporated the need both to support smallholders and to provide cheap food for urban populations (Jayne et al. 1999).

The Historical Role of the State in Food Markets

Throughout history, governments in all parts of the world have intervened in food marketing, from the procurement of grain by the Roman Empire to the provision of milled wheat to the bakeries of Paris in the eighteenth century to the ubiquitous cereal boards in developing countries in the latter half of the twentieth century. State intervention was justified on the basis of the economic rationale that producers are highly vulnerable to climactic fluctuations and to price uncertainty, and its objectives were to maintain low food prices while supporting agricultural incomes (Duncan and Jones 1993). In Africa, government intervention in food markets dates to at least the 1930s, though in varying forms and to different extents (Jayne and Jones 1997). State involvement in food markets had the primary intention of keeping urban consumer prices low and stable, while a secondary objective was to protect smallholders from private traders (Sahn, Dorosh, and Younger 1997).

At the same time, the nature and extent of state intervention have varied widely among the countries of Sub-Saharan Africa, in part as a result of their colonial legacies. State intervention prior to market reform can be distinguished according to whether agricultural policies were generally favorable or discriminatory toward agricultural production. Thus, in countries favoring agriculture, such as Kenya, Malawi, Zambia, and Zimbabwe, policies were oriented to controlling prices, providing market infrastructure, subsidizing consumption, and limiting private activities. In these countries, food market reform has been incremental, characterized by policy reversals and resistance to reforms by governments (Beynon, Jones, and Yao 1992). In countries whose pre-reform policies were strongly biased against agriculture, such as Somalia, Ethiopia, and Tanzania, reform has been relatively rapid, with a dramatic collapse of the market share of the state enterprises.

State intervention experiences can be classified into three categories, according to the extent of involvement: (1) a relatively open food market with limited parastatal involvement in the market; (2) price intervention without explicit food rationing; and (3) extensive involvement in pricing, procurement, and quantitative controls (Sahn, Dorosh, and Younger 1997). Much of West Africa, notably countries in which a single food crop does not dominate, such as Ghana, Cameroon, the Gambia, and Niger, falls into the first category. In these countries, liberalization has not represented a threat to food security through increasing food prices and has instead contributed to improved efficiency, reduced price volatility, and welfare gains (Alderman and Shively 1996). A number of countries in eastern and southern Africa intervened heavily in food markets, particularly maize, without resorting to quantitative restrictions—for example, Tanzania and Malawi, which fall into the second category. In these countries, liberalization has been slow, subject to reversal, and subject to official skepticism that private traders can ensure food security. Finally, in the third category, governments in Madagascar, Mozambique, Guinea, and Ethiopia, prior to reform, banned private trade and were engaged in direct food distribution through rationing. In these countries, parallel markets played an important role. Thus, the degree of reform is strongly influenced by prior conditions and the extent of state intervention (Sahn, Dorosh, and Younger 1997).

In countries with heavy government intervention and a commitment to supporting agriculture, such as Kenya, Zambia, and Zimbabwe, the use of input subsidies, commodity pricing that subsidized transport costs, and subsidized credit programs successfully promoted smallholder incomes and consumer welfare. However, gains in smallholder incomes were potentially eroded by currency overvaluation and protection of domestic industry. The high cost of these programs and the ensuing drain on public budgets proved unsustainable and led to the pressure by donors to reduce state intervention (Jayne et al. 1999). Thus, the support of inefficient marketing parastatals and the explicit subsidies not only were fiscally unsustainable but also often did not achieve the stated food security objectives (Sahn, Dorosh, and Younger 1997). Prior to reform, producer price subsidies were inadequate in many instances, resulting in producer prices far below prices on the parallel market. The wedge between the official producer price and the parallel market price can be explained by four external factors (Seppälä 1997). These factors are the attempt to reduce risks to farmers through floor pricing and secure market access; pan-territorial pricing; the extended scope of parastatal activities such as the provision of inputs, extension, and roads; and sales to consumers at below-procurement prices. These noncommercial functions led to the inefficiency of the government agencies.

In contrast, liberalization has had a more limited impact in countries with a limited state role, mainly in West Africa (Sahn, Dorosh, and Younger 1997). Generally, despite the original economic rationale of state intervention, interest group politics and rent-seeking behavior are judged to have influenced the largely anti-agricultural bias characterizing Africa's economic policies in the modern era (Bates 1981; Krueger, Schiff, and Valdes 1991).

Objectives and Organization of the Chapter

This chapter aims to review the food market reform experiences and their impact in selected countries in Sub-Saharan Africa. In reviewing the country case studies, the analysis addresses the following questions: How has the process of reform itself mattered for the outcome? Why has food reform not achieved the desired effects on agricultural production? What should be the role of the state in the wake of reform?

The chapter synthesizes empirical studies in 10 countries in Sub-Saharan Africa, of which 3 are in eastern Africa (Kenya, Tanzania, and Ethiopia), 4 are in southern Africa (Malawi, Zambia, Zimbabwe, and Madagascar), and 3 are in West Africa (Mali, Ghana, and Benin). These countries were selected to capture a range of reform experiences as well as to reflect geographic diversity. Building on the schematic representation of market reform linkages in Figure 2.1, the chapter first discusses the pre-reform position of governments and the process of food market reform in the selected countries. We then review the impact of reforms on food markets in terms of market integration, price stabilization, changes in marketing or transaction costs, and traders' investment. The following section takes up the impact of food market reforms on agricultural production, including general supply response and smallholder issues. Next we address welfare concerns, poverty, and food security. Finally, from an institutional economics perspective, we look at the remaining issues or constraints in the wake of market reform.

The Reform Process

The influence of European involvement in food production in the early colonial period appears to be a key determinant of the extent of state intervention in food marketing in the post-independence era (Jayne and Jones 1997). At one extreme, countries such as South Africa and Zimbabwe developed highly dualistic production and marketing structures, which served to support and stabilize maize prices to European farmers. Countries such as Tanzania, which experienced little European settlement, had relatively less state intervention in food markets. Further along the spectrum, countries with even fewer colonial settlements and without a single dominant crop, such as Ghana, hardly intervened in food markets. Production instability and the ensuing large price fluctuations played a major role in influencing the design of food marketing systems.

The main food marketing reforms over the past decade have several key features (Jayne and Jones 1997). Reforms started with attempts to reduce the level of marketing subsidies. This widened the margins between producer and selling prices, and reduced public purchases and the size of stockpiles. Subsequently, changes were made to the regulatory structure. The removal of official pricing of food products is often a slow process. In a number of countries, state agencies continue to exist, with a redefined role. Finally, very few initiatives to support private trading and to develop public institutions have been made (Jones 1996).

A closer investigation of the specific reform experiences of the selected countries reveals that the majority of countries started the 1980s with marketing boards holding an official monopoly in the procurement and distribution of grain, with prices set pan-territorially. Table 4.1 summarizes the scope of reforms for the 10 selected countries, in light of the extent of state intervention in food markets before and after reform, for both locally produced and imported

TABLE 4.1 Scope of food marketing reform in selected countries

Country	Crop	Output market Before	Output market After	Wheat imports Before	Wheat imports After	Rice imports Before	Rice imports After
Benin	Tubers	●	○	✪	✪	✪	✪
Ethiopia	*Teff;* maize; wheat	●	○	✳	✪	✳	✪
Ghana	Tubers	○	○	✳	✳	✪	✪
Kenya	Maize	●	●	✳	✳	✳	✪
Madagascar	Rice	●	○	✳	✳	n.a.	✪
Malawi	Maize	●	▶	✪	✪	✪	✪
Mali	Millet; sorghum	●	○	✳	✪	✳	✪
Tanzania	Maize	●	○	✳	✪	✳	✪
Zambia	Maize	●	▶	n.a.	n.a.	n.a.	n.a.
Zimbabwe	Maize	●	●	✳	✳	✳	✪

SOURCES: World Bank (1994) in Seppälä (1997); Lirenso (1993) for Ethiopia.

NOTES n.a. means not available. ● = major restrictions on purchases and sales; ▶ = limited intervention by state buying agency; ○ = no intervention except food security stocks; ✳ = state monopoly; ✪ = no monopoly.

foods. Both Benin and Ghana, with no dominant crop, were relatively more open before reform and have continued to be so. Countries with heavy intervention prior to reform but without a policy regime strongly biased toward agriculture, such as Ethiopia, Madagascar, Mali, and Tanzania, have implemented food market reform quite extensively.

Benin

The Office National des Céréales (ONC), created in 1983, with the help of local organizations known as the Centres d'Action Régionales pour le Développement Rural (CARDER) attempted unsuccessfully to control 25 percent of the cereals market, reaching only 5 percent in 1990 because of a lack of human and financial resources (Badiane et al. 1997). Even prior to liberalization, with the exception of the 1976–77 period, market prices of cereals were never controlled and private traders largely dominated food markets. The market reforms launched in 1990 effectively dismantled the ONA and CARDER, transforming the ONA into the Office National d'Appui à la Sécurité Alimentaire (ONASA), which is responsible for supporting food security and providing market information and extension to farmers. ONASA's role in the market is extremely small in the wake of market reforms, controlling only 0.15 percent of the annual volume of maize traded.

Ethiopia

Between 1976 and 1990, grain trade was strictly controlled by a government parastatal, the Agricultural Marketing Corporation (AMC), which administered a highly distorted trade regime in which official prices set by the parastatal were below producer prices. Thus, at official prices, producers lost 24 percent of the market value for wheat and 52 percent for *teff* (Amha 1994). Marketing policy in this period included the administration of a compulsory delivery system with fixed quotas per producer, bans on private trade (with the exception of a few licensed traders who were given delivery quotas), uniform pricing, restricted interregional transport of grain, and grain rationing to urban consumers. In this period, the AMC built 2,202 warehouses around the country to serve as grain collection centers.

In response to external pressures, a radical and abrupt market reform was enacted literally overnight in March 1990, taking the government parastatal as well as private traders by surprise (Fisseha 1994). The following excerpt from the proclamation of March 1990 reveals the extent of the reform.

> In the trade sector of the economy, private entrepreneurs will be able to compete with state-run trade enterprises in agriculture or industrial commodities as well as in import–export trade. In the area of trade in grain products in particular, trade exchange will henceforth be conducted on the basis of free market pricing while the grain control situation and the quota system will cease. The Agricultural Marketing Corporation (AMC) will enter the free market and operate as a state trading organization.

Thus, in a single move, the reform of 1990 resulted in the restoration of private trade, the removal of official pricing, the removal of quotas, free movement of grain, and the transformation of the parastatal, renamed the Ethiopian Grain Trade Enterprise, into a buffer stock scheme.

Ghana

Starting from a situation in which the private sector was relatively free to trade and store grain, Ghana's period of structural adjustment began by *increasing* the role of the state in the maize marketing system (Coulter 1994). In the face of a major drought in 1982–83, the government sought to increase the role of the Ghana Food Distribution Corporation (GFDC). However, owing to a deteriorating financial position, the GFDC's policy of minimum prices to farmers was abandoned. The Economic Recovery Program (ERP), started in 1983, resulted in the liberalization of the foreign exchange market, liberalization of agricultural marketing, elimination of the Guaranteed Minimum Price program, and the promotion of the private sector (Badiane et al. 1997). However, even prior to reform, small independent traders dominated 95 percent of the marketable surplus. In the wake of reforms, the GFDC has taken the role of providing drying and storage services to maize farmers and traders, and investments have been channeled into new infrastructure, such as the construction of feeder roads and upgrading of storage and sanitary facilities.

Kenya

The slow and uneven pace of grain market reforms in Kenya in the period since 1980 reflects the government's reluctance to bow to external pressure (Beynon, Jones, and Yao 1992). Initially, pricing reform was undertaken in the first structural adjustment program in 1980, in which domestic producer prices were linked to import parity prices (Seppälä 1997). However, pressure to reform the role of the National Cereals and Produce Board (NCPB) met with considerable resistance. In response to pressure, the government allowed private trade up to a 4 ton maximum. In 1984, the government allowed the state-organized Kenya Grain Growers Cooperative Union (KGGCU) to market maize in competition with the NCPB. In 1988–89, further modifications were made to allow a few licensed buyers to enter the market, but these licenses were revoked in 1992. In 1992, field studies revealed that the NCPB, the KGGCU, and a few individuals controlled official maize marketing. In this period, police continued to seize private movements of maize. Starting in 1993, serious efforts to liberalize were made in the removal of inter-district trade restrictions and imports were liberalized. A total liberalization of grain trade was announced in 1994, resulting in the restriction of financing to the NCPB. In October 1998, the government announced that the NCPB would no longer procure maize domestically or support maize prices. However, the NCPB resumed price supports in December 1998 (Jayne et al. 1999).

The combined effects of population growth and stagnant production have led Kenya to become a net maize importer in most years. At present, commercial imports of maize are undertaken entirely by the private sector, although the legislative rules allowing the NCPB to import maize at a future date have not changed (Jayne et al. 1999).

Madagascar

Starting in 1976, the socialist regime nationalized private agricultural enterprises and totally dominated the collection, marketing, processing, transport, and distribution of rice. New state organizations were created at each administrative and regional level to market rice. Consumer prices were subsidized and producers received minimum paddy prices (Badiane et al. 1997). In 1982, the government implemented a structural adjustment program in which the private sector was allowed to operate in agricultural marketing. In 1986, large state-owned enterprises were opened up to the private sector, and in 1991 prices were liberalized. In 1994, the Malagasy franc was devalued, and in 1995 import tariffs on imported rice were reduced from 30 percent to 10 percent.

Malawi

The government established the Agricultural Development and Marketing Corporation (ADMARC) as a monopsonistic buying agent for smallholders' maize, at guaranteed fixed prices. ADMARC provided pan-territorial and pan-seasonal prices for farmers, requiring it to subsidize maize prices with export earnings from tobacco. With the world prices for tobacco deteriorating, its ability to continue maize subsidies was eroded in the early 1980s.

In 1981, Malawi embarked on a series of structural adjustment programs, which entailed adopting a flexible exchange rate regime and moving slowly toward liberalizing its price and marketing policies. Although the World Bank initially supported ADMARC's activities, it disagreed on the level of food prices relative to export prices (Seppälä 1997). In 1987, a new series of structural adjustment loans were launched, with the conditionality of complete privatization of maize marketing. However, although private trading was allowed in this period, producer prices remained fixed by the government until as late as 1995, when a price band was established (Badiane et al. 1997). ADMARC administers the price band and acts as buyer of last resort. Despite privatization and the closing of a number of ADMARC buying centers, ADMARC remains dominant in the maize market, with private traders engaged in bulking for delivery to ADMARC (Beynon, Jones, and Yao 1992).

Mali

The liberalization of Mali's coarse grain marketing was conducted in a unique fashion, with the support of a donor consortium, the Programme de Restructuration du Marché Céréalier (PRMC).[1] The PRMC was funded by the donors' each pledging food aid to be used for free distribution or to be sold locally to generate "counterpart funds," in order to finance the liberalization process (Coulter 1994).

In the first phase of the reform program, between 1981 and 1987, the official monopoly of the state agency, the Office des Produits Agricoles du Mali (OPAM), was abandoned and private traders were allowed to operate. However, an official price scale (*barème*) continued in effect and OPAM maintained an important role of regulating prices through market operations. In the wake of two successive bumper crops in 1986 and 1987, the OPAM exhausted its funds and could not maintain its price stabilization role. From 1987, in the second phase, official price support was abandoned and OPAM's commercial role was reduced to managing a strategic food reserve, distributing food aid, and sales of grain to remote areas.

---

1. The PRMC is coordinated under the Ministry of Finance and controls its own budget. Decisions are taken by unanimity between the government and the donor representatives from France, Germany, Canada, the United States, the Netherlands, the European Union, and the World Food Programme. The PRMC has played a key role in the reform process by building consensus both between the government and donors and between donors.

Unlike the reform of coarse grain marketing, the reform of rice marketing in Mali has had mixed success. In 1987, marketing restrictions were removed and farmers were allowed to sell to either private mills or large parastatal mills, operating under the Office du Niger (ON). However, despite these reforms, the parastatal milling enterprises remained inefficient, overstaffed, and non-viable (Coulter 1994). Through 1992, parastatals continued to set official prices, and import duties were set at levels that allowed the parastatals to break even, resulting in oligopolistic trade in rice dominated by a few large traders. Since 1992, the ON's commercial role has been reduced to irrigation activities, water management, and extension, and milling has gradually been privatized.

Tanzania

Prior to the liberalization of maize trading in 1984, widespread parallel marketing developed in the early 1980s in response to the inability of the parastatal, the National Milling Corporation (NMC), to meet urban demand at subsidized consumer prices and low producer prices (Beynon, Jones, and Yao 1992). The NMC, which had replaced the National Agricultural Produce Board in the 1970s, administered pan-territorial prices, which resulted in subsidies to producers in peripheral areas (Seppälä 1997). In the course of its structural adjustment program, the government removed subsidies for maize flour and engaged in currency devaluation. Between 1987 and 1990, restrictions on interregional trade were removed. Although the government favored cooperative marketing over private trading, private trading was liberalized in 1990 and the NMC was restricted to milling maize (Beynon, Jones, and Yao 1992; Coulter 1994). However, a dual economy existed in this period; in some remote producing zones, the NMC continued to play a role in procuring and distributing grain and maintained pan-territorial pricing alongside private trade in other parts of the country.

Zambia

An important aspect of the Zambian maize economy is the need to import maize during most years because locally produced maize is generally exhausted 8–10 months after harvest (Jayne et al. 1999). Despite extensive market intervention since the colonial period, the Zambian government has made significant attempts to move to a market-oriented economy in recent years. Prior to 1990, the government administered pan-territorial and pan-seasonal prices, and the procurement, distribution, and processing of maize were undertaken solely by state-owned enterprises and cooperatives. Moreover, marketing agencies were subsidized in order to keep marketing margins below the total marketing costs of these agencies. This resulted in an increasing share of subsidy costs in the government budget, rising from 5.5 percent in 1984 to 13 percent in 1990.

The government undertook a partial liberalization in 1990, granting market entry to private traders in local maize markets, while continuing to control international trade and long-distance trade between government depots. At these depots, the government continued to administer uniform prices, although margins were widened to reduce subsidy levels. However, this approach proved unsustainable as the economy deteriorated in the 1990s, leading to reform legislation that proposed to liberalize all domestic product and input marketing.

The state marketing board was abolished in the early 1990s and the national milling industry, which had been nationalized in 1986, was privatized in 1995. Private multinational firms are currently active in maize and fertilizer marketing and private importation of maize has been allowed, although export bans continue to remain in place (Jayne et al. 1999). Despite the important strides toward reform, liberalization objectives appear to be in conflict with market stabilization objectives. Thus, the Food Reserve Agency (FRA), established in 1995, sold maize in late 1997 to industrial millers at prices that were 25 percent below market prices, giving certain actors a major advantage and disrupting private trade (Jayne et al. 1999). Similarly, the FRA sold 140 percent of the Eastern Province maize requirement at 30 percent below the market price (Johansson 1999). These stabilization measures, designed to reduce consumer prices, selectively benefit large-scale millers with access to FRA reserves while undermining the small-scale traders and millers. The FRA activities have exacerbated the uncertainty within the private sector over public policy, reducing the private sector's incentives to import maize and to invest in the marketing system.

Zimbabwe

At independence in 1980, Zimbabwe inherited a set of parastatal marketing boards created by the colonial government (Masters and Nuppenau 1993). Thus, the Grain Marketing Board (GMB), which procured and sold maize at a single pan-territorial price, was maintained. In addition, the government chose to expand the intake network to better serve smallholder farmers in communal areas; it thus tripled the number of buying stations between 1983 and 1985. With this expansion, along with the increased extension and credit services, marketed surplus rose from 87,000 tons in 1980–81 to 390,000 tons in 1984–85 to a peak of 750,000 tons in 1988–89. During this period, Zimbabwe was a regular exporter of maize and hailed for its smallholder Green Revolution (Coulter and Poulton 2001).

However, as the depot network expanded, it became increasingly difficult to defend the pan-territorial prices; the GMB's operating costs rose sharply, reaching 45 percent of the producer price. Over all crops, marketing subsidies reached 50 percent of the agricultural budget. Subsequently, as a result of budgetary pressures and negative per capita growth in agriculture, the government announced its commitment to market reforms in 1990. These reforms were primarily aimed at reducing budget deficits through a series of cost-cutting measures. At the same time, the government retained several major policy objectives, namely, the control of maize meal prices, the protection of smallholder farmers from exploitation by private traders, and price support for communal maize producers. The reforms included opening up local trade to private traders in 1992, although the GMB retained its monopoly over external trade, in addition to allowing private milling and abolishing maize meal subsidies to consumers in 1993.

In stark contrast even to the experiences of Kenya and Zambia, where state intervention has been high, Zimbabwe's approach to food security and consumer price stability is unique. Although the GMB's market share has fallen, it remains a major player in domestic maize marketing and is the sole legal importer and exporter of maize. Indeed, the GMB has expanded its range of marketing activities during the reform period and continues to administer fixed pan-territorial and pan-seasonal prices (Jayne et al. 1999). The government's fiscal objectives and the commitment to price support in communal areas pulled the GMB in opposite directions. Thus, private traders began trading and transporting to and from accessible districts, leaving the high-cost areas to be covered by the GMB. In 1993, with a bumper crop, the GMB received huge quantities of grain for storage, running up a deficit equal to nearly 3 percent of GNP (Jayne and Jones 1997). In 1995–96, in contrast, GMB's fixed purchasing price was too low, resulting in on-farm storage and a sharp increase in prices once official stocks were exhausted; this was followed by a 70 percent real increase in the purchasing price the next year.

In mid-1998, continuing economy-wide budget deficits, alongside inflationary pressures and a poor harvest, led the government to reintroduce price controls on maize meal for the first time since 1993. An important factor in this decision was the perception that the industrial milling sector operates as a cartel, dominated by three major large-scale millers (Jayne et al. 1999). In response, the GMB has vertically integrated into milling to compete with the large millers, raising significant questions about the ability of the GMB's pricing structure to adjust in a flexible manner to market conditions and about the more fundamental effect of weakening the position of the smaller millers, who face higher procurement costs of maize (Jayne et al. 1999).

Summary

Reform experiences vary significantly across selected countries. In both the scope and pace of reform, Kenya, Zimbabwe, Zambia, and Malawi emerge as the most interventionist and least committed to a complete reform agenda (Seppälä 1997; Jayne et al. 1999). In contrast, Ethiopia, Madagascar, and Tanzania provide examples of pervasive reforms, undertaken in a relatively short time. Table 4.2 presents the status of food marketing in the wake of reforms. Thus, whereas seven of the case-study countries have eliminated official pricing of foodgrains, price controls are still in place in the eastern and southern African states of Malawi, Tanzania, and Zimbabwe. With the exception of Madagascar,

TABLE 4.2 Current status of food market reforms in the case-study countries

Country	Reform year	Crop	Pricing policies	Marketing board	Movement restrictions	Licenses	Import taxes	Trade bans
Benin	1990	Tubers	No	Yes	Yes	No	Yes	Yes
Ethiopia	1990	*Teff*; maize; wheat	No	Yes	No	Yes	Yes	No
Ghana	1983	Tubers	No	Yes	Yes	Yes	n.a.	No
Kenya	1988–present	Maize	No	Yes	No	n.a.	Yes	Yes/no
Madagascar	1986	Rice	No	No	Yes	Yes	Yes	Yes
Malawi	1987	Maize	Yes	Yes	No	Yes	No	Yes
Mali	1981–87	Millet; sorghum	No	Yes	No	Yes	n.a.	n.a.
Tanzania	1984	Maize	Yes	Yes	Yes	n.a.	n.a.	No
Zambia	1985–94	Maize	No	Yes	No	n.a.	Yes	n.a.
Zimbabwe	1986–present	Maize	Yes	Yes	No	Yes	n.a.	Yes

SOURCES: Coulter (1994); Gebre-Meskel (1996); Seppälä (1997); Badiane et al. (1997); Jayne et al. (1999).

NOTE: n.a. means not available.

marketing boards continue to exist in all countries, although with a modified role.

The Impact on Market Performance

In recent years, a vast economic literature has arisen that explores the impact of market reforms in Sub-Saharan countries on various aspects of market performance. Among these, a number of studies have reviewed the extent of the private sector's response to market reform throughout Sub-Saharan Africa, including trader entry, competitiveness, and investment behavior (Staatz, Dioné, and Dembele 1989; Amani and Kapunda 1990; Beynon, Jones, and Yao 1992; Coulter and Golob 1992; Santorum and Tibaijuka 1992; Takavarasha 1993; Dembele 1994; Vaze et al. 1996; Badiane et al. 1997; Barrett 1997). Other studies have focused on quantitative assessments of the effect of market liberalization on increased market efficiency, measured by the degree of market integration or the co-movement of prices across space and time (Alderman 1993; Argwings-Kodhek, Mukumbu, and Monke 1993; Masters and Nuppenau 1993; Goletti and Babu 1994; Dercon 1995; Minten and Kyle 1995; Mwanaumo, Masters, and Preckel 1997; Badiane and Shively 1998; Jayne, Negassa, and Myers 1998; Bassolet and Lutz 1999). In addition, studies have sought to measure the impact of market reform on market price volatility, consumer prices, and the size of marketing margins (Adekanye 1982; Gabre-Madhin 1991; Bryceson 1992; Dadi, Negassa, and Franzel 1992; Jayne and Rubey 1993; Pinckney 1993; Alderman and Shively 1996; Barrett and Dorosh 1996; Jayne et al. 1996; Shively 1996; Jones and Wickrema 1998). Finally, analysts have increasingly turned their attention to the examination of the institutional arrangements underlying private trade and, more broadly, the impact of liberalization on market development, that is, the emergence of private trading networks and institutions to provide market information and ensure contract enforcement (Thompson 1991; Sahn and Sarris 1992; Bryceson 1993; Fafchamps 1996; Jayne et al. 1997a; Gabre-Madhin 1999).

Several general themes emerge from this broad literature. First, studies suggest that private traders have responded in large part to increased market opportunities, evidenced by private sector entry in the wake of reform. At the same time, private sector operations are characterized by limited capital, a low degree of specialization, and little long-term investment. Factors seen to constrain the behavior of traders are limited access to credit, continued uncertainty about the state's commitment to reform, and policy reversals in many instances. In countries of eastern and southern Africa, in particular, this had led to a vicious cycle in which the government's uncertainty about the private sector's capacity has triggered intervention that in turn has caused uncertainty in the private sector about the role of the state, leading to what amounts to speculative behavior by the private sector, which in turn confirms the worst fears of the state.

Second, empirical studies document a trend toward long-term market integration and the increasing efficiency of price transmission in the wake of reform, indicating that urban markets in particular are well integrated. However, rural markets are often segmented in the short term owing to weak information and transport infrastructure.

Third, marketing margins, defined as the spread between producer and consumer prices, have been reduced from pre-reform levels. This reduction appears to be primarily due to the lowering of consumer prices in many countries. Available research indicates that consumers have overwhelmingly gained from market liberalization, with a significant decline in real consumer prices for both grain and meal. This decline is attributed to increased competition and lower costs in food marketing and processing, as marketing margins have shrunk, as well as to more effective transmission of declining real world prices and increased food aid flows in the reform period (Jayne et al. 1996). The lowering of marketing margins across countries suggests that the private sector is in effect engaging in spatial arbitrage, although margins still remain high relative to producer prices, owing to the high costs of inland transport.

Fourth, market prices in the post-reform period remain highly volatile. In comparison with markets in Asia, where real average annual variations in the retail price of rice in Indonesia, for example, are 10.5 percent of the prices in the cheapest months, in African countries variations are often in excess of 40 percent (Ellis, Trotter, and Magrath 1992). Much of this level of variation has to do with the extent of storage. In parts of Ghana where maize is grown mainly as a cash crop, with very little on-farm storage, the variation in the wholesale maize price in real terms is over 90 percent. Seasonal price variation in Indonesia is mitigated by the presence of large rice millers with access to formal finance who are actively engaged in inter-seasonal storage of rice and who are willing to bear even negative returns on storage in return for the benefits of guaranteeing their operating stocks. Thus, the atomistic nature of private trade in most African countries and the lack of formal financing mechanisms result in few traders or millers engaging in temporal arbitrage, which would serve to stabilize prices (Coulter 1994).

Finally, available research addressing market development suggests that reform has prompted the emergence of large numbers of informal traders. Although these traders behave competitively in a static sense, they have dynamic disadvantages because their capacity to innovate is limited by their small scale and limited resources and educational levels (Coulter and Poulton 2001). These informal traders are unlikely to obtain bank finance or to engage in long-term contractual arrangements and generally store for very short periods. For this reason, despite initial trader entry, more complex marketing arrangements involving mechanisms such as forward contracting and quality premia have not emerged (Beynon, Jones, and Yao 1992). Moreover, private traders tend to rely on social, ethnic-based networks and personalized, trust-based exchange in order to circumvent the high transaction costs of obtaining market information, searching for reliable partners, and enforcing contracts (Fafchamps and Minten 2001). In a number of instances, age-old practices of intermediation have re-emerged, with some traders operating exclusively as brokers, specialized in matching grain buyers and sellers. This practice enables some degree of anonymous exchange between long-distance partners, thus reducing the transaction costs of searching and enforcing contracts (Gabre-Madhin 1998).

The following sections will examine the above themes more closely, drawing on the empirical literature in the context of the selected case countries: Benin, Ethiopia, Ghana, Kenya, Madagascar, Malawi, Mali, Tanzania, Zambia, and Zimbabwe.

Market Integration

The success of market reform depends in large part on the strength of the transmission of price signals among markets, or the integration of these markets. Market integration is important for predicting the effect of price changes in a given market on other markets, particularly in areas of chronic food deficit. According to Sexton, Kling, and Carman (1991), three factors may contribute to a lack of market integration: (1) markets are not linked by arbitrage because transaction costs are prohibitively high; (2) there may be impediments to efficient arbitrage such as trade barriers or risk aversion; and (3) imperfect competition exists arising from collusion or preferential access.

Traditional tests of market integration focused on bivariate correlation coefficients of spatial prices (Lele 1971; Jones 1972), but this approach received early criticism by Blyn (1973) and Harriss (1979) because these coefficients do not distinguish the presence of other synchronous factors such as inflation and seasonality. A larger body of literature has emerged that focuses on time series using ARCH methods as well as cointegration techniques to study the relationship between nonstationary price series (Engle and Granger 1987; Goodwin and Schroeder 1991; Palaskas and Harriss-White 1993). Recent efforts on spatial price transmission have focused on integration using cointegration techniques (Alderman 1993; Alexander and Wyeth 1994; Dercon 1995; Abdulai 2000). If price movements in a given market are completely irrelevant for forecasting markets in another market, the two markets are said to be segmented. If, in contrast, prices in both markets have a constant linear relation, they are cointegrated. In the event of cointegration, it is generally understood that some causality runs from one market to another that enables the prediction of prices in the second market. However, it is important to note the methodological issues associated with cointegration analysis. Although the accepted practice is that cointegrated prices are interpreted as indicating market integration, cointegration is neither necessary nor sufficient for market integration (Barrett 1996). In the presence of nonstationary transaction costs, failure to find cointegration may be consistent with market integration. This has led to criticism of exclusively price-based models of market integration, because they do not account for discontinuity in trade flows or for transfer costs, and generally do not rely on microeconomic analysis of market behavior (Dercon 1995; Harriss-White 1999). Recent work by Minten and Kyle (2000) demonstrates that the presence of transaction costs related to search and supervision and other coordination-related transaction costs results in greater price asymmetry and reduced price transmission.

Whereas cointegration models generally assume that transaction costs are constant between markets, a relatively new class of models, known as parity bounds models, uses transfer costs as a proxy for transaction costs and makes the analysis of integration dependent on the variation of transfer costs with quantities transacted and across agents (Baulch 1997). Fafchamps and Gavian (1996) applied this method in the context of livestock markets in Niger. Their results indicate that, although prices are seldom cointegrated, a parity bounds approach assuming high transportation costs and quality differentials reconciles the data with efficient spatial arbitrage.

An issue of concern to policymakers, beyond whether markets are perfectly integrated or segmented, is the speed of price transmission. The extent of market integration can thus be determined by considering both the magnitude of price adjustment, estimated with dynamic multipliers, and the time needed to adjust.

MALAWI.　Goletti and Babu (1994) conclude that almost all maize markets studied in Malawi are cointegrated in the long term, evidenced by a stable long-term relation among their prices. Moreover, the number of cointegrated markets increased after liberalization in July 1987. In the post-reform period, three major markets appear to be pivotal for the transmission of price signals to other markets. However, Goletti and Babu also note that the degree of integration is not perfect, in that the adjustment of price changes to external shocks is not 100 percent and for most markets is below 50 percent. The time required for adjustment is an average of close to 6 months, indicating that markets are not integrated in the very short term. Overall, they conclude that, although liberalization has enhanced market integration, the extent and speed of price transmission still remain low, which they attribute to the need for investments in market infrastructure.

BENIN.　In contrast to Malawi, the maize market in Benin was not affected by significant government intervention in recent decades. Thus, tests of cointegration in this context are less concerned with the effects of market reform than with whether there remain characteristics of agricultural production, marketing, and consumption that inhibit the effective transmission of price signals. Using cointegration analysis, Lutz, van Tilburg, and van der Kamp (1995) confirm that long-run price integration exists between pairs of maize markets. However, they use an error-correction model to test the speed of adjustment and find that no full short-run integration can be found within a market cycle of four

TABLE 4.3 The speed of adjustment of prices between pairs of maize markets

		Cumulative partial multiplier (percent of price transmitted)					
A_t	B_t	Same day	After 4 days	After 8 days	After 12 days	After 16 days	After 20 days
Azove (r)	Azove (w)	65	76	83	89	92	91
Azove (w)	Bohicon (w)	43	68	93	87	89	91
Dogbo (r)	Dogbo (w)	81	94	98	99	100	100
Dogbo (w)	Azove (w)	28	39	48	56	63	69
Dassa (r)	Dassa (w)	81	86	91	90	92	93
Dassa (w)	Bohicon (w)	−9	10	25	38	48	57
Bohicon (r)	Bohicon (w)	47	64	76	83	89	92

SOURCE: Lutz, van Tilburg, and van der Kamp (1995).

NOTE: (r) means retail market and (w) means wholesale market.

days. They further determine that, with a few exceptions, roughly 90 percent of the price in the central market is transmitted to the rural market within 16 days (see Table 4.3). Thus, arbitrage takes place in a relatively short time frame in the Benin market, particularly in comparison with the Malawian case.

ETHIOPIA. Negassa (1998) exhaustively tests for the direction of price causality between wholesale and retail prices (that is, vertical integration) for seven markets in Ethiopia, as well as between wholesale and producer prices (that is, horizontal or spatial integration) for five markets. In terms of vertical integration within given markets, the causality from producer to wholesale price was found to be stronger than that from wholesale to producer in the case of *teff,* wheat, and maize. In terms of spatial integration, tests of causality between the central market of Addis Ababa and other markets reveal that in the majority of cases either the Addis Ababa wholesale price caused wholesale prices in other markets or there was a two-way causality. Generally, for the three cereals considered, the results indicate a high degree of transmission of prices between levels of the marketing chain as well as evidence of spatial price transmission.

Marketing Margins

The transport and marketing of foodgrains in Africa can cost up to 70 percent of product values, far more than elsewhere, even in the developing world (Ahmed and Rustagi 1987). In particular, transport costs are high because of Africa's relatively low population density and weak infrastructure. This implies that spatial price differences have a significant influence on market performance and will counteract any potential benefits of market reform (Mwanaumo, Masters, and Preckel 1997). In many instances, prior to market reform, prices were set by governments to be uniform across space and time (pan-territorially and pan-seasonally) and the procurement and distribution of marketed grains were undertaken solely by government-owned agencies. In this period, the margin between official buying and selling prices was smaller than total marketing costs, resulting in unsustainably increasing government subsidies. An important objective of market liberalization and the opening of local markets to private traders was the reduction of marketing costs and the shrinking of price differentials, leading to the expansion of marketed volumes.

TANZANIA.   Maro (1999) points to the rapid increase in the quantity of food marketed to Dar-es-Salaam from outlying areas following liberalization: 13 percent of the marketed surplus of maize, 70 percent of rice, and 95 percent of beans was sold to Dar-es-Salaam in the 1992–98 period. In a recent study of Tanzania's agricultural markets, Delgado and Minot (2000) track the evolution of price spreads between Dar-es-Salaam and different parts of the country between 1986 and 1998. Assuming that relative wholesale-to-retail markups do not differ significantly across markets, the spatial price spread between Dar-es-Salaam and 43 other markets is considered an indicator of total marketing costs and is used as a dependent variable in the regression analysis. The explanatory variables include a time trend, road distance, road distance squared, and monthly dummy variables (see Table 4.4). The results of this analysis for wheat, rice, and maize reveal that spatial price spreads have declined over the study period, mostly as a result of liberalization. However, transport costs remain

TABLE 4.4 Determinants of spatial price spreads between Dar-es-Salaam monthly retail prices and interior market retail prices, 1986–98

	Wheat	Rice	Maize
Mean real spread over period	174.09	135.30	45.88
Continuous time trend	−1.35	−0.06	−0.09
Road distance from Dar	0.11	0.11	0.05
Road distance squared	−0.00	−0.00	−0.00
Market is on rail line	−12.41	21.32	−3.71
Market is isolated	n.s.	n.s.	10.87
Market is port city	−20.25	−32.04	−5.53
Lowest 2 of 12 monthly dummies	November, January	December, January	October, November
N	3,504	4,861	4,721
Adjusted R^2	.67	.68	.71

SOURCE: Delgado and Minot (2000).

NOTES: Prices are in December 1998 Tanzania shillings per kilogram. All coefficients are statistically significant at 5 percent or better unless n.s. is shown. N.s. indicates not statistically significant at 5 percent.

high, representing 60 percent of total marketing costs, and thus absolute spatial margins are still high. The implication of high margins is that one-quarter of Tanzania's maize supply appears still to behave as a nontradable crop.

ETHIOPIA. In Ethiopia, market integration appears to coexist with high spatial price differentials, which is indicative of poor market infrastructure in terms of transport, storage, and market information. In particular, the wholesale price spread between the Addis Ababa market and other selected markets was found to be very high, with spreads greater than 20 percent of the wholesale Addis Ababa price in one-third of cases. In addition, both vertical and spatial price differentials are characterized by high volatility. Thus, in terms of vertical spreads, the coefficient of variation of the wholesale and retail price spread for selected markets varied from 26 percent to 39 percent. In terms of spatial price spreads between Addis Ababa and selected markets, the coefficient of variation of the wholesale price spread was greater than 50 percent in one-third of all cases. The volatility of spatial price spreads may be attributed to the continuing high risk of spatial arbitrage, owing to uncertainties such as the imposition of road taxes.

CHANGES IN SPATIAL MARGINS IN THE POST-REFORM PERIOD. From the perspective of country-level market reforms and their expected objectives, changes in marketing costs in the wake of market liberalization are expected to be transmitted to prices, and thus reflected in the spatial margin between local prices. For the sake of comparison between countries, Badiane et al. (1997) use relative price spreads, calculated as the proportion of the origin market price (the lower price of each market pair). Relative price spreads range from 20 to 30 percent in Benin and Ghana, from 10 to 20 percent in Malawi, and around 10 percent in Madagascar. The lower price spreads in Malawi may be due to the higher presence of the government parastatal, ADMARC, which continued to operate a price band policy through 1996.

Spatial price trends have declined considerably across local markets in Benin, where the unit marketing costs per ton per kilometer are the lowest among the selected countries (US$0.17 per ton per kilometer in comparison with US$0.59 per ton per kilometer for Malawi). Absolute price spreads have declined in all studied markets and have also fallen significantly in relative terms for the majority of markets (Badiane et al. 1997). In contrast, no significant change in spreads is seen in Malawi, perhaps because of the continued domination of ADMARC in the study period. In general, effective market liberalization is associated with lower spatial price spreads, though to varying degrees (see Figure 4.1).

TEMPORAL MARKETING MARGINS. Analogously to the expected reduction in transport costs, market liberalization is expected to lower the cost of holding grain stocks over time and thus reduce the temporal price spread between markets, as private traders engage in temporal arbitrage. Comparing temporal price spreads across selected countries, price spreads are very high in Ghana and relatively low in Madagascar (Badiane et al. 1997).

FIGURE 4.1 Spatial marketing margins in Benin, Malawi, and Ethiopia

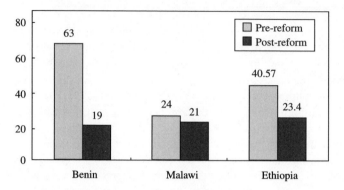

SOURCES: Badiane et al. (1997); Negassa and Jayne (1997).
NOTES: With the exception of Ethiopia, margins are the relative margin, defined as the price spread divided by the producer price. For Benin, the price spread for maize is between Parakou and Cotonou for the periods 1985–89 and 1990–95. For Malawi, the price spread for maize is between Nkhotakota and Lilongwe for the periods 1984–87 and 1988–91. For Ethiopia, the price spread for *teff* is the absolute margin between Addis Ababa and Bako for the period 1986–96.

FIGURE 4.2 Temporal percentage price spreads in Benin and Malawi

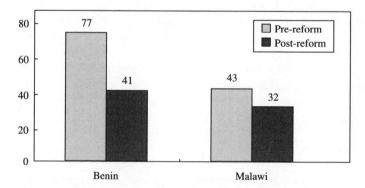

SOURCES: Badiane et al. (1997); Negassa and Jayne (1997).
NOTES: The percentage price spread is calculated as the ratio of the spread between the minimum and maximum price over the minimum price. For Benin, the price spread for maize is for Cotonou between the periods 1984–89 and 1990–95. For Malawi, the price spread for maize is for Lilongwe for the periods 1984–87 and 1988–91.

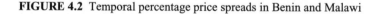

Changes in temporal margins in the wake of reform are mixed. Temporal price spreads have continuously declined in Ghana and Benin, with the most dramatic changes in Benin (see Figure 4.2), where margins have declined by between 10 percent and 80 percent. In the case of Ghana, price spreads in the early 1990s were well below the 10-year averages for the period 1987–96. In Malawi, in contrast, temporal price spreads have exhibited a constant or an upward trend, even after the exclusion of drought periods when prices tend to rise more rapidly over time.

Market Price Levels and Volatility

A major concern of the debate on structural adjustment programs (SAPs) and market reform, in particular, has been the effect on food prices in low-income countries. At the heart of these concerns is the recognition that the macroeconomic environment influences the levels and the volatility of agricultural prices and that, in the absence of hedging mechanisms, increased price variability can have adverse consequences for both consumers and producers of agricultural goods (Shively 1996).

Although the objective of market liberalization is to raise food prices and stimulate agricultural growth and incomes, the record of implementation and subsequent results have been mixed (Barrett and Dorosh 1996). An important issue is the extent to which farmers are net food buyers, in which case their real incomes may decline as food prices increase. If a substantial proportion of farmers are smallholders who are net food buyers, then real income gains from reform accrue mainly to large farmers producing a surplus for market (Weber et al. 1988).

MAIZE MEAL PRICES IN KENYA, ZIMBABWE, AND ZAMBIA.   A relatively neglected aspect of research on market reform has been its effect on the distribution of prices facing consumers. In the eastern and southern African context, Jayne et al. (1999) note that this issue is complicated by major changes in the composition of maize meal consumption as a result of reforms. Prior to reforms, in urban and grain-deficit areas maize meal consumption was in the form of refined sifted meal processed by a small number of large, roller milling firms. Roller meal, also referred to as sifted meal, has an 80–85 percent extraction rate. Registered milling firms were integrated into the state marketing channel, and milling and retailing margins were fixed by the government. In rural grain-surplus areas, whole or "posho" meal was consumed, produced by small-scale hammer mills. Hammer-milled whole meal contains the entire maize seed, with a 100 percent extraction rate. Despite the fact that the unit processing costs of hammer milling are less than half of the roller-milled meal, government subsidies in the pre-reform era kept refined meal prices below those of whole meal.

During the course of market reform, governments eliminated subsidies to registered millers. This resulted in increased roller meal prices and the rapid expansion of whole meal processing by smaller mills (Jayne et al. 1999). Prior to reforms, 90 percent of urban meal consumption was roller meal from large mills. This percentage declined to 40–60 percent in 1994 in Zimbabwe, Zambia, and Kenya (Jayne et al. 1995). Thus, with the elimination of subsidies to large mills, households switched to buying meal from smaller, hammer mills where maize meal was cheaper. A comparison of the actual price dispersions of industrial roller meal and hammer-milled meal between the pre-reform periods (January 1985 to April 1993 for Zimbabwe and Zambia and January 1985 to December 1993 for Kenya) and the reform periods (May 1993 to September 1998 for Zimbabwe and Zambia and January 1994 to September 1998 for Kenya) reveals that real roller meal prices increased significantly for Zambia and Zimbabwe. However, average whole meal prices in the reform period are lower than or roughly equal to the price of subsidized roller meal in the pre-reform period in these countries. Moreover, the availability of hammer-milled meal has resulted in the reduction of upside price risk for consumers. Since roller meal prices were not heavily subsidized in Kenya, real roller meal prices have declined, although their volatility has increased.

GHANA: FOOD PRICE VARIABILITY.   An important policy concern regarding food market reforms has been their effect not only on price levels, but also on the variability of food prices. In the absence of hedging mechanisms, increased price volatility can be detrimental to both consumers and producers. In Ghana, prior to reform, both direct and indirect state interventions in the maize market historically reduced price variability. After market reform in 1983, average wholesale maize prices declined but prices remained volatile during the mid-1980s, both seasonally and randomly (Alderman and Shively 1996).

Although maize marketing had relatively little state intervention, an important aspect of Ghana's economic reform was the rapid and massive currency devaluation that occurred between 1983 and 1985, when Ghana moved from a fixed exchange rate regime to a managed float. The value of the Ghanaian cedi was reduced from 2.75 cedis per U.S. dollar in April 1983 to 60 cedis per dollar in October 1985. The devaluation in effect shut out maize imports, resulting in an increased vulnerability to movements in domestic storage and production as well as possible border exports (Shively 1996). Over the 1978–93 period, a summary view of maize price variability, as measured by the coefficient of variation, skewness, and kurtosis, reveals that deflated wholesale maize prices remained volatile (Table 4.5). In addition, this period is characterized by a clearly upward trend in maize production, with the exception of the sharp drop in production in the major drought year of 1983.

Formal analysis of maize price variance and levels in the 1978–93 period, using an ARCH regression model, indicates that the hypothesis that market reform increased price volatility in Ghana is largely incorrect (Shively 1996). After controlling for production and the effects of devaluation and informal border exports, the analysis reveals that price variability did increase in the reform year, 1983, but that it decreased in the subsequent period. This reduction

TABLE 4.5 Summary of monthly maize prices in Ghana, 1978–93 (excluding 1983)

Market	Coefficient of variation	Skewness	Kurtosis
Bolgatanga	33	1.30	3.29
Cape Coast	14	0.64	0.49

SOURCE: Shively (1996).

NOTE: Skewness is calculated as $M_3 / (M_2)^{3/2}$; kurtosis is calculated as $[M_4 / (M_2)^2]^{-3}$ (where M_r is the rth central moment).

is attributed to increased domestic maize stocks, brought about by investments in road rehabilitation and infrastructure, as well as the reduction of the black market trade brought about by devaluation.

ETHIOPIA.   In a study of the effects of liberalization on grain prices in Ethiopia, Negassa and Jayne (1997) find that, for given markets, the share of the producer price in the retail price after reform averaged 93 percent for white *teff,* 91 percent for wheat, and 86 percent for maize, representing an increase of between 32 and 42 percent from the pre-reform period. A comparison of price levels and price variability before and after market reform in Ethiopia reveals that real average prices have fallen in terminal markets such as Addis Ababa and have risen in markets located in grain-surplus zones (see Figure 4.3). Similarly, the coefficient of variation of grain prices, based on the annual mean, has fallen significantly in the case of Addis Ababa while rising slightly in the surplus-region markets.

The Impact on Food Production

In large part, the aim of structural adjustment, and in particular the reform of domestic food markets, has been to improve the performance of the smallholder sector. Thus, the emphasis of reform efforts has been the expansion of marketed surplus, primarily through the effect of increased producer prices. However, this raises the issue of whether a boost in producer prices can provide an adequate incentive for producers to invest increasing resources in food production. Platteau (1996) argues that higher prices generate only a "once-and-for-all" upward supply response that is not sustained. Others have also questioned whether higher producer prices are indeed the primary objective of structural adjustment efforts (Krueger, Schiff, and Valdes 1991; Killick 1993). Although, initially, the aim was to provide price incentives to rural producers, pressures emerged later on to keep consumer prices low. The contradictory effects of the two objectives led to a third objective, decreasing the costs of marketing. Domestic price deregulation can thus have different effects on these three objectives, depending on the type of crop—importable, competitive, and nontradable (Table

FIGURE 4.3 Real average grain prices and temporal price variability in Ethiopia, 1986–96

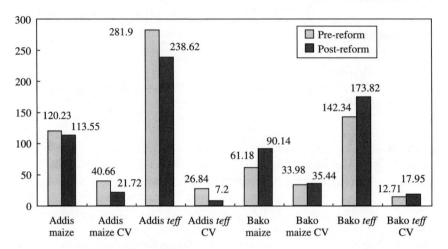

SOURCE: Negassa and Jayne (1997).

NOTES: Real prices are obtained by deflating by non-food CPI (1995 = 100) for Addis Ababa. CV is the percentage by which real monthly prices vary around the annual mean.

TABLE 4.6 Effects of liberalization measures on producer profits, consumer prices, and marketing costs

Reform measure	Producer profits			Consumer prices			Marketing costs		
	I	II	III	I	II	III	I	II	III
Domestic price deregulation	...	↑↓	↑↓	↑↓	↑↓	↑↓	...	↓	↓
Input price deregulation[a]	...	↓	↓	...	↑	↑	...	...	...
Reduced food security intervention[b]	...	↑	...	↑	↑	↑	↓	↑↓	↑↓
Liberalized food import	...	↓	→	↓	↓	→	↓	↓	→
Exchange rate depreciation	...	↑	→	↑	↑	→	...	...	...

SOURCE: Seppälä (1997).

NOTES: I—importable crop, II—competitive crop, III—nontradable crop.

[a]Input price deregulation is the end of subsidized input prices.

[b]Reduced food security interventions imply less food aid at concessional prices and stricter criteria for food security interventions.

4.6). Moreover, the effect of price reform on producer profits and consumer prices is often difficult to separate from that of concomitant reform measures such as input price deregulation and exchange rate depreciation.

Seppälä (1997) and others have argued that the effects of domestic market reform are difficult to separate from other policy changes, related or unrelated to structural adjustment, or from changes in the external environment. This suggests that the most accurate measure of the success of marketing reform is the producer/consumer price ratio, for which there are very few primary data that enable pre- and post-reform comparisons.

The Supply Response

Has liberalization increased food production? In addressing this question, Seppälä (1997) notes the following caveats. First, the period of analysis (1980–95) may be too short given that there can be a lag of 5 to 10 years between policy reform, price changes, and supply response. Second, countries vary with respect to their production efficiency. That is, liberalization has less impact on supply if production is already using land and labor relatively efficiently. Seppälä's analysis relies on the World Bank classification of 27 Sub-Saharan African countries according to a liberalization score, which reflects policy changes between the "before SAP" and "after SAP" periods. The liberalization score takes four values: "private marketing" denotes no intervention before or after SAP; "liberalized food marketing" identifies countries in which interventions had been removed by 1992; "limited intervention" indicates countries in which some interventions remained in place after 1992; "major restrictions" signals countries in which major state intervention existed after 1992. For the purposes of this analysis, countries relying on private marketing are the West African countries of Côte d'Ivoire, Gabon, Ghana, and Sierra Leone, as well as Chad and Burundi. Countries that liberalized food markets are Benin, Burkina Faso, Cameroon, Congo, Central African Republic, the Gambia, Guinea, Guinea Bissau, Madagascar, Mali, Mozambique, Niger, Senegal, Tanzania, and Togo. Countries maintaining limited intervention are Malawi, Mauritania, and Zambia, and countries with major intervention are Kenya and Zimbabwe.

Noting that growth figures are sensitive to the study period selected, a comparison of the growth in key food crop production between 1985–89 and 1990–94 by country groups, grouped according to their liberalization scores, suggests that growth was highest in countries with private marketing before and after SAP whereas production declined significantly in the interventionist countries (Table 4.7). The population-weighted average increase in countries with private marketing was 1.0 percent, compared with a 4.5 percent decline for liberalizing countries, and a 28 percent and 26 percent decline for countries retaining limited and major intervention, respectively. Among the liberalizing countries, positive growth is seen in Guinea, Togo, and Benin, while Tanzania and the Gambia have the poorest performance. Among the interventionist coun-

TABLE 4.7 Growth in per capita food production between 1985–89 and 1990–94, by liberalization score

Liberalization score	Growth in per capita food production (percent)[a]	Number of countries	Population in 1990 (million)
Private marketing	1.0	6	43
Liberalized food marketing, 1980–92	−4.5	15	116
Limited intervention in 1992	−28.0	3	20
Major restrictions in 1992	−26.0	2	33

SOURCE: Seppälä (1997).

[a] Based on average values for each period, weighted by 1990 population. With drought years excluded, the figures are 1.0 percent, −2.4 percent, −17.4 percent and −20 percent, respectively.

tries, food production in Malawi, Zambia, and Zimbabwe was very adversely affected by drought in 1992; drought again hit Zimbabwe's food production in 1994. When drought years are omitted in countries facing severe drought (mainly in East Africa), the decline in the country group average growth for the liberalizing countries changes from −4.5 percent to −2.4 percent.

Extending the analysis to find out whether producer prices in countries with liberalized food markets are substantially higher than they were before reforms, Seppälä (1997) uses real producer prices that have been indexed using 1990 as the base year. The results for the country groups are ambiguous in that no simple distinctions between liberalized and interventionist countries can be made in terms of price development in the study period and there are larger variations within country groups than between groups. The results also suggest that the importability of a crop is an important explanatory variable. Thus, coarse grains such as millet and sorghum have had good producer prices whereas maize and rice prices are more vulnerable to competition.

Overall, according to official figures, per capita grain production in Sub-Saharan Africa has remained more or less static over the past 20 years. However, the aggregate trend hides regional differences. In eastern and southern Africa, where countries used their marketing boards to promote the production of high-yielding maize varieties, production has been most affected by the partial withdrawal of state services (Coulter 1994). Viewing country cases individually, per capita production has risen significantly in Ghana, where reform was least pronounced given the relative absence of state intervention. Production has risen slightly in Mali and declined in Zimbabwe and Tanzania, where intervention was significantly greater. Out of six countries surveyed by Jayne and Jones (1997), only Tanzania saw an increase in total production between the periods 1980–89 and 1990–95, and all countries experienced declines in per capita grain production ranging from 18 to 39 percent.

In sum, it appears that the relationship between market reform and supply response in Sub-Saharan Africa is tenuous, at least over the relatively short time span following full liberalization. Drought, wars, and the substitutability of food crops for traded crops are among the factors that intervene in this relationship. Thus, although interventionist countries experienced significant declines in production between 1985–89 and 1990–94, this can be partly explained by overproduction in the 1980s and drought in the 1990s. The effect of reform on prices is also complex. In instances where real producer prices declined, this may be owing to the removal of guaranteed floor prices within pan-territorial pricing schemes as well as to the simultaneous opening of imports.

Smallholder Agriculture

How have smallholders responded to market reform? An empirical study of the aggregate productivity of smallholder farms in India, Kenya, and the Sudan by von Oppen, Njehia, and Ijaimi (1997) finds that improved market access results in increased on-farm productivity. In the Nakuru district of Kenya, a 10 percent improvement in market access resulted in an increase of 1.5 percent in aggregate productivity, of which 0.4 percent was achieved through specialization and 1.1 percent through intensification. It also appears that, in Kenya, large farmers gain the most from improved market access (Kamara and von Oppen 1999).

Jayne and Jones (1997) argue that the "smallholder Green Revolution" achieved in the 1980s in parts of eastern and southern Africa, which featured state-led investments in inputs, credit, and purchasing centers, may be over with the advance of market reforms. Up to the initial reforms, a large proportion of smallholders benefited from implicit transport subsidies in pan-territorial pricing alongside input subsidies and concessional credit. In Zimbabwe and Zambia, per capita smallholder grain production increased by 51 percent and 47 percent, respectively, between the late 1970s and late 1980s. In Kenya and Tanzania, it rose 30 percent and 69 percent, respectively, between the 1970–74 and 1980–84 periods (Figure 4.4). At the same time, production growth in this region was achieved at a cost greater than the value of the output, and state-led provision of services to smallholders proved both politically and economically unsustainable (Jayne and Jones 1997). With the partial or complete removal of explicit subsidies to smallholders, hybrid maize seed purchases and fertilizer use declined in the early 1990s in this region, and population growth has outpaced grain production growth in most of eastern and southern Africa. Although part of the food output decline in the early 1990s was due to the 1992 drought, the downward trend in production growth since the 1980s remains (Figure 4.5).

Despite improved incentives to smallholder agriculture from the currency devaluations and other macroeconomic and sectoral reforms, production has

FIGURE 4.4 Trends in per capita coarse grain production between 1970–74 and 1990–95

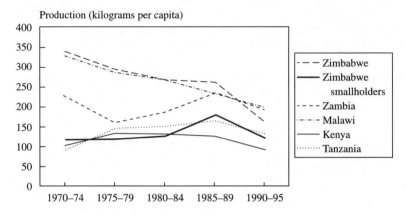

SOURCE: Data from Jayne and Jones (1997).

declined in the post-reform era in the highly interventionist countries of the region (Jayne and Jones 1997). In contrast, liberalization promoted the removal of agricultural taxation and provided a boost to smallholder agriculture in other parts of Africa, notably West Africa.

Alternatively, Sahn and Arulpragasam (1994) argue that production in Malawi has failed to rise primarily because real producer prices have not risen. Moreover, smallholders exhibit price responsiveness by reallocating resources

FIGURE 4.5 Trends in coarse grain production between 1970–74 and 1990–95

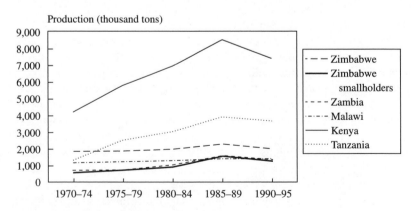

SOURCE: Data from Jayne and Jones (1997).

among crops. Thus, existing data suggest that an inverse relationship exists between maize production and the relative price of cash crops. This effect explains the lack of intensification of maize production above population growth in Malawi.

In Zambia, the results of a survey of smallholders in the post-reform era (Kalinda, Shute, and Filson 1998) suggest that, although the majority of rural households had access to agricultural extension and credit services, smallholders faced problems in marketing their output under the liberalized system. Smallholders became more vulnerable relative to private agents because their cash liquidity constraints forced them to sell at the harvest rather than store output on-farm. Similarly, credit constraints led to barter transactions on disadvantageous terms for smallholders. In Tanzania, Ghana, and Mali, liberalization has increased the smallholders' role in storing maize, although storage losses are considerable (Coulter 1994).

In the Malian context, three factors appear to influence households' ability to produce a net surplus of coarse grains for the market: rainfall and soil conditions, household access to farm technology, and institutional support in the form of extension services and credit (Staatz, Dioné, and Dembele 1989). Thus, although farmers have benefited from market reform, their capacity to respond has been limited by their restricted access to technology and services; this is similar to the case of rice producers in Madagascar (Berg 1989). This finding is consistent with studies in other parts of the Sahel, which suggest very low short-run price elasticities of supply for coarse grains (Jayne and Minot 1989).

In sum, the effect of market reforms on smallholders depends in large part on the extent to which pre-reform governments taxed or subsidized smallholder production. In the eastern and southern African context, market reforms have resulted in the removal of input and credit subsidies, whose positive effects have not been offset in the short run by the gains from lower-cost, private distribution systems. In contrast, reform in contexts such as West Africa and elsewhere where smallholders were taxed heavily has had an initially positive, although limited, impact on production. Generally, it appears that market reforms have improved the distribution of inputs and outputs but have not led to increased demand by farmers for modern inputs. The increased costs of inputs after reforms are partly offset by increased output prices and an improved input distribution system. However, modern input use and, consequently, gains in productivity remain low, owing mainly to lack of access to credit (Badiane et al. 1997).

Poverty, Welfare, and Food Security Impacts

Unlike export crops, food crops serve both as a source of income for rural producers and as a wage good for urban and rural households. The conflict between these two roles defines the classic food policy dilemma confronting reform efforts: the need to restore producer price incentives while keeping consumer prices low. Historically, government intervention in food markets in Africa was primarily intended to keep urban consumer prices low and stable, with a secondary objective to protect farmers from the vagaries of private market actors (Sahn, Dorosh, and Younger 1997). The poor performance of agriculture lies at the heart of the push for market reforms. Fundamentally, reforms have aimed to remove the restrictions impeding the transmission of market prices from the farm gate to consumers.

As noted by Sahn, Dorosh, and Younger (1997), the process of state disengagement from food markets raises two major concerns. In the case of farmers, the key issue is whether and how private sector agents will fill the gap left by the parastatal agency. The two main concerns are (1) whether farmers benefit or are penalized by their reliance on parastatals, and (2) whether private food markets function well or not. In the case of consumers, the key issue is whether they had access to food at subsidized prices prior to reform and whether liberalization will harm the poor as subsidies are removed.

In order to address these issues, the extent to which food was rationed at the official price in the pre-reform era must be determined. If the parastatal guarantees universal access to consumers and the marginal price is equal to the official price, the benefits of the subsidy accrue to households in proportion to their consumption. If the subsidy is implicit, procurement at below the parity price will keep farm-gate prices low and depress producer incomes. In the case of an explicit subsidy from the treasury, which drives a wedge between producer and consumer prices, the financial costs are borne by those who pay the taxes that finance the budget.

Further, when state procurement and imports fail to meet demand at the official price, rationing is likely to occur. In the implicit subsidy case, if the cost of keeping prices low is borne by the farmer, the incentives to produce and market food crops is reduced. If the treasury pays the cost of an explicit subsidy, constrained budgets may result in rationing at the official price and in consideration of who gets access to the subsidized good at the lower price.

Ghana: Limited Parastatal Involvement prior to Reform

In Ghana, no foodgrain dominates consumption—domestically produced root crops and coarse grain account for most of food consumption. The diversity of the national diet reduces the impact of intervention in any one crop. State intervention in Ghana was relatively limited prior to reform and government purchases of grain were too small to influence producer prices. However, the extent of the impact of the devaluation on food prices, particularly of imported foods, remained a concern. Alderman and Shively (1996) find that the prices of major staple foods declined between 1984 and 1990. They find that a devaluation of 100 percent translated into only an 8 percent increase in food prices, owing to the existence of a parallel market premium prior to reforms and to the fact that few food items are traded internationally.

Malawi: State Intervention without Rationing

Prior to reform, the agricultural parastatal, ADMARC, was engaged in both procurement and distribution of maize. As seen in Table 4.8, the explicit subsidy of consumers was substantial, representing between 0.74 and 3.19 percent of total government spending, and there was little taxation of producers (Sahn, Dorosh, and Younger 1997). The government did not reduce subsidies through increasing consumer prices until the 1990s, during the second decade of economic reforms. Prior to reforms, an active parallel market for maize purchases existed, with prices from 20 to 75 percent below the official ADMARC price.

However, it is likely that the rural poor had limited access to the lower official maize prices, for several reasons. First, ADMARC sold maize in larger quantities than were generally purchased by the poor. Second, the distance to ADMARC distribution centers limited access by those with financial and time constraints. Finally, during periods of peak demand, when the price divergence would be greatest, rural smallholders were most adversely affected relative to urban households (Sahn, Dorosh, and Younger 1997). Thus, in welfare terms, it would appear that the universal subsidy scheme in place prior to reform resulted in a disproportionate share of benefits going to the non-poor.

At the same time, an important question remains whether market reforms have benefited the poor. According to Chilowa (1998), structural adjustment

TABLE 4.8 Maize subsidy in Malawi, 1980–88

Year	Subsidy (1980 MK per metric ton)	Quantity of ADMARC sales (metric tons)	Total subsidy (1980 MK thousand)	Subsidy as percentage of	
				GDP	Total expenditure
1980	55.40	136,849	7,581	0.75	2.45
1981	57.32	95,821	5,492	0.56	1.66
1982	67.76	84,212	5,705	0.45	2.17
1983	16.72	134,885	2,555	0.22	0.74
1984	31.83	174,678	5,559	0.54	1.98
1985	38.93	115,460	4,495	0.43	1.54
1986	15.35	246,860	3,789	0.36	1.35
1987	49.31	198,108	9,769	0.94	3.19
1988	62.28	102,399	6,377	0.55	2.87

SOURCES: Kandoole, Kaluwa, and Buccola (1988); Reserve Bank of Malawi 1987, 1988 in Sahn, Dorosh, and Younger (1997).

NOTE: MK refers to Malawi kwacha.

policies have concentrated on liberalizing markets rather than addressing production constraints. Thus, the losers from market reforms are the net food buyers among smallholder farmers, low-income urban consumers, and remote smallholders, while the winners are the net food sellers among smallholders and traders, and ADMARC itself. The food insecurity of rural households, which normally experience a maize deficit, has been exacerbated by the high and volatile producer and consumer prices in the wake of reforms (Ministry of Economic Planning and Development 1995, in Chilowa 1998).

Peters (1996) similarly concludes that structural adjustment reforms have not benefited the rural poor disproportionately. Whereas liberalization has provided new income opportunities for relatively better-off households in terms of expanded tobacco and maize sales, the poorest 25 percent of rural households studied experienced a relative worsening of income and food security. Between 1986–87 and 1990–91, in response to rising consumer prices and price volatility, this income group reduced its share of maize sales and increased the proportion of its cash budget going to maize purchases (Table 4.9). Further, analysis of maize prices in the local markets suggests that producer prices fell by just over 25 percent in real terms between 1986 and 1991 owing to high inflation. The lower real producer price combined with a higher consumer price led to an increase of 44 percent in the actual cost of maize, with a corresponding decline in real minimum wages in this period.

Zimbabwe: The Food Insecurity Paradox

In the pre-reform era, the threefold expansion of marketed grain by smallholders from 1980 was hailed as Zimbabwe's smallholder miracle (Mabeza-Chimedza 1998). At the same time, overflowing state grain reserves throughout the 1980s and widespread chronic malnutrition together constituted Zimbabwe's food insecurity paradox (Jayne and Chisvo 1991). This paradox was attributed to the structure of the grain market, in which the one-way distribution of grain by the state siphoned grain out of semi-arid rural areas early in the harvest season. Controls on private transfers of maize, on resale, and on pricing restricted rural consumers from obtaining maize, thus creating shortages in producing areas later in the season. This had the further result of reducing rural consumers' cash incomes by as much as 30 percent (Jayne and Chisvo 1991). A key question now is whether market reform in Zimbabwe has successfully resolved this paradox.

Zimbabwe has diverged very significantly from other countries in the region in its approach to enhancing food security and reducing consumer price instability. The parastatal agency, the Grain Marketing Board (GMB), remains a major player in the domestic procurement and sales of maize as well as the monopoly importer and exporter. Over the reform period, GMB has expanded its marketing activities and continues to maintain pan-territorial and pan-seasonal prices. In May 1998, the government reinstated price controls on roller

TABLE 4.9 Comparison of welfare indicators for sample rural households in Malawi, 1986–87 and 1990–91

	1st income quartile		2nd income quartile		3rd income quartile		4th income quartile	
	1986–87	1990–91	1986–87	1990–91	1986–87	1990–91	1986–87	1990–91
Income per capita (1987 MK)	37.49	31.39	64.49	57.76	87.66	93.78	184.56	288.39
Percentage change		–16.0		–10.0		7.0		56.0
Percentage of income from food crops	19.1	12.6	16.6	17.3	18.2	18.1	14.4	16.5
Percentage of income for home consumption	34.6	38.3	32.6	33.6	32.4	29.8	28.8	21.8
Maize harvest (kilograms per capita)	73.2	86.8	110.9	152.9	146.1	228.6	248.9	408.3
Maize sales (kilograms per capita)	8.5	4.7	3.6	17.4	8.5	28.4	17.2	89.9
Maize purchases (kilograms per capita)	22.8	16.9	32.4	26.1	34.6	29.6	36.8	24.7
Percentage of cash budget spent on maize	25	36	23	24	19	19	13	9

SOURCE: Peters (1996).

NOTE: MK refers to Malawi kwacha.

meal for the first time since reforms began in 1993 (Jayne et al. 1999). Although the return to maize meal price controls was a response to the perceived oligopolistic behavior of the three major industrial milling firms, the GMB's selling price for maize in 1998 was 20–35 percent below market prices. Thus, the government has implicitly reintroduced subsidies on industrial roller meal because the large firms have better access to the relatively cheap GMB maize stocks. Since the roller meal subsidy may result in increased demand for roller meal, it will disproportionately benefit high-income consumers. Major losers potentially are small-scale, informal millers and private traders, as well as the treasury (Jayne et al. 1999).

Beyond Market Reform: The Road Ahead

In Sub-Saharan Africa, 15 out of 28 countries classified by the World Bank as undertaking structural adjustment had significant controls on food marketing in the 1980s, and an additional 5 had state intervention in food procurement. By 1994, all of these countries had lifted the main restrictions on market participation (Jones 1995). In the nearly two decades since reforms began, economic reform and structural adjustment have tended to draw polarized responses either in favor or against reform. Related to this is the tendency to treat structural adjustment as a single, well-understood, empirically observable process rather than as an abstract concept with diverse, and often contradictory, empirical references (Booth 1994).

THE PREMISE OF REFORM.   Market reform was largely predicated on the premise among donors that marketing boards in Africa depressed food production by taxing agriculture (Bates 1981; World Bank 1981). This was generally true in the case of coarse grains in West and Central Africa and in the non-maize-based regions of eastern Africa. In these countries, food policy was designed primarily to meet urban consumption needs, a large share of which depended on cheap imports of rice and wheat, achieved by exchange rate overvaluation (Bates 1981; Jayne et al. 1997b). Food policy was fundamentally different in the maize-dependent countries of eastern and southern Africa, where state intervention was greater and based on extensive subsidization of European settler producers as well as of African smallholders (Jayne and Jones 1997). In these countries, urban food security depended to a greater extent on domestically produced white maize, rather than on imported grains. Given the importance of the state in providing credit and input and output markets, it is argued that the prediction that market reform would lead to increased production was less accurate. It is increasingly recognized that sectoral reform prescriptions have been based in large part on superficial knowledge of the prevailing economic institutions and how they influence economic outcomes (Jayne et al. 1997a).

THE PROCESS OF REFORM.   The process of market reform can encompass at least seven distinct types of sectoral measure affecting price incentives: regulatory reform (liberalization); price reform; cost-saving measures; privatization of state agencies; the replacement of universal subsidies with targeting; external trade policy; and measures to foster new marketing channels (Jones 1995). To date, market reform has focused mainly on domestic and external trade liberalization and on privatization; less progress has been made in defining the new role that governments should play and the appropriate instruments to undertake that role, and how donor support and state resources can best be used.

In this section, we begin by summarizing the achievements and failures of market reforms in Sub-Saharan Africa, based on the extensive literature surveyed in this chapter. Second, we review the lessons of the reform experience of the past two decades and highlight the constraints to effective liberalization. Third, we discuss emerging policy issues in market development; in particular, we raise the importance of institutions. Finally, we discuss the appropriate role of the state and effective donor support in the post-reform era.

Has Market Reform Succeeded?

To begin, an important issue is whether market reform has been fully implemented. The most important obstacle to reform implementation has been the lack of genuine commitment by decisionmakers (Coulter and Poulton 2001). This is particularly the case in Zimbabwe, where controls over trade, the use of food reserves to maintain pan-territorial pricing, and a reluctance to eliminate marketing boards are observed. Similarly, Zambia's reform process was halted by the creation of the Food Reserve Agency for commercial imports of grain and fertilizer. Badiane et al. (1997) also raise the pervasive problem of partial liberalization, which occurs when the policies and regulations of other sectors that directly affect agricultural markets are not included in the reforms. The apparent lack of commitment by policymakers may be rooted in ideology, vested interests, or bureaucratic failure. Kenya is a particular example of vested interests—the liberalization experience has been marked by the influence of rent-seeking.

The context of market reforms and the process by which reforms have been implemented both vary widely among countries in Sub-Saharan Africa. In eastern and southern African countries with a significant reliance on white maize and a dualistic agrarian structure, reform has taken place in the context of donor conditionality and intense macroeconomic difficulties. In these countries, where pre-reform policies were generally favorable to agriculture and state intervention was extensive, reform has tended to be partial, with the state retaining some role in the food marketing system. In contrast, in the Sahelian countries, where there is a greater reliance on coarse grains and rice, and where food aid pricing policy and exchange rate and trade policies created a strong bias against agriculture, parastatal marketing agencies had a limited role in the market. Elsewhere in West Africa and other forest zone countries in Central

Africa, root and other non-grain crops dominate staple food markets. These countries are characterized by a relatively private marketing system prior to reforms, and policy interventions were generally focused on trade and storage.

Generally, market reform in Sub-Saharan Africa was motivated by the need to address agricultural production incentives and promote supply, to increase smallholder incomes and consumer welfare, to remove distortions in the agricultural economy caused by rent-seeking and biases, and to reduce or eliminate the unsustainable fiscal costs of state intervention. In light of these objectives, how successful has market reform in Sub-Saharan Africa been? Jones (1998) notes that the main results of reform include

- A significant reduction in marketing and processing costs,
- Improvement in the spatial integration of markets,
- A wider range of marketed products, such as less refined maize meal,
- A reduction in the fiscal costs of the marketing system, to the extent that official prices are aligned with the market or parastatal marketing has been eliminated,
- Limited impact on grain production and agricultural productivity,
- Efficiency gains for consumers and mainly large-scale producers,
- Increased price instability for both producers and consumers.

In this study, we separate the impact of reform into three categories: the impact on market performance, the impact on production, and the impact on poverty and welfare. A consensus is emerging that market reform has been most successful in the first category, with the narrowing of marketing margins and the increased transmission of prices (Badiane et al. 1997). Unresolved issues are the low level of investment and specialization by private traders, the lack of market development into more sophisticated arrangements such as forward trading and quality premia, and high transport costs (Beynon, Jones, and Yao 1992). Almost universally, private sector agents are constrained by limited access to credit and storage facilities, as well as by problems in securing transport (Beynon, Jones, and Yao 1992; Badiane et al. 1997). As a result, turnover of stocks is rapid and seasonal storage is rare, which serves to exacerbate the volatility of prices.

In terms of the second type of impact, advocates of market reform argued that liberalization would raise farm productivity by raising farm profitability through increased average output costs and reduced input costs spurring investments and commercialization. However, the results of reform are mixed and often inconsistent with expected productivity increases. Jayne et al. (1997b) use national-level data from seven countries and find that partial measures of agricultural labor productivity increased in only three cases and partial measures of land productivity rose in four cases. Badiane et al. (1997) use micro-level household data from five countries and conclude that, although reform has succeeded in improving the distribution system for inputs and outputs, it has not created increased demand for the modern inputs that could lead to productivity gains. Increased input costs, owing mainly to the removal of universal state subsidies, have been partially compensated by the simultaneous increase in output prices and improvements in input distribution, but the main constraint to smallholder farmers is access to credit.

In reviewing the reform experiences of four widely divergent countries (Kenya, Zambia, Mozambique, and Zimbabwe), Jayne et al. (1999) conclude that food market liberalization has generated more successes than is generally recognized. Examples of these successes are the efficiency gains in maize milling and retailing in eastern and southern Africa, the greater availability of maize grain in rural deficit areas, and the rise of regional trade patterns. Furthermore, consumer vulnerability to price instability has not been as severe as portrayed because improved grain distribution, processing, and border trade have expanded consumers' options and enhanced their ability to stabilize maize meal expenditures.

Constraints to Effective Liberalization

Throughout the reform process, critics both in Africa and among development economists in Europe have expressed unease about liberalization and its potential benefits. Questions were raised as to whether the approach was thought out; whether implementation was adequately phased; whether too much emphasis was placed on pricing policy rather than on complementary investments in infrastructure and services (Coulter 1994). A literature review of cereal market reform experiences by Coulter and Compton (1991) reveals the emergence of several constraints in the operation of liberalized marketing systems in Africa:

- Inadequate roads and vehicles
- Lack of availability of trade credit
- Lack of storage chemicals
- Lack of market information
- Unsupportive legal framework
- Lack of commitment by governments
- Inconsistent donor support

Among these factors, the lack of government commitment presents the most significant obstacle. Coulter (1994) identifies two principal reasons for governments' resistance to reform. First, liberalization is perceived to be a risky process. African policymakers may be concerned about the potential for market failure, the emergence of oligopolistic structures, the vulnerability of farmers at the hands of speculative middlemen, and ensuing price volatility. There may also be a credibility issue because, at the time of reforms, policymakers had not witnessed a fully liberalized system in operation, compounded by donor countries' failure to liberalize their own agricultural trade. A second main source of resistance is a vested interest in the command economy stemming from the "patrimonial order," in which leaders maintain patron–client relationships based on familial and ethnic loyalties (Bates 1981; Killick 1994).

It appears that donors have varied in their enthusiasm for and approach to reform. Thus, some donors' approach, for example in Tanzania and Zambia, has been to support state-dominated cooperatives. Similarly, marketing boards have been favored for infrastructural support throughout the adjustment period, for example in Ghana and Kenya. In Tanzania, donors continued building warehouses for the parastatal up to 1992, two years after the government had stopped its trading role and despite the fact that the NMC had over 400,000 tons of surplus storage capacity (Coulter 1994).

The market reform process has been characterized by frequent policy reversals, interventions, and inconsistent official policies. These can be attributed to

- Mistrust of markets by policymakers, particularly in formerly socialist states such as Tanzania and Mozambique,
- Governments' commitment, under the guise of a "social contract," to provide input subsidies and assured markets at pan-territorial prices, and
- Political processes in which politicians respond to local interests and pressures (Coulter and Poulton 2001).

Emerging Lessons and Key Policy Issues

Important lessons emerge from the nearly two decades of reform experiences across Sub-Saharan Africa. Liberalization of food markets was both necessary and inevitable given the costly nature of state intervention and the financially unsustainable expectations embedded in the "social contract" (Jayne and Jones 1997; Coulter and Poulton 2001). Liberalization accelerated the demise of the state-led smallholder Green Revolution in certain countries in southern and eastern Africa, which was inherently a temporary and unsustainable phenomenon owing to the high level of subsidies involved (Jayne and Jones 1997). The challenge is to find more sustainable ways to support productivity growth. Liberalization has been severely constrained by the lack of domestic political consensus (Booth 1994; Badiane et al. 1997; Jones 1998).

The review of experiences suggests that reforms have resulted in increased competition, leading to reduced marketing costs, with benefits to both producers and consumers' welfare; reduced non-productive, rent-seeking activities; and rationalized pricing policies that allow more productive use of agricultural resources and lower fiscal burdens (Jones 1998). Thus, it can be concluded that liberalization itself has not jeopardized food security or agricultural growth.

At the same time, what are the key policy issues emerging from the reform experiences? Coulter and Poulton (2001) suggest the main elements of a guiding framework for improving the operations of liberalized marketing systems are

- To minimize the costs of producing and distributing grain,
- To free up cross-border trade.
- To provide a clear legal basis for liberalization, and
- To promote market-based diversification.

Jones (1998) identifies four key policy issues that have emerged across a wide range of countries:

1. The central importance of physical infrastructure, especially the network of rural feeder roads.
2. The limited capacity of the small-scale private sector to deepen and expand its operations beyond small-scale processing and assembly, wholesale and retail activities, pointing to the need for effective systems of credit and input supply, as well as of market regulation to promote the supply of public goods such as information and contracts.
3. The need for new instruments and approaches to price stabilization that combine the private sector's marketing efficiency with either greater price stability or means of reducing price volatility.
4. The potentially increasing importance of trade policy and the impact of international trade agreements on domestic marketing policy.

From Market Reform to Market Development: The Importance of Institutions

As Jayne et al. (1997a) note, market reform is not an end in itself. Liberalization may have brought about a more efficient foodgrain distribution system, but Schultz's "efficient but poor" hypothesis may also be applied to the functioning of food markets. Although margins may have been reduced to the level of marketing costs, these costs are prohibitively high throughout Sub-Saharan Africa, inhibiting private investment in markets. Food markets in Africa are characterized by small-scale trader operations, limited trader investment in transport and storage, and the slow development of private markets. Despite an initially dynamic response to reform, more complex marketing arrangements such as forward trading and quality premia have emerged very slowly, if at all. Thus, private food markets have a limited capacity to reduce risks for producers, consumers, and traders (Beynon, Jones, and Yao 1992).

Recent institutional research on the structure of food markets in Africa reveals that markets are characterized by primary forms of exchange involving high transaction costs, such as the costs of searching for buyers and sellers, of monitoring and enforcing contracts, and of obtaining market information

(Jayne et al. 1997a; Dorward, Kydd, and Poulton 1998; Gabre-Madhin 1998; Fafchamps 1999). In addition, markets rely on the use of personalized trading networks, which reduce transaction costs but also limit the scope of marketing activities (Fafchamps 1996; Robison and Siles 1997). Other important institutional issues remain:

- The existence of high market risks and ineffective coordination, which inhibit private investment in developing more reliable markets.
- Uncertain property rights and their enforcement, creating further risk in the marketing environment.
- Limited vertical coordination between input delivery, farm finance, and crop sales, owing to the lack of trust and the absence of institutions governing business practices and providing contract enforcement at low cost.
- Limited public market information, resulting in asymmetric information.
- Limited product grades and standards, requiring visual inspection of products at the time of exchange and contributing to higher transaction costs.
- Transport constraints, as a result of which import parity prices are two to four times higher than export parity prices, leading to increased price instability and market concentration (Shaffer et al. 1985; Jayne et al. 1997b; Gabre-Madhin 1998; Fafchamps 1999).

The Appropriate Role of the State and Donor Support

In most African countries undertaking reform, the World Bank and, to a lesser extent, other donors have played a significant role (Jones 1995). Although the reform agenda has taken a negative view of the role of the state, a consensus is emerging that the state can, and should, play a positive role in enhancing market development beyond reform. The review of reform experiences suggests that conditionality is a blunt instrument: although the IMF's budgetary conditions have proved decisive in accelerating implementation of pricing reform, they do so in a way that compromises good reform management (Jones 1998). Other issues include conflicts between donor agencies' objectives.

As the food security agenda moves beyond market reform to market development, Jones (1995) identifies three main problems that must be resolved:

1. *Defining the role of the state.* Market failures arise in the absence of an institutional infrastructure or regulatory framework to reduce transaction costs. This framework would include legal and social conventions to define and allocate property rights; rules about transactions and contracts between individuals; rules about liability; and a system to enforce these rules. The state can play a central part in sustaining the regulatory framework underlying markets, if the distortion of enforcement by local political pressure can be avoided.

2. *Establishing a policy for price instability.* In many instances, there is a complete absence of market instruments to reduce or pool price risk. This may present an opportunity for the state to act, especially in terms of delivering income support to targeted vulnerable groups. A further policy issue is that, in order not to preclude the private sector from undertaking seasonal and inter-annual storage, the state withdrawal from stabilization must be perceived as irreversible. A program for price stabilization must emphasize the development of forward contracting and futures markets, as well as trade policy issues.

3. *Determining how to deliver support services to the private sector.* Whereas state investment in marketing has primarily focused on permanent storage facilities, with the assumption of high losses in traditional forms of storage, liberalization has resulted in grain storage being increasingly on farm. Thus, an important area of state support is physical investment, research, and extension for on-farm storage (Tyler and Bennett 1993). Credit is another critically important area of support. The state must take into consideration the particular needs facing the large number of small-scale private sector participants, for example by designing group lending schemes. The state can also play a key role in the provision of market information, notwithstanding the danger of relying on donor funds to maintain information systems. Finally, establishing and maintaining quality standards would reduce transaction costs and facilitate the development of forward contracting (Gabre-Madhin 1998).

5   Market Reforms for Export Crops

At least 90 percent of export cropping in Sub-Saharan Africa (excluding South Africa) since the late 1970s has been carried out by smallholders, the same ones responsible for the vast majority of food supply (Delgado 1995). The industrial palm, rubber, and fruit plantations in the humid coastal belt of West Africa and the large farms of East Africa were the exception, rather than the rule, for export cropping prior to the reform era of the 1980s. Millions of small-scale producers have been directly affected by liberalization in export crop markets as well as food crop markets over the past 15 to 20 years.

Yet the effects and timing of export crop liberalization were quite different from those of food crop liberalization, for four main reasons. First, public revenue from price taxation of agricultural exports has historically been a major source of domestic funding for government activities. Second, because of the importance of export crops in the commercialization of subsistence agriculture, export crop price policies were akin to a rural incomes policy. Third, export crops were typically more dependent on credit and purchased inputs than were food crops. Fourth, African governments tended to have a much greater degree of control over export crop marketing than over food crop marketing, especially in West Africa (Delgado 1995).

This chapter aims to review market reform experiences in the export crop sector and their impact in selected countries of Sub-Saharan Africa. In reviewing the country case studies, the analysis addresses the following questions: What has been the role of market reforms over the past 20 years in changing the fundamental relationship of the state to smallholders, and how have outcomes differed across countries and crops? What institutions have sprung up to promote the input supply and marketing functions previously carried out by parastatals? How have reforms affected the levels, composition, timing, and quality of traditional export crop sales by producers in the context of changing external markets for these products? How have producers and private traders fared during the reform period in terms of the level and stability of their incomes? What remains to be done to strengthen the positive impact of existing reforms?

116

   The chapter synthesizes empirical studies in 11 countries in Sub-Saharan Africa, of which 2 are in southern Africa (Malawi and Mozambique), 2 are in eastern Africa (Tanzania and Uganda), 2 are in Anglophone West Africa (Nigeria and Ghana), and 5 are in Francophone West Africa (Benin, Cameroon, Côte d'Ivoire, Mali, and Senegal). These countries were selected to capture diversity in reform experience, institutional heritage, and traditional export crops. The markets studied include both perennial tree crops (cocoa, coffee, and cashew) and field crops (cotton, peanuts, and tobacco).

The Historical Role of Export Crops in Africa and Their Place in the Market Reforms of the 1980s and 1990s

The rise of export cropping in Africa has been extensively documented by historians (Crowder 1968; Suret-Canale 1977).[1] It began around 1910 in most areas, then took off in earnest after the Second World War with the rapid expansion of cash-cropped area per agricultural worker (Anthony et al. 1979). In colonial times, export cropping was seen as a way to make the colonies pay the costs of military and civilian occupation. After independence it was one of the few sources available for new governments to finance rapidly expanding national budgets (Bates 1981). As shown in Table 5.1, agricultural exports accounted for 37 percent of all Sub-Saharan merchandise export receipts as late as 1985–87. Their share was significantly lower but still substantial at 27 percent in 1995–97 (excluding Nigeria and South Africa).

   Agricultural production prior to and during the colonial era was constrained primarily by lack of access to markets and services and seasonal labor bottlenecks in indigenous farming systems. The commercialization-via-export-cropping economic development model pursued until recently combined narrowly focused schemes for boosting the output of specific crops with the introduction of seeds that had different seasonal labor profiles than the traditional food crops. These changes overcame seasonal bottlenecks and permitted expansion of output with existing resources. In this sense, the expansion of cash crops such as peanuts, cotton, and cocoa was a manifestation as much of technical change as of commercialization (Delgado and Ranade 1987).

   The heyday of cash crop expansion was the 1960s. This period saw secular improvement in world commodity prices, fueled by the postwar expansion in world trade. It was also a time when many African smallholders first obtained access to cropping opportunities previously reserved for colonial farmers (Heyer, Maitha, and Senga 1975).

   The issue of the state's role in the marketing and processing of export crops was not very prominent in Africa in the 1960s and early 1970s. Compared with alternatives, the surplus generated by new export activities was large

---

1. This section draws heavily on Delgado (1998).

TABLE 5.1 Agriculture's share in selected African economies (percent)

Country	In GDP		In total merchandise export		In 1990 total labor force	
	1986–88	1996–98	1985–87	1995–97	Males	Females
Benin	36	35	22	48	65	86
Cameroon	24	41	30	32	62	83
Côte d'Ivoire	30	26	73	57[a]	54	72
Ghana	50	21	65	36	64	55
Malawi	44	33	93	80	78	96
Mali	44	41	87	60	83	89
Nigeria	36	31	4	3	43	44
Senegal	19	19	18	9	70	86
Tanzania	46	43	85	65	78	91
Uganda	54	42	96	74	81	88
Sub-Saharan Africa excluding Nigeria and South Africa	30	28	37	27	72	85

SOURCES: World Bank (1992, 2000).
[a]Two-year average of 1995 and 1996 because 1997 data were not available.

enough to provide a respectable share for producers, even after marketing parastatals, rural notables, fiscal authorities, and domestic and foreign processors had taken large margins (Anthony et al. 1979; Delgado and Jammeh 1991).

Questions about the role of the state in agriculture began to arise after Africa's commodity exports began to decline following the oil shock of 1973 (Lewis 1980). The reaction was delayed for tropical beverage crops because of a tripling of their prices in the 1976–77 marketing season. This price rise was due to the domination in the 1970s of world markets for cocoa, coffee, and tea by a small number of sellers and purchasers, under conditions of price-inelastic demand managed by international buffer stocks. The stock decline responsible for the 1977 event was only 29,000 metric tons (Gbetibouo and Delgado 1984). By 1979, however, commodity prices were widely in decline for the same reason, once the effects had set in from good weather, technological change, investment in response to high prices, and income compression in terminal markets from rising oil prices (Gbetibouo and Delgado 1984). These commodity price swings contributed hugely to the inauguration of structural adjustment program (SAP) lending by the World Bank in that year (World Bank 1981).

Even as the need for market-oriented economic reform in Africa's export-cropping schemes became widely accepted during the 1980s, it was increasingly apparent that specific strategies were being developed only very slowly, if at all. Agricultural policies of the 1970s were often preserved by vested interests that were still in control in the 1980s (Bates 1981). In many cases, reform was complicated by concern about the impact of reforms on the rural poor, who were facing declining real world prices for agricultural exports (of the order of 60 percent—Table 1.2), declining per capita incomes, and drought.

African countries accounted for large world market shares of tropical beverage crops in the 1970s (and still account for two-thirds of world cocoa production), and they were heavily dependent on only a few commodities per country (Delgado 1995). Thus they had a large stake in the operation of the international buffer stock agreements that ruled several of these markets in the 1970s and hung on through the 1980s. In particular, the buffer stock agreements of the International Cocoa Organization (ICCO) and the quota mechanism of the International Coffee Organization (ICO) provided important rents to commodity export parastatals in Africa during the 1970s, because they allocated export quotas. With the collapse of cocoa and coffee prices in the early 1980s, the international buffer stocks grew to unsustainable sizes in the late 1980s, leading to their demise at the end of the decade. African parastatals, which were in part the logical extension of these schemes, quickly followed suit in many cases (Akiyama et al. 2001).

The large rents, the real importance of export cropping in the existing economic structure, and the lack of governance strong enough to deal with the redistribution of income inherent in institutional change meant that reforms were delayed in many cases. Many African countries went from a situation where export agriculture was a net source of revenue to a situation where it was a net drain. Whereas food markets were largely liberalized during the 1980s (other than in a few countries in southern Africa), export crop activities showed widely varying degrees of liberalization into the 1990s, and in some cases have not been liberalized at all.

Issues Related to the Reform of Export Crop Markets

Market reform in Africa was motivated by the inability of governments to maintain parastatals and producer prices at a time of falling world prices. Reforms were complicated by the political difficulty of changing the status quo. Changes in policies have trade-offs that are specific to each case. As a general rule, however, overall macroeconomic reform in Africa was associated with a reduction in public expenditures, leading to declines not only in social services but also in public goods support to agricultural production, such as research, extension, and road construction and maintenance. This led to debates about the implications of reform for public revenue, for the structure and performance of agriculture, and for rural incomes.

PUBLIC REVENUE. Liberalization of export crop parastatals has raised anew the issue of agriculture's appropriate tax contribution to the national economy (Townsend 1999). Surveys of African countries suggest a negative relationship between the share of public revenue collected from price taxation of commodity exports and the total amount of revenue collected (World Bank 1994). One explanation is that net revenue rises when money-losing parastatals are closed. In other cases, a Laffer-type increase in total tax revenues may be made possible by faster growth under a lower tax rate.

Unfortunately, price taxation through direct control of crop marketing is sometimes replaced by other forms of export taxation in reforming countries. In Tanzania, for example, the decline in price taxation by parastatals was accompanied by devolution of taxing authority from central authorities and a rapid proliferation in local taxes and cesses. Calculations show that the total tax burden borne by most export crop producers in Tanzania did not significantly decrease during the reform period, even though direct price taxation declined markedly (Delgado and Minot 2000).

EXPORT MARKET STRUCTURE AND PERFORMANCE.   A major motivation for reform is the disincentive effect of high marketing margins and low producer prices in unreformed systems. The ability of the private sector to cut margins and raise producer prices is a major benchmark of the success of reform. Beyond the average level of producer prices, there is the issue of whether private sector marketing leads to greater variability in export crop prices. If it does, it is necessary to see whether the greater variability is outweighed by higher expected prices.

The higher producer prices offered by independent traders encourage producers to invest. Yet the dissolution of parastatals may result in lower input use, causing yields and output quality to fall. Research and extension provided by parastatals will also disappear. Private agents do not have the incentive to provide such activities because of the incomplete capturability of benefits.

A specific concern about export crop liberalization is whether the necessary funds will be available to private traders to finance crop purchases. Traders are typically expected to pay for delivered crops in full at the time of delivery, whereas a parastatal may make a series of delayed payments to farmers. Another issue is whether the private sector will be able to supply the human and physical infrastructure—field buyers and other agents, transportation equipment, and storage facilities—to move the crop physically from farm to free-on-board (f.o.b.) status. Besides the issues of market entry and investment, there is also the question of what happens to the thousands of redundant employees of parastatals.

Still within marketing issues, there is the question of what happens to linked markets for inputs when major changes are occurring in the marketing institutions for export crops. Most parastatal forms of export crop marketing also provide inputs such as fertilizer and chemicals on credit to farmers. Moral hazard is created for input credit loans to producers once there is no exclusive outlet for output. Buyers may be unwilling to offer credit when farmers are no longer obliged to sell to their lender.

In the effort to increase value-added from national agricultural production, many African countries encouraged private or public investments in the processing of exported crops, using crops procured by the export parastatals as inputs. It may be that these vertically coordinated industries will suffer once they have to compete with foreign buyers for supplies of raw material.

Another question is whether ending the parastatal marketing systems will increase or decrease diversification among agricultural exports. In the 1980s, the top three agricultural exports in 11 of 15 African countries examined by Delgado (1995) accounted for more than 98 percent of export receipts from significant agricultural exports; in the other 4 cases they accounted for 85–94 percent of significant agricultural export receipts. Without doubt, most African countries in the 1980s were too dependent on too small a number of agricultural export crops. Unless this effect of comparative advantage at work in relatively small and only partially commercialized countries is so strong as to wipe out other forms of market-oriented domestic resource use, liberalization is expected to lead to greater diversification of production patterns.

PRODUCER INCOMES.   Producer incomes depend on both direct and indirect effects of export crop activities. Direct effects concern the level of payments per unit of output, their timing and reliability, and the variation of these effects over years (price stability) and across locations. Indirect effects involve the amount of liquidity available for other activities in a region. The impact of reform on direct and indirect income effects may differ across time and regions.

The spatial dimension is particularly important in countries where parastatals apply pan-territorial procurement prices. Such systems tax producers near ports and subsidize those in remote areas. Liberalization can be expected to raise producer prices in the more favorable export crop zones that are well served by infrastructure and to lower them in more remote, less favorable zones.

Export crops play a key role in introducing liquidity into demand-constrained rural areas (Delgado et al. 1998). Liberalization that affects the timing and volume of producer payments for export crop deliveries will affect the liquidity of rural areas. Such areas often have substantial amounts of underused labor and land that can be used to produce items for local sale if people have both the desire and the liquidity to purchase them. These items include goods and services that either do not travel (services performed locally) or are too perishable or bulky (local processed foods, local beer, bulk starch) to export out of local areas. Export crop sales increase local purchasing power and can have multiplied effects on local income under these conditions. This effect can cut both ways: a decrease in local liquidity in remote areas owing to the removal of pan-territorial pricing can have multiplied negative effects in such zones.

Overview of Case Studies and Commodities

More than 90 percent of Africa's agricultural exports are accounted for by 10 commodities: cocoa, coffee, cotton, tobacco, sugar, tea, palm oil, rubber, bananas, and peanuts (Delgado 1995). The remaining 10 percent is split among a number of minor and non-traditional exports. These cover specialty products important for some countries (such as cashews in Tanzania and Mozambique, pineapples and bananas in Côte d'Ivoire, Cameroon, and Ghana, cut flowers in Kenya, and vanilla in Madagascar), small exports of declining traditional products (such as sisal in Kenya, Madagascar, and Tanzania, or rubber in Liberia and Gabon), or rising exports of high-value specialty items such as Nile perch fillets from Uganda, Tanzania, and Kenya.

Minor traditional exports such as sisal, like the major traditional agricultural exports, were historically subject to parastatal marketing. Non-traditional high-value exports such as fruits, flowers, and fish rely on private sector distribution channels capable of meeting the stringent health and timeliness needs of these demanding perishable exports (Jaffee and Morton 1995). This review focuses on the liberalization of traditional agricultural exports.

The cases under review focus on 11 countries, 5 English speaking, 5 French speaking, and 1 Portuguese speaking, and cover six commodities. The cases are: Benin (cotton); Cameroon (cocoa); Côte d'Ivoire (cocoa); Ghana (cocoa); Malawi (tobacco); Mali (cotton); Mozambique (cashew); Nigeria (cocoa); Senegal (peanuts); Tanzania (coffee, cotton, cashews); and Uganda (coffee). This mixture covers a broad spectrum of liberalization experiences with regard to timing, extent, and impacts. The country-specific cases below are presented in approximate order of speed of liberalization, with the fastest and most complete cases first.[2]

Overview of World Price Trends for the Six Traditional Commodities

COCOA.   World cocoa real prices have been on a secular downward trend for many years. They spiked by a factor of two-and-a-half following the Brazilian freeze in 1977, but fell back to their trend level by 1980. By 1984 cocoa prices had increased by 20 percent, but followed a sharp downward trend to about one-third of their long-term trend value by 1992. They recovered by about 20 percent by 1997, then fell again. As of late 1999, they were US$920 per metric ton, or 54 percent of their December 1997 value in nominal terms (World Bank 2000).

COFFEE.   Coffee world real prices followed an evolution similar to that of cocoa prices. The two crops are tightly bound by substitutability in both consumption and production. However, coffee prices fell even further than cocoa

---

2. These sections draw heavily on Shepherd and Farolfi (1999), Townsend (1999), and Akiyama et al. (2001).

prices in 1991, increased by a factor of two-and-a-half by 1995, then fell to 20 percent less than their 1991 levels by the end of 1999. The volatility of both coffee and cocoa prices, as measured by their coefficients of variation across seven adjoining years in each direction (Townsend 1999), has increased significantly since the early 1970s because of the breakdown of international commodity agreements covering these crops.

COTTON. Cotton world real prices have trended downwards since the 1960s, owing to the introduction of synthetics and China's change from an importer to an exporter. The fall in the early 1980s was especially sharp, causing severe problems for a number of parastatals that had tried to justify their existence in terms of producer price stabilization. There was some appreciable recovery from 1992 through 1996. As of late 1999, prices had fallen to less than half their value in the early 1990s in real terms. The volatility of cotton prices, as measured above, increased sharply from the 1970s to the late 1980s but, until recently, seemed to have declined somewhat since the early 1990s.

TOBACCO. Tobacco real world prices have also trended downwards from the 1960s. They experienced significant strengthening in the mid-1990s, but a 60 percent decline since then. Tobacco price volatility has actually weakened somewhat compared with the 1960s, but the long-term prospects for this crop are poor owing to health concerns.

PEANUTS. Peanut prices in Africa are currently driven primarily by the price of vegetable oil, which in turn is driven mostly by policy decisions in the European Union. As a raw commodity with many substitutes and facing competition from subsidized exports, its prospects are not good. Producers are shifting from small peanut varieties used for oil to larger varieties used for specialty exports of cocktail peanuts.

CASHEW NUTS. The one specialty crop included in the review, raw cashew nut, has also gone through wild price gyrations over the reform period. With the exception of 1993, world prices rose steadily from the early 1980s to the mid-1990s, then fell to mid-1980s' levels (Delgado and Minot 2000). World prices are heavily influenced by India, a major producer and processor.

Nigeria (Cocoa)

This case represents the "cold turkey" approach to liberalization. In December 1986 the cocoa board was abruptly dissolved, along with the parastatals for oil palm, rubber, coffee, and peanuts. Parastatal procurement, quality control, processing, storage, and marketing disappeared, along with administered prices. The private sector was not immediately able to assume the quality control and storage functions formerly fulfilled by government, although there was a great deal of private capital inflow into the cocoa sector from outside agriculture.

At the same time, the naira became increasingly overvalued and domestic inflation rose. Cocoa became a much sought after hedge that also allowed owners access to foreign exchange under Nigeria's foreign exchange retention scheme. This allowed exporters to keep half the foreign exchange they generated. As a result, producer prices in domestic currency were driven very high, in some cases above the world price at official exchange rates. In the 1989–90 season, Nigerian exporters reportedly made forward contracts equivalent to four times the available harvest, leading to default and loss of confidence (Shepherd and Farolfi 1999).

After the defaults, cocoa bean exports were banned to ensure a supply for domestic processors. This led to oversupply and further disruption of the market. When the ban was lifted it became apparent that many individuals who had become prominent in the cocoa trade had no long-term commitment to the sector. These disruptions and the lack of traders with long-term perspectives on the industry resulted in a market lacking in the private institutions necessary to manage the cocoa trade effectively (Shepherd and Farolfi 1999).

Cameroon (Cocoa)

In Cameroon, the parastatal Office National de Commercialisation des Produits Bruts (ONCPB) controlled the marketing of cocoa until 1990. It functioned as a *caisse de stabilisation,* regulating prices and transactions but not handling actual cocoa. Agents were licensed for specific areas, within which they had no competition. Pan-territorial producer prices were set at low levels, and specific margins were prescribed for each stage of the market.

Reform began in 1989 when the licensing of agents ceased. In 1991 price stabilization efforts ended and the ONCPB was replaced with the Office National du Cacao et du Café (ONCC) and the Conseil Inter-Professionelle Café-Cacao (CICC). The CICC functioned as an industry board, bringing producer representatives face to face with representatives of different parts of the marketing chain. In practice, the new system experienced many of the same problems as the old one, with the added twist that private exporters could exploit the fact that compensation from the stabilization board was based on submitted contracts and not on monitoring actual shipments. Exporters could choose to submit only their low-price contracts, and the fund would lose out on taxing the high-price ones. This led to the insolvency of the fund in 1994 (Varangis and Schreiber 2001).

A free-market export system was instituted after 1994. Producer prices reportedly rose significantly. After initially high market entry, by 1998 only two traders accounted for 80 percent of exports, with these firms accounting for much of the forward sales to Dutch processors (Varangis and Schreiber 2001). Transfer of quality control functions from the government to the private sector quickly followed the 1994 liberalization, and quality reportedly declined (Shepherd and Farolfi 1999).

Uganda (Coffee)

Until 1991, the coffee sector in Uganda was under the complete control of the parastatal Coffee Marketing Board (CMB) and official cooperative societies that together fixed and administered producer prices, which were very low relative to f.o.b. prices. Production in a country that 25 years before had been East Africa's most prized supplier of coffee had fallen on very hard times following two decades of civil war. Producer prices were highly taxed throughout the period, declining a further 50 percent in real terms between 1986 and 1989 alone. A fall in the world price in 1989 could not be passed on under these conditions to producers, and further price taxation became untenable (Akiyama 2001).

After 1991, the government adopted a sequential approach to liberalization. First, the export monopoly of CMB was removed. Then the regulatory and development functions of CMB were transferred to a new body, the Ugandan Coffee Development Authority (UCDA), which had purely regulatory powers. Parastatal control of prices and margins ended; previously fixed prices were replaced with a floor price for exports announced daily by UCDA.

Subsidized government credit facilities were withdrawn from the official producer cooperatives, forcing them to compete with the private sector. In the course of 1992, exporters were permitted to receive export market proceeds in domestic currency at the open market rate, and the export tax on coffee was removed. Finally, the minimum export price was replaced by an indicative export price (Shepherd and Farolfi 1999). By 1998, 50 private exporters were registered, late payments for crops had declined, and producer prices had risen substantially.

Tanzania (Coffee, Cotton, Cashews)

The liberalization of export crop parastatals in Tanzania was complex and different for each crop. In 1984, the commodity marketing boards were initially replaced by cooperative unions as monopoly buyers of outputs and monopsonistic sellers of inputs. Although the cooperative unions were ostensibly independent associations of hundreds of primary cooperatives, in fact they were parallel parastatal marketing boards. Since the old boards were maintained, the cooperative unions added a further layer to the bureaucracy without additional efficiencies.

In theory, the pricing, marketing, and processing of coffee were liberalized in 1990–91. The old Tanzanian Coffee Marketing Board (TCMB), a parastatal, was renamed the Tanzanian Coffee Board (TCB), an industry board, and given purely regulatory functions. In fact, liberalization did not occur until the 1994–95 cropping season, when private traders were finally able to operate legally. The cooperative unions remained active, although in competition with the private sector. In 1997–98, private traders handled about 75 percent of the coffee, including most of the better grades. Input supply reportedly became a major problem, with regard to both suppliers' credits and the quality of inputs. The quality of Tanzanian coffee exports suffered because of falling input use and a lack of uniform grading.

Input problems began to be sorted out in the arabica zone in 1998–99 with the adoption of an approved input list by the Kilimanjaro Cooperative Bank.

The bank began a pilot program to provide 30-day suppliers' credits to primary cooperatives (Delgado and Minot 2000). The quality of output is improving with the arrival of 11 private coffee-curing factories, in addition to 4 owned by the cooperative unions.

The cashew nut industry was also liberalized in the same period. Liberalization was an act of desperation because the industry had virtually ceased to exist. Private traders were allowed into marketing in 1991 and into export in 1992. As of 1997–98, 28 of 62 licensed private traders accounted for 90 percent of the crop; 2 of 5 cooperative unions in the sector handled 6.5 percent. Since 1992, the use of sulfur blowers—essential to quality—has expanded rapidly, as have cashew exports, which are primarily in raw nut form to India (Dorward, Kydd, and Poulton 1999). All 12 state-owned cashew-processing factories are currently idle, because costs far exceed returns.

The Tanzanian Cotton Marketing Board operated as the supervisor and rule-setter of the cooperative unions and primary cooperatives dealing with cotton until 1994, when it was replaced by the Tanzanian Cotton Lint and Seed Board (TCLSB). The Cotton Marketing Company (CMC), a subsidiary of TCLSB, continues direct state involvement in cotton marketing. Although market entry to the cotton trading sector was high, the TCLSB denied private traders access to CMC-operated ginneries. Subsequently, 21 private ginneries were set up, but there was much foot-dragging on drawing up appropriate rules and regulations for private sector involvement in procurement and processing, with severe downward effects on the overall quality of the crop in terms of color and staple length (Shepherd and Farolfi 1999). In 1998, private operators bought and processed 60 percent of the crop and the rest was processed and sold by two cooperative unions.

Mozambique (Cashew Nuts)

Cashew nuts are Mozambique's most important crop export in terms of export revenue. They also provide income for 1 million smallholder farmers. Prior to the liberalization of the agricultural sector in 1997, the government maintained a ban on exports of raw nuts in order to protect the domestic processing industry, which employed 10,000 workers. Under external reform pressure, the government replaced the export ban with an export tax on raw nut exports. This tax was intended to be progressively phased out, and did see an initial reduction in 1998. Elimination of the export ban and the subsequent reduction in the export tax provoked significant losses in the inefficient large-scale processing factories, as they had in Tanzania earlier in the 1990s. The formerly state-owned or subsidized processors could no longer compete with cheaper processing facilities in India.

Small farmers, in contrast, benefited from the liberalization of trade and the reduction in the export tax, because they were able to export their raw nuts through private traders with direct channels to India. Producer prices increased by 8 to 15 percent between 1997–98 and 1998–99 (Mole and Weber 1999). Smallholders also received a larger share of f.o.b. prices, increasing from 45 percent in 1996 to 52 percent in 1997, but falling to 48 percent in 1998. In 1999, in an attempt to revive the local processing industry, the tax on direct exports of raw nuts was increased again to 14 percent. Since then, there has been a re-emergence of smaller manual processing factories, which are more cost-effective than the large-scale capital-intensive factories protected by the export tax. Furthermore, domestic processors are coping with declining nut quality associated with low use of sulfur to control mildew, early harvesting to avoid disease, and low replanting rates by small farmers.

Côte d'Ivoire (Cocoa)

Cocoa in Côte d'Ivoire has long been big business, with the state heavily involved. Early on, the cocoa marketing board was a prototype for market intervention throughout Francophone Africa. Officially known as the Caisse de Stabilisation et de Soutien des Prix des Produits Agricoles, it was universally referred to as CAISTAB.

From the beginning, CAISTAB was primarily in business to fix and enforce guaranteed producer prices, with differentials by grade. It also set a reference export price, based on averaged regular forward sales for about two-thirds of the crop and forecast spot sales of the remainder (Varangis and Schreiber 2001). Working backwards on a mark-down basis, price norms were fixed down to the producer level according to a schedule known as *le barème*. CAISTAB licensed market agents and regulated internal trade based on the *barème* pricing norms. It engaged in direct export, but did not enforce a monopoly on export sales. CAISTAB had its own warehouses and collection agents, and would typically compete with the private sector for exporting part of the harvest. Even before reforms, however, the private sector did most of the actual physical handling of the crop, and there were over 700 licensed traders (Varangis and Schreiber 2001).

If the actual foreign price received by one of the country's private exporters exceeded the reference price, the difference was payable back to CAISTAB. If not, CAISTAB made up the difference to the export house. Thus the price stabilization applied to private exporters as well as to the farmers. The surplus generated in the stabilization fund was very low during the 1960s and early 1970s. It became quite high during the cocoa/coffee boom of the late 1970s, but then dropped into negative territory in the 1980s as the authorities resisted lowering producer prices as long as they could (Gbetibouo and Delgado 1984).

At first, like other export parastatals in Francophone Africa, CAISTAB tried to use the domestic currency benefits of the January 1994 devaluation of the CFA (Communauté Financière Africaine) franc to rebuild the stabilization fund. However, by 1995, an agreement was negotiated with the World Bank to revise the way that the *barème* prices were calculated and to make them indicative rather than binding. After 1995, the share of the crop directly handled by CAISTAB was limited by fiat to 15 percent, and the number of approved direct exporters was enlarged to 32.

Interestingly, although pan-territorial producer pricing was abandoned in 1995–96, significant geographic differences did not emerge in producer prices (Varangis and Schreiber 2001), suggesting that infrastructure constraints in the cocoa areas were not the central issue, and perhaps also that there was more leeway in the system to compress trade margins than there was to compress producer margins even further. By 1998, 5 large operators and 62 smaller licensed exporters handled the whole of the crop. In 1999, CAISTAB lost its price-fixing authority and reverted to the role of a purely regulatory agency. This led to complete liberalization of the sector in the 2000 market year.

Malawi (Tobacco)

Tobacco-growing in Malawi is a slightly different case from the others considered. Only recently have smallholders been allowed to become involved in growing and selling burley tobacco. Previously it was grown on large estates. Between 1981 and 1988, problems with the all-encompassing agricultural parastatal, the Agricultural Development and Marketing Corporation (ADMARC), led Malawi to create alternative forms of funding mechanisms to work within ADMARC's infrastructure to deliver inputs to smallholders. In 1990, smallholders were granted permission to grow burley tobacco under a quota system; the quotas were abolished in 1997–98 (Minot, Kherallah, and Berry 2000). Since 1994, tobacco marketing for smallholders, as for the large estates previously, has been handled by privately run auctions under state license and supervision. Auction sales are reportedly characterized by a low degree of price competition (Townsend 1999).

Following the liberalization of burley tobacco production and marketing in Malawi, tobacco production by smallholder farmers increased dramatically, from 33,000 hectares in 1990–91 to 100,000 hectares in 1996–97. The success of smallholder tobacco production in Malawi is in large part a consequence of allowing smallholder participation in tobacco auction floors, either through farmer clubs or through sales to licensed traders. The number of smallholders growing tobacco more than doubled between the 1993–94 and 1994–95 growing seasons (Zeller, Diagne, and Mataya 1997). There is also some indication that tobacco production has contributed to increasing smallholder farmers' cash income. However, claims have also been made that liberalization in Malawi has primarily benefited relatively well-to-do households that already produced a substantial marketed surplus, thus aggravating rural income inequality (Peters 1996; Chilowa 1998).

Benin (Cotton)

As of 1997–98, cotton marketing in Benin continued to be entirely handled by a government parastatal, as is the case in the rest of the CFA franc zone countries. The government announces pan-seasonal and pan-territorial prices before the planting period. The Société Nationale pour la Promotion Agricole (SONAPRA) handles the distribution of seed cotton, chemicals, and fertilizers, extension, procurement at the village level, transport, ginning, and marketing. It also operates six of its own ginneries. As in the rest of the CFA franc zone, technical assistance to SONAPRA is handled under contract between the government and the Compagnie Française pour le Développement du Textile (CFDT).

Since 1995–96, six new private ginneries have been allocated part of SONAPRA's collected seed cotton, and the resulting output was marketed by SONAPRA. Starting in 1998–99, under substantial World Bank pressure, the six private ginneries were permitted to purchase SONAPRA seed cotton at auction, as a way of allocating 386,000 metric tons of production among ginneries with a capacity of 500,000 metric tons. Since 1997, one private company has also been permitted to market 25,000 metric tons of cotton lint abroad.

Debate over further liberalization of SONAPRA's functions continues. The likely outcome is the sale of shares in the company to both domestic and foreign stakeholders in the cotton subsector, with one-third being retained by the state (Soulé 1999).

Senegal (Peanuts)

The Senegalese case is different from the other countries' primarily because of the extreme importance of peanuts to Senegal's agricultural economy.[3] In 1994–95, the Peanut Basin accounted for 85 percent of the national cropped area, and about half of the cropped area in the Basin was devoted to peanuts. The government has multiple, evolving instruments of control over the peanut sector.

Prior to 1965, private peanut traders coexisted with government trade, and the main processing factories were private. In 1965, the Office National de Commercialisation et d'Assistance pour le Développement (ONCAD) was created to take over all peanut marketing for the state, gradually to take over processing from private sector mills that were essentially French owned, to take over the input supply and extension functions for peanuts, and to provide producer credit.

In the face of crippling debts, falling world vegetable oil prices, internal governance problems, and non-repayment of loans by farmers, ONCAD was dissolved in 1980. Its procurement, processing, and output marketing functions

---

3. This subsection draws heavily on Badiane and Gaye (1999).

were transferred to the new Société Nationale de Commercialisation des Oléagineux du Sénégal (SONACOS); its input supply, credit, and extension functions were transferred to the new Société Nationale d'Approvisionnement du Monde Rural (SONAR). Facing similar problems to those affecting the old ONCAD, SONAR imploded in 1985. The key seed multiplication and distribution function and the seed credit system were transferred to the new Société Nationale de Graines de Semence du Sénégal (SONAGRAINES). The procurement function was transferred to official cooperatives and licensed traders, called *organismes privés de stockage* (OPS). In reality, both the cooperatives and OPS were agents of SONACOS rather than independent and competing traders.

In theory, the monopoly of SONACOS over private peanut trade was abolished by decree in 1988, but in fact SONACOS still handles most of the unshelled peanut trade (for oil). Through SONACOS and SONAGRAINES, the state continues to control a large share of the input supply, marketing, and processing of oil peanuts in Senegal. Pan-territorial and pan-seasonal producer prices are set, and many movement restrictions remain. Private traders now handle part of the shelled peanut trade (mostly for table use). Regulatory controls over the procurement and sale of unshelled peanuts are also still in place. Despite SONACOS's dominance of the formal trade in unshelled peanuts for oil, a lively parallel trade exists for local and artisanal-processing demand, which is quite important in growing areas. The simultaneous existence of official and unofficial marketing systems for oil peanuts has resulted in relatively high variation in the price of unshelled peanuts, across both locations in the growing zone and time periods. The partial reforms embarked upon appear not to have led to the emergence of an efficient marketing system. Badiane and Gaye (1999) conclude that, without efforts to reduce the unit cost of processing groundnuts, Senegal may not be able to compete in international markets for very long.

Ghana (Cocoa)

Ghana was the world's largest cocoa producer in the 1970s. Production declined throughout the decade into the 1980s, for a variety of reasons, the most important of which was that the producer share of the export price in the late 1970s had declined to about 10 percent (Gbetibouo and Delgado 1984). Producers began to get some relief with the beginnings of macroeconomic reforms in 1983. Producer prices rose to about half of export prices after 1987, dipped again in the mid-1990s, and recovered to about 50 percent in 1998 and an estimated 67 percent in 2000 (Varangis and Schreiber 2001).

Until 1992–93 the Ghana Cocoa Board (COCOBOD) controlled all phases of cocoa marketing, from procurement at the farm gate to sales to domestic processors and exports. A fixed producer price was set in advance for the entire year by the governmental Producer Price Review Committee. Reforms permitting domestic procurement (but not export) of cocoa were introduced in

1993, but the Produce Buying Company (PBC), a subsidiary of COCOBOD, still directly procured 43.5 percent of all cocoa in 1999–2000. COCOBOD regularly sells 60–70 percent of the crop forward, to hedge its procurement operations and to provide operating capital (Varangis and Schreiber 2001).

Because the Cocoa Marketing Company (CMC), a subsidiary of COCOBOD, continued to be the sole authorized exporter of cocoa until 2000, domestic cocoa buyers other than the PBC could not easily access loans from abroad for procurement (Shepherd and Farolfi 1999). Foreign firms had little incentive to provide capital or to contract forward with entities that could not guarantee a supply of exports. Thus private sector traders in Ghana lacked the access to foreign capital markets that their peers in other countries seem to have when they procure cocoa for export, which makes it hard to compete with COCOBOD on procurement. On the positive side, Ghana maintained high standards of quality control, unlike some more liberalized systems in West Africa, and CMC regularly received quality premia for its cocoa (Shepherd and Farolfi 1999). Further reforms in 1999 and 2000 have led to the privatization of PBC into a publicly traded stock company. Starting in 2001, private firms are allowed to export up to 30 percent of their domestic procurement of cocoa (Varangis and Schreiber 2001).

Mali (Cotton)

The cotton sector in Mali is run by the Compagnie Malienne pour le Développement du Textile (CMDT), about one-third of whose share capital remains in the hands of the mother house, the Compagnie Française pour le Développement du Textile (CFDT), as is common in the cotton sector of Francophone West Africa (Baffes 2001). Unlike in Benin, only marginal changes have occurred in the Malian cotton sector during the reform era. The government sets pan-seasonal, pan-territorial prices in advance of planting. CMDT is the sole supplier of inputs to and the sole purchaser of cotton from farmers' associations, the sole contractor of transport services for cotton, the sole buyer of seed cotton, the sole operator of ginneries, and the sole exporter. Since 1992, the farmers' associations in each locality, which were largely created by CMDT in the 1970s, became more involved in an intermediary role between CMDT and individual farmers (previously CMDT employed its own agents to handle these tasks). As in Benin, CFDT and the Centre de Coopération International en Recherche Agronomique pour le Développement (CIRAD), France's main overseas agricultural research parastatal, continue to play advisory roles. Also as in Benin, producer prices have been kept to a relatively low share of the f.o.b. price.

One reason the CMDT monopsony/monopoly has been able to persevere is that on the whole it has been well run and had good results. Vertical integration of the supply chain through marketing contracts with the French Compagnie Cotonnière (COPACO) provides reliable access to foreign capital and expertise. Furthermore, CMDT was a pioneer in the use of genuine farmers' associations, which increased the participatory nature of local decisionmaking (if not national policy). Finally, although CMDT aggressively promoted cotton cultivation, it also adopted a system approach that helped farmers with food cultivation through fertilizer provision and manure pits, and livestock health and feed maintenance. The downside is that these effective non-price interventions have come at a cost: producers received only 25–30 percent of the f.o.b. price of cotton (adjusted for ginning) throughout the 1990s (Baffes 2001).

Impacts on the Performance of Markets for Export Crops

State-Owned Enterprises

Before assessing measures of impact, it is necessary to see whether very much has changed. In the food crop sector examined in Chapter 4, it is pretty clear that private marketing is nearly ubiquitous. It became so de facto as early as the second half of the 1980s in most countries, including those such as Tanzania where food was officially controlled, and it is certainly here to stay. The evidence presented above shows that this is far from the case for export crops. In Mali, Benin, Côte d'Ivoire, and Senegal, the parastatal organizations that traditionally have been involved in the export crop sector are alive and well, and still handling the majority of the crop. The degree of liberalization is significantly higher in the Anglophone cases and Cameroon, although, even in the Francophone cases, there is now a degree of competition from the private sector that did not exist in the pre-reform period. On the other hand, in both Francophone and Anglophone Africa, public goods provision for agricultural research, extension, and the maintenance of rural roads has declined over the reform period (Akiyama et al. 2001).

The Financing of Crop Procurement and Forward Sales

One of the widespread surprises in the experience of export crop reform in Africa is that, where liberalization has allowed private sector entry into all parts of the marketing chain, the availability of capital to procure, process, and sell the crop has not been a problem. Overseas buyers of these commodities in world markets, typically large multinationals such as Lonrho and Nestlé, have quickly built a vertically integrated chain of local agents stretching down to the village level, providing funding through each link of the chain (Shepherd and Farolfi 1999). The overseas buyer finances the domestic exporter, who finances the processor, who finances traders. Domestic traders who do not deliver as contracted quickly lose their business opportunities under this scheme of things, so the incentives for compliance are strong and the willingness of foreign lenders is accordingly greater.

In the Ghana case, credit for cocoa procurement was scarce. This was because, despite the presence of the private sector in the domestic trading of cocoa, the monopoly of the Cocoa Marketing Company—a COCOBOD subsidiary—on actual export sales broke the vertical chain that facilitated outside loans for cocoa procurement (Shepherd and Farolfi 1999). As before, COCOBOD could continue to borrow internationally to secure operating capital for procurement from farmers. Private traders, on the other hand, were not attractive candidates for foreign loans because they were not directly involved in export markets. Under these conditions, domestic traders had less incentive to repay loans on time and there was no guarantee that making such loans would help the outside company procure supplies of cocoa. In the CFA franc zone countries, where relatively little liberalization has occurred, procurement credit (*crédit de campagne*) continues to be provided as previously through public sector or quasi-public sector banking institutions domiciled in the franc zone such as the West African Development Bank (BOAD) and the regional CFA zone central banks with links to the French Treasury.

Both CAISTAB in Côte d'Ivoire and COCOBOD in Ghana also engaged heavily in forward sales of the following year's cocoa crop. This both hedged the profit on the future crop and financed their current procurement activities. Their ability to sell forward was based on their reputation and known ability to deliver. The ability to deliver is a problem for the smaller traders since liberalization, because the incentive not to deliver when the spot price rises is high and enforcement mechanisms weak. Under these conditions, multinationals have a greater incentive to assure throughput through vertical integration and direct investment rather than through forward contracts. As will be seen in the next section, this aspect of world commodity trade imposes certain limitations on the degree of competition that can be expected in domestic markets for exportables under liberalization.

Market Entry and Thinness

The country cases above suggest that market entry into licensed trader positions, where available, has been rapid following liberalization of exports. Where monopoly trading rights have been lifted, as in Tanzania, market entry in favorable production areas with good transportation infrastructure has been strong. However, the private sector has been much slower to penetrate into remoter and more difficult areas. Market entry in Cameroon was also strong in the 1990s, as in all the other countries where controls were lifted.

In countries where both parastatals and the private sector compete, it is almost always in different regions. In Tanzania, for example, the 21 new private ginneries established by the private sector following liberalization operate in only 5 out of 9 regions. These are the regions where a reasonable density of quality cotton is produced. The parastatal TCLSB now buys in the less favorable regions where there is no other buyer. The relatively small size of African production in most cases has led to a relatively small number of private agents handling the majority of the crop. In the case of cashew nuts in Tanzania, for example, only 28 out of 62 licensed agents handled 90 percent of exports in 1997–98. This number may still be large enough to avoid collusion, but this is not always the case in some crops and in some areas. In any event, a cartel of eight may still be preferable to a monopsony of one in the case of the old system.

There is also widespread evidence from other countries that rapid entry into export commodity trade following liberalization has led to rapid concentration in the numbers of export traders. In Cameroon for example, liberalization of the cocoa sector in 1994 saw the registration of 200 licensed exporters, but by 1997 only 2 companies with direct links to Dutch processors handled 80 percent of export cocoa, with the rest divided between domestic processors (15 percent) and the 50 remaining private traders (5 percent) (Varangis and Schreiber 2001). Although a variety of explanations have been advanced for this widespread phenomenon, it seems clear that the dysfunctional banking systems of many countries and the problems of contract enforcement have led to a situation where a few favored companies with international links can quickly out-compete local companies that cannot as easily secure access to operating capital.

Marketing Margins

Marketing margins for export crops, including the share remaining with market agents, have clearly shrunk in countries where liberalization has proceeded and remained large in countries where it has not. As shown in Table 5.2, the producer's share of the free-on-board (f.o.b.) price is of the order of 64–98 percent in Cameroon, Malawi, Nigeria, Tanzania, and Uganda, and of the order of 37–62 percent in Benin, Côte d'Ivoire, Ghana, and Senegal, where reform has been slow or nonexistent. The producer's share of the f.o.b. price is the best measure of how well the reforms have succeeded in passing on the benefits of liberalization to the producer. These percentages were typically much lower in Cameroon, Malawi, Nigeria, Tanzania, and Uganda in the early 1980s (Townsend 1999). They were about the same in Benin, Côte d'Ivoire, Ghana, and Senegal.

Domestic liberalization affects not only domestic marketing, but also the relationship between the country's f.o.b. price and the world price. Differences between f.o.b. border prices and world prices are also shown as ratios in Table 5.2. Ratios below 80 percent reflect either especially high transport costs (as for landlocked Uganda) or low domestic quality compared with available benchmarks (as in Senegal). Although this ratio has improved since 1990 for some African countries and commodities, it has declined for others, suggesting no firm trend over the period (Townsend 1999).

TABLE 5.2 The situation in 1996–97: Selected traditional exports

Country	Commodity	Commodity's share of agricultural exports (percent)	Producers' share of f.o.b. border price (percent)	Border price as percentage of world price	Marketing channel
Benin	Cotton	94	37	95	Full parastatal control of prices, marketing, and input.
Cameroon	Cocoa	25	76	86	Liberalized marketing and export starting in 1994.
	Coffee	26	73	87	
Côte d'Ivoire	Cocoa	56	46	96	*Caisse de stabilisation* system until 1998–99; liberalized thereafter.
Ghana	Cocoa	92	39	96	Full parastatal control of prices and marketing.
Malawi	Tobacco	75	82	86	All marketing through private auctions with low competition.
Mali	Cotton	57	44	82	Full parastatal control of prices, marketing, and inputs.
Nigeria	Cocoa	51	98	92	Complete liberalization in a short period.
Senegal	Peanuts	4	62	75	Most peanuts exported as oil (not shown). Marketing and processing only partially liberalized.
Tanzania	Coffee	30	77	98	Coffee largely liberalized starting in 1990–91. Cotton partially liberalized at first, now fully, as is cashew. State-run cooperative unions continue to compete with the private sector, but handle only a small share of the crop.
	Cotton	29	64	83	
	Cashews	21	64[a]	78[b]	
Uganda	Coffee	77	72	78	Full liberalization, with parastatal primarily playing regulatory function now.

SOURCES: Compiled from Townsend (1999), various locations; cashew data for Tanzania from Delgado and Minot (2000).
[a]1994–97. [b]1997–98.

Producer Price Levels

Real producer prices for African export croppers definitely improved by a substantial margin over the 1990–97 period, as shown by the positive and sometimes high growth rates for our country cases in Table 5.3. Except for tobacco, this was a period of solid growth in real prices on world commodity markets, as shown by the second column of Table 5.3.

Changes in real producer prices can be decomposed into contributing components: changes in the nominal producer price, changes in the nominal exchange rate, changes in domestic inflation, changes in the marketing margin between producers and world prices, and changes in world prices themselves. The third column of Table 5.3 shows how the wedge between producers' and f.o.b. prices changed as a result of policies. The effects of exchange rate and inflation changes, which summarize the outcome of macroeconomic policies, are summed up in the inflation-adjusted, or real, exchange rate (RER). Exchange rate pass-through then refers to the degree to which changes in the RER— summarizing the impact of macro and trade policy reforms on the economy—are passed through to producers in the crop sector under consideration (Townsend 1999). This is shown in the last column of Table 5.3. In some cases, such as cocoa in Nigeria (73 percent) and tobacco in Malawi (54 percent), the degree of pass-through of benefits from macroeconomic policies to producers was quite high. However, in the case of peanuts in Senegal (–42 percent) and cocoa in Cameroon (–37 percent) and in Côte d'Ivoire (–30 percent), not only did producers not reap any benefits from macroeconomic reform, but they actually lost ground owing to unfavorable sectoral policies that more than overcame any benefits from macroeconomic reform.

The actual decomposition of real producer prices for a weighted composite of crops in our case study countries is given in Table 5.4 for two time periods, essentially the 1980s and the 1990s through 1997. The first column is the change in real producer prices. This is equal to the sum of the other three columns, which are the contributing components: changes in real world prices (the external factor), changes in macroeconomic and trade regime policy (RER), and changes in sectoral policy (the ratio of the producer price to the f.o.b. price). For example, in Benin between 1981–83 and 1989–91, real producer prices in domestic currency increased a total of 22 percent: 5 percent came from increases in world prices, 15 percent from macro policies (devaluation of the real exchange rate), and 2 percent from sectoral policies in agriculture that cut domestic marketing margins. In the 1990s, the CFA devaluation added a much larger improvement to producer prices, but this was largely offset by a big increase in marketing margins because the parastatals in Benin declined to pass on the benefits of the devaluation in domestic currency to the producer.

Generally, the 1980s was a period of modest or poor trends in real producer prices in the CFA franc zone, owing to weak macroeconomic adjustment

TABLE 5.3 Price trends and incentives effects for selected export cases, 1990–96/97 (percent)

Country	Commodity	Annual growth in real producer price	Annual growth in real world price	Total change in producer's share of world price	Net pass-through to producer of real exchange rate devaluation
Benin	Cotton	2.0	0.5	−10	−18
Cameroon	Cocoa	2.5	2.8	3	−37
	Coffee	9.8	9.9	11	14
Côte d'Ivoire	Cocoa	3.2	2.8	21	−30
Ghana	Cocoa	0.7	2.8	−15	−9
Malawi	Tobacco	4.2	−3.1	5	54
Mali	Cotton	0.8	0.5	−8	−34
Nigeria	Cocoa	6.8	2.8	17	73
Senegal	Peanuts	4.0	0.8	−6	−42
	Coffee	14.1	9.9	19	17
Tanzania	Cotton	5.9	0.5	11	20
	Cashews	1.7	...	18	...
Uganda	Coffee	8.8	9.9	38	19

SOURCE: Compiled from Townsend (1999), various locations.

TABLE 5.4 Decomposition of external and internal effects on export crop producer prices in selected countries, 1981–83 to 1989–91 and 1989–91 to 1995–97 (percent)

Country	Period	Total change over period in:			
		Real producer price, domestic currency	Real world price (US$)	Real exchange rate	Nominal protection coefficient
Benin	1981–83 to 1989–91	22	5	15	2
	1989–91 to 1995–97	8	2	40	−34
Cameroon	1981–83 to 1989–91	−48	−56	−33	41
	1989–91 to 1995–97	36	0	33	3
Côte d'Ivoire	1981–83 to 1989–91	−63	−71	16	−8
	1989–91 to 1995–97	15	13	2	0
Ghana	1981–83 to 1989–91	102	−75	227	−50
	1989–91 to 1995–97	3	−11	21	−8
Malawi	1981–83 to 1989–91	−9	−33	2	22
	1989–91 to 1995–97	7	−39	31	15
Mali	1981–83 to 1989–91	4	−12	4	12
	1989–91 to 1995–97	7	−12	21	−2
Nigeria	1981–83 to 1989–91	31	−111	151	−9
	1989–91 to 1995–97	41	14	−58	85
Senegal	1981–83 to 1989–91	−13	−81	9	59
	1989–91 to 1995–97	22	−21	44	−1
Tanzania	1981–83 to 1989–91	9	−90	106	−7
	1989–91 to 1995–97	49	34	−5	20
Uganda	1981–83 to 1989–91	−76	−88	44	−32
	1989–91 to 1995–97	44	11	13	20

SOURCE: Extracted from Townsend (1999:Table A.8).

to a substantial slide in real world prices. This was somewhat compensated by improvements in sectoral policies (except in Côte d'Ivoire). Experience in the 1990s was better, but not nearly as much as might have been thought during the huge stimulus offered by the 1994 CFA devaluation.

The 1989–91 to 1995–97 period offered more hope to producers in the Anglophone countries, because of improvements in both macro and sectoral policies that boosted incentives to export crop farmers.

Producer Price Stability

Parastatal price interventions, and especially those of the *caisse de stabilisation* type, are frequently justified as contributing to the stability of income of poor farmers. However, there is little doubt that they achieve that stability by lowering prices overall. This raises the question of how much price stability is worth to poor farmers.

Townsend (1999) addresses this head-on for African export cropping. He uses the algorithm suggested by Newberry and Stiglitz (1981) to decompose the extra benefit of price stability to farmers into a hypothetical positive risk premium that farmers would pay to stabilize prices (calculated as a function of the farmers' aversion to risk and the variation in income they would experience from price variation) and a hypothetical cost of achieving stable incomes (calculated as a function of the income change from stabilization divided by expected income). To apply this to a sample of African countries, Townsend assumes that the cost of stabilization is the difference between the share of the f.o.b. price garnered by producers in countries with and without stabilization schemes. He finds (as also suggested by the analysis in the previous subsection) that this cost is about 30–45 percent of the f.o.b. price, for a range of African cases over the 1975–97 period. On the side of the risk premium, using a variety of assumptions about the degree of risk aversion of African producers, Townsend estimates a benefit to the producer from stable prices of about 2–8 percent. The stark conclusion is that the net cost of stabilization to export crop producers is unacceptably high.

Indirect Impacts on Food Grain and Input Markets

Finally, it is clear that the parastatal mode of promoting smallholder export crop development, when it is done well, can be useful for promoting the growth of input markets and food production. It does so by paying for the infrastructure and input distribution systems and giving farmers credit from crops that can be used as collateral while in the ground, since the farmer would have difficulty selling the harvest elsewhere (von Braun and Kennedy 1994; Kelly et al. 1996; Govereh and Jayne 1999; Strasberg 1999). However, when farmers have good alternatives for selling the export crop, credit becomes a problem.

It could be argued that these are separate issues from liberalization per se. Indeed, it could be argued that the lack of development of viable, nongovernment input and rural finance institutions over time was in part caused by the alternative offered by the export crop parastatals. This review will be limited to considering the direct impact of the market liberalization of export crops on production practices involving export crops, recognizing that a larger issue of its impact on food crop production is possible. In all likelihood, liberalization of export cropping, *ceteris paribus,* will reduce food production for a time until fertilizer use and other key indicators return to previous levels. This seeming trade-off between rising export crop production and decreasing food production has been noted across Africa (Lamb 2000). However, it is probably erroneous to conclude from this, as Lamb does, that food production is declining because producers are shifting labor and land to export crops. A far more likely explanation is the decline in input use—and especially fertilizer use—with the drying up of credit under export crop liberalization.

Impacts on the Production of Export Crops

Supply Response and Growth of Output

Townsend (1999) reports that in the period 1989–90 to 1996–97, the production and sale of African agricultural exports grew by 30 percent in volume. This is equivalent to a compound annual rate of growth of 3.8 percent, which exceeds the high population growth rate of 3 percent per annum seen in the region. Although weather is a big factor in year-to-year fluctuations, there is no doubt that the trend in overall volume was sharply negative from 1971 to 1984 and sharply positive thereafter (Townsend 1999), which can only be explained by responses to improvements in farm-level incentives.

Such responses can be expected to be even stronger on a crop-by-crop basis because the production substitution effect among crops comes into play as well as the overall incentive effect. Delgado and Minot (2000) separately regressed data on outputs of coffee, cotton, and cashews from 1985 to 1997 across zones in Tanzania against real producer prices and a variety of other determinants of output. They found significant short-run price responses for output for cotton and cashews, both of which are very responsive to purchased inputs use. The estimate at sample means for cotton indicated that a 1.00 percent increase in the expected producer price of cotton would lead to a 0.73 percent increase in the production of seed cotton. The short-run elasticity for cashews was 0.78 (Delgado and Minot 2000).

For coffee in Tanzania, the significant response was to prices lagged three years, the time it takes for new bushes to begin to yield. It is likely that the supply response of a perennial such as coffee shows up largely in acreage planted. There is strong evidence that arabica coffee plantings in Tanzania and Uganda increased significantly after the 1995 price spike, as they did throughout East Africa after the 1977 price spike.

The performance of the agricultural export sector as a whole for our sample countries is shown in Table 5.5. Although real agricultural GDP growth was quite variable across the sample over the 1990–97 period (from 6.5 percent per annum in Malawi to 2.5 percent per annum in Senegal), in all cases it was close to or comfortably above the rate of population growth. More significantly, annual growth over the period in the net income terms of trade—the price of exports divided by the price of imports multiplied by the growth in exports—ranged from –2.7 percent in Ghana to 22.2 percent in Uganda. However, most growth rates were strongly positive, implying significant real growth in the contribution of export cropping to the balance of trade. From the macroeconomic perspective this is a very favorable outcome of structural adjustment.

Productivity data in Table 5.5 are mixed over the 1990–97 period. Productivity per worker is an important gauge of productivity growth in export cropping in much of Africa, at least outside the East African coffee zones where land pressures have become very severe. Table 5.5 shows large increases in value-added per agricultural worker in Benin and Nigeria over the 1990–97 period, and significant losses in productivity in Côte d'Ivoire and Ghana during the same period.

Export market liberalization affects productivity not only through investments, as in new coffee plantings, but also through its impact on the use of fertilizers, insecticides, and other purchased inputs. Although the generally favorable evolution of price incentives over the 1990–97 period encouraged investment, the dissolution of parastatal institutions in some cases made access to inputs difficult, and this had an adverse impact on quality, as will be seen below (Shepherd and Farolfi 1999).

Diversification of Agricultural Output

The heavy concentration of Africa's traditional exports in agriculture and within agriculture has been a perennial concern of development economists working on African issues (Delgado 1995). Indeed, a large part of the United Nations Economic Commission for Africa's statement of opposition to the Berg report's opening statement on the need for structural adjustment (World Bank 1981) was that it was perceived as a strategy led by agricultural exports, which some saw as further concentrating resources in an overinvested area (Browne and Cummings 1984). Since market liberalization is designed to facilitate both market entry and market exit, and to increase the flexibility of producer responses generally, it is interesting to ask whether Africa's exports have become more concentrated in agriculture or if exports have become more diversified during the reform era.

The aggregate evidence on diversification from our sample countries, shown in Table 5.1 above, is mixed. Between 1987 and 1997, the share of agriculture in GDP grew only in Cameroon; it fell elsewhere. Similarly, the share of agriculture in total merchandise exports grew between 1987 and 1997 only

TABLE 5.5 Changes in the agricultural export performance of selected countries, 1990–96/97 (percent)

Country	Growth per year in real agricultural GDP	Total increase in real annual value added per worker, 1979–81 to 1994–96	Growth per year in the net income terms of trade[a]	Growth per year in agricultural export volume
Benin	5.2	51	n.a.	n.a.
Cameroon	4.5	–4	12.9	1.0
Côte d'Ivoire	2.6	–11	6.8	2.9
Ghana	2.7	–16	–2.7	3.2
Malawi	6.5	–4	–0.8	1.5
Mali	3.4	3	1.4	2.8
Nigeria	2.9	43	10.5	3.5
Senegal	2.5	9	n.a.	n.a.
Tanzania	3.7	n.a.	8.7	7.7
Uganda	3.8	n.a.	22.2	13.9

SOURCE: Compiled from Townsend (1999), various locations.

NOTE: n.a. means not available.

[a]The net income terms of trade are defined by Townsend (1999) as an index of agricultural export prices divided by an index of food import prices times the volume of exports.

in Benin and Cameroon, and fell elsewhere. The shrinking share of agriculture in GDP and exports supports the view that SAP as a whole has probably favored the diversification of economies somewhat out of agriculture.

Countries that embraced the diversification of agricultural exports were successful at expanding production in the first half of the 1990s. In Uganda, for example, nontraditional agricultural exports increased from US$1.4 million in 1988 to US$75 million in 1993 (World Bank 1996). However, almost US$20 million of this was in bean and maize exports to Kenya that could not be sustained once the rains picked up again in that country. Another big component, fish exports to Europe, has not been sustained because of health bans imposed by the European Union.

Optimism about nontraditional agricultural exports from Tanzania in the early 1990s was not borne out in the late 1990s. This was in spite of Tanzania's varied menu of traditional agricultural exports made possible by extreme variation in its micro-climates (Delgado and Minot 2000). Generally, nontraditional exports such as spices and horticulture continue to offer promise, but numerically are not likely to be large enough to offer an alternative to traditional agricultural exports for some time to come. Overall, there is some evidence that export market liberalization promotes diversification of total exports, reducing over-reliance on agricultural commodity exports, and it clearly does promote overall growth. That growth in turn will help diversify domestic food demand out of overconsumption of starchy staples and into animal products and horticulture.

Credit, Input Use, and Productivity

Other than improving producer prices, the big impact of export crop market liberalization on production has been through inputs markets. Under parastatal marketing arrangements, farmers often received seed, pesticides, and fertilizers from the parastatal. The cost of those inputs was later deducted from what the parastatal paid for the crop. With multiple outlets now available, the farmer is not obliged to sell the crop to the entity that advanced funds for inputs. This moral hazard prevents input credits from being offered. This happened in Tanzania between 1995 and 1999: input use by coffee producers declined and coffee yields fell from 250 to 200 kilograms per hectare, even as the coffee area planted expanded. There are also cases of parastatals not doing their jobs, and liberalization coincided with increased access to inputs and higher yields. In Uganda, fertilizer was hard to obtain before liberalization began, even though the official price was low (Shepherd and Farolfi 1999).

Problems with falling use of inputs under liberalization have been reported in the Cameroon cocoa areas, Tanzanian cotton and cashew areas, and Ghana cocoa area (Dorward, Kydd, and Poulton 1998; Shepherd and Farolfi 1999). Efforts to separate input supply parastatals from output procuring parastatals (as in Senegal, where SONACOS purchased peanuts and SONAR supplied credit, fertilizer, and seed) have tended not to work very well because the advantages provided by linking the two functions are lost, without gaining the advantages of a competitive market.

Quality and Processing

Maintaining parastatal control of export marketing channels is often justified by the need to assure quality. In Ghana, COCOBOD's quality control division inspects shipments both at the cocoa buying points and prior to purchase by CMC, the export subsidiary (Shepherd and Farolfi 1999). These controls pertain to both COCOBOD-procured cocoa and that of private traders. Private traders therefore have their cocoa inspected by a competitor at the farm level and by the monopoly at the export level (Shepherd and Farolfi 1999). Shepherd and Onumah (1997) report that Ghanaian cocoa sold at a premium of US$80 per metric ton over average world prices compared with a discount of US$20 per metric ton on Ivorian cocoa and a discount of US$60 per metric ton on Nigerian cocoa in the 1996 season (cited in Shepherd and Farolfi 1999). Neither the CAISTAB in Côte d'Ivoire nor private vendors in Nigeria were able to maintain the same standards as the parastatal in Ghana did.

In Cameroon, producer cooperatives undertook pre-commercialization controls of cocoa quality before selling to the parastatal. Currently, the transaction involves only the buyer and the seller. Quality depends on whether private traders have an economic incentive to preserve existing quality grades. Cotton quality has declined so much in Tanzania since the liberalization of ginning that two grades are no longer maintained. A possible explanation for this is that the structure of local taxation greatly reduces the incentive for processors to produce the higher grade. They do better to lump all grades together to face the lower tax rate (Shepherd and Farolfi 1999).

Nigerian cocoa quality dropped so much following liberalization in 1986 that the International Cocoa Organization (ICCO) at one time suspended Nigeria for exporting poor-quality cocoa. According to Shepherd and Farolfi (1999), the exporters were not merchants interested in developing a long-term market, but people seeking to obtain foreign exchange at a time of restrictive exchange controls.

Liberalization was also affected by conflict arising in the processing of higher-value agricultural exports. In some cases, governments slowed liberalization to ensure cheap inputs for state-owned factories. In other cases, parastatals denied private traders access to processing facilities as a way to resist privatization. In Tanzania, private cotton ginneries and coffee curing factories sprang up after parastatals would not process cotton and arabica coffee owned by private traders. Similarly, resistance by the coffee parastatal in Uganda to processing private traders' coffee led to the rapid creation of 23 hulling factories with private funds (Shepherd and Farolfi 1999). In both of these cases the private sector found ways around barriers created by parastatals, but they had to recreate infrastructure that already existed.

Impacts on the Level and Distribution of Incomes

Direct Impacts on Producer Incomes

Between 1990 and 1997 there was uniformly positive (minimum 3 percent) and generally high (up to 49 percent) real growth in agricultural export producer prices in the sample countries (Table 5.4). Over the same period there was between 25 and 40 percent aggregate growth in the volume of agricultural exports from those countries (consistent with the annual growth rates shown in Table 5.5). Growth of both real prices and volume leaves little doubt that real producer incomes rose substantially in the agricultural export sector in the 1990–97 period. Admittedly, this was a time of rising world commodity prices, as well as a period of liberalization in marketing arrangements, yet, even while real prices fell in the 1980s, the sample countries that liberalized early (Nigeria and Ghana, for example) tended to do better than those that put off the day of reckoning (Côte d'Ivoire, Uganda, and Cameroon).

Initial problems with sorting out processing arrangements and assuring supplies of inputs may have reduced the benefits to producers relative to what they could have been. Nevertheless, on average, market liberalization appears to have boosted producer incomes. To this average direct boost should be added an average spin-off effect from pumping extra liquidity into rural areas. Such spin-off effects are often left out of the estimation of benefits from policies that increase tradable incomes in rural areas. Finally, in any average there are losers and winners. The next two sections will examine the spin-off effects on income levels and distribution in households that produce export crops.

Indirect (Spin-Off) Effects on Incomes

The literature on agricultural growth linkages in Africa shows fairly conclusively that one impact of increasing incomes for export cropping is to increase farmer spending for both investment (in export crop and food crop production capacity) and consumption. Even consumption expenditure adds to growth in rural areas if it is spent on locally produced goods and services that would otherwise not have been sold and that are produced with underused local labor, land, or capital. Examples are perishable processed foods (such as local beer), services, or bulky items. A number of independent studies around Africa have shown that local inflows of income from export crop sales have a multiplied effect on overall local production when there are underused local resources. The results of seven of these studies are summarized in Table 5.6.

The first column of Table 5.6 shows the total potential extra production of local nontradables from household spending of an extra unit of outside-sourced income in the local market (Delgado et al. 1998). It shows, for example, that re-spending of an extra dollar of export crop income in Madagascar can result in a further US$1.13 of local income generated from new production of non-

TABLE 5.6 Multiplier effects on rural incomes from promoting agricultural exports in seven African countries

Country	Year	Extra income from nontradables[a] (US$)	Range of values[b] (US$)	Percentage of extra income from consumption[c]	Source[d]
Burkina Faso	1984–85	1.88	0.31–3.33	93	Delgado et al. (1998)
Madagascar	1984	1.13	0.99–1.66	80	Dorosh and Haggblade (1993)
Malawi	1986–87	0.66	0.41–2.08	94	Simler (1994)
Niger	1989–90	0.96	0.77–2.34	79	Delgado et al. (1998)
Senegal	1988–89	1.36	0.75–2.11	42	Delgado et al. (1998)
Tanzania	1992	0.80	0.80–1.40	...	Delgado and Minot (2000)
Zambia	1985–86	1.48	0.41–1.48	98	Delgado et al. (1998)

[a]The net additional income estimated to result from spending on demand-constrained locally produced goods and services after an initial income shock of US$1 in the tradable agriculture sector.

[b]The range of values obtained for extra income under different parameter assumptions.

[c]The share of total net additions to income attributable to consumer spending alone (not including backward production linkages).

[d] Within the sources given, there is variation in tools used and authorship. The Burkina Faso results are derived from fixed-price multiplier (FPM) work using semi-input–output models based on the work of Bell and Hazell (1980), carried out in the Burkina case by Delgado and Sil; Madagascar results are based on work using a social accounting matrix (SAM) by Dorosh and Haggblade; Malawi results are based on FPM work by Simler; Niger results are based on FPM work by Hopkins, Delgado, and Gruhn; Senegal results are based on FPM work by Kelly, Delgado, and Alfano; Tanzania results are based on work using a SAM by Wobst, reported in Delgado and Minot (2000); and Zambia results are based on FPM work by Hazell and Hojjati.

tradable goods and services. As a rule of thumb, any policy that sustainably increases producer incomes from agricultural exports will increase local rural income by twice the amount of the increased exports.[4]

Impacts on the Distribution of Incomes

Market liberalization may affect income patterns in three key ways. The first is by encouraging households to switch from food production to export crop production. This could cause nutritional and food security problems as well as affect the amount and distribution of income. But most poor regions in Africa have unemployed capacity for local food production; what they lack is liquidity to bring those resources into production. An increase in export crop output can increase local incomes, which in turn will be spent on locally produced food. The extent to which this happens depends on the availability of underutilized local resources.

A second way liberalization will affect incomes is through the elimination of pan-territorial pricing. Pan-territorial pricing is seen as an equity policy. It transfers income from farmers in areas with better infrastructure and higher population density to farmers in less developed, more remote areas. Although the elimination of pan-territorial pricing is likely to leave remote areas less well off, it is clear that parastatal procurement of crops at administered prices is a very inefficient way of assuring regional income transfers. It is unsustainable and therefore not a solution. Growth made possible by prices that encourage trade will have a greater long-term effect on remote regions.

Third, conventional wisdom holds that export cropping is largely if not exclusively a male activity in Africa (von Braun and Kennedy 1994; Delgado 1995). Similarly, food cropping is assumed to be largely a female activity. Some have suggested that, if liberalization increases payments to export crop producers, then men will benefit more than women. But women also benefit from the re-spending of export crop revenues in local markets. The new local liquidity would not otherwise appear, as illustrated by the following example from Burkina Faso.

Reardon, Delgado, and Matlon (1992) found that, out of three agroecological zones of Burkina Faso in the 1980s, women had higher relative and absolute incomes in the cotton zone than in the other two zones surveyed. All cotton payments went to men, but they spent most of that income locally on local processed food and beer and handicrafts made by local women. Those women would not otherwise have had an outlet for their wares. There is every reason to think that increased export crop revenues from market liberalization were spread around during the 1990s.

---

4. This argument is now widely admitted. The details and caveats are contained in Delgado et al. (1998).

Conclusions: Problems and Lessons from the Export Crop Liberalizations of the 1980s and 1990s

Overall Appreciation of Export Crop Liberalization since 1986

The literature surveyed in this chapter suggests the presence of steady structural change in African export cropping that is contributing to building market-led economies. The production response to the favorable evolution of incentives in the first seven years of the 1990s is uncontestable. Furthermore, despite foot-dragging and turf-protection by parastatals and other vested interests, the private sector has prevailed wherever it was given a chance.

The prospects for the immediate future are less certain. The nearly simultaneous disasters for world commodity markets arising from the Asian economic crisis starting in July 1997 and the Russian financial crisis starting in August 1998 pose challenges for even the best laid liberalization schemes. Although the prospects for worldwide recovery are good (World Bank 2000), price slides for Africa's main exports of the order of 50–60 percent since 1997 will take time to erase.

Furthermore, many institutional and marketing incentive problems remain. First, for those channels that are completely liberalized, some major issues still to be resolved include small trader access to operating capital, producer access to credit and inputs, quality control, and public revenue generation. Second, there is the issue of how to replace the export crop parastatals' equity functions. Third, for those channels that are only partly liberalized, it is becoming apparent that partial liberalization can have perverse incentives effects that are potentially worse for export cropping than are either full parastatal control or full liberalization. We will address these issues in turn.

Finding New Institutions for Dealing with Previously Linked Transactions

Issues concerning the maintenance of a sufficient number of export traders to ensure competition in crop procurement, as seen above, arise from the difficulties posed by poor banking systems, high domestic credit costs, and the underlying difficulties of formal sector contract enforcement for small traders in Africa.

A discussion of banking issues in development goes beyond the scope of this book, but it is clear that it will be difficult to expect too much in the way of lasting market entry from market liberalization in export crops until banking and legal issues in contract enforcement are addressed. A possible solution might include bonding of members of a trader association that can provide collective guarantees of contract delivery; however, this also requires a degree of oversight by government to prevent collusion in procurement, a difficult task in the best of institutional circumstances.

The discussion above also revealed the wide-ranging problem in Africa of producer access to quality inputs on credit. Unlike parastatals, private traders are unlikely to provide credit because they cannot ensure that farmers will deliver the crop to them (including repayment in kind). Farmers typically have nothing but their crop to offer as collateral. Under liberalization, another solution must be sought. The literature on the topic tends to stress the need for institutions that emphasize the commercial value of "trust and reputation" (Fafchamps 1999).

One approach to this is to recreate aspects of the ongoing relationship that smallholders had with export cropping parastatals. Contract farming is a solution. Farmers receive inputs, credit, and extension in return for selling their output at a guaranteed price to a known outlet (the trader). Contract farming occurs widely in Africa for items with relatively high value-added. Because such items are often perishable or require special handling to preserve quality, they tend to have high transaction costs associated with them. These costs act as information and asset barriers to market participation by smallholders (Delgado 1999). As an institution, export crop parastatals got around these barriers by contracting with the farmer, and it is possible that private sector traders, large farms, or processing firms could do the same. Whether or not contract farming is favorable for the smallholder depends a great deal on the balance of power between traders/processors and farmers (Delgado 1999). This issue has been explored in the literature on the liberalization of smallholder export cropping. Establishing a balance that provides appropriate incentives to all agents is critical to the success of market liberalization.

Empowering the Poor to Remain Part of the Agricultural Growth Strategy

Because of asset and information barriers to participation in high-value markets, there is concern that the poor will be left out of export crop liberalization. If this happens, it will be for purely organizational reasons, because in general there are few economies of scale in production but many in processing and marketing. In remote areas, alternative equity strategies may need to be pursued.

Dorward, Kydd, and Poulton (1999) identify five conditions for evolving a beneficial set of arrangements (i.e. institutions) between small farmers and a trader/processor. First, there must be a "seller's market," in the sense that the trader/processor does not have easy access to alternative sources of supply. Second, there must be real competition among traders for available supply. Third, farmers need to have something valuable to lose if they do not honor their contracts. Dorward, Kydd, and Poulton (1999) stress trust and reputation in this context. Shepherd and Farolfi (1999), addressing the same issue, stress the need for trust and reputation among traders rather than farmers. On this view, traders' associations could help bind traders together to police themselves against rogues who buy up crops financed by other traders. Public oversight would be necessary to ensure that the traders' associations did not collude to split the market and limit competition. Fourth, farmers must have reliable information about regional prices, such as from radio broadcasts. Fifth, the region in question must have a minimum density of producers, to keep collection costs within reasonable bounds.

Where these five conditions are fulfilled, it should be possible for mutually beneficial contractual arrangements to emerge that allow private sector agents to take over the input supply, credit, and quality control functions previously exercised by the parastatal. However, accountability of actors to a viable local judiciary remains important, and thus this mode is most likely to work where rural democratization and decentralization are proceeding.

Cutting Corners: The Problems of Partial Sectoral Liberalization

The final three sets of lessons concern the costs of partial liberalization. First, liberalization may leave some vital part of the market channel in state hands, such as CMC's monopoly on cocoa exports from Ghana. In this case, outside buyers had little guarantee that financing private domestic traders in Ghana would give them (the outside buyer) access to either more cocoa or quality cocoa. It also weakened the link between the source of funds and the agent using them, lessening the likelihood of repayment. This rupture of the channel prevented the inflow of external capital to Ghana, to the detriment of the internal trading class.

Second, refusal to liberalize any part of a sector, such as cotton in Mali, can backfire if other reforms, such as exchange devaluation and liberalization of the livestock trade, make other pursuits more profitable. CMDT appears to have managed to maintain its position relatively well, in part because the organization is run well and is of use to farmers. Experience with the otherwise similar Société de Développement des Fibres Textiles (SODEFITEX) in Senegal has not been as good (Townsend 1999).

Third, completely liberalizing an export overnight (such as cocoa in Nigeria) while other controls remain in place (such as on foreign exchange) can provoke short-term behaviors on the part of nonmarket participants that are not favorable to the long-run development of the industry. Short-term participants may damage the reputation of the national product in foreign markets. This stands in contrast to the measured sequencing of the coffee liberalization in Uganda, which was highly successful in progressively replacing public functions with private actors throughout the marketing chain.

6 Conclusions and Policy Implications

The implementation of the market reforms and their impact on agricultural production and income growth have varied substantially across countries and crop sectors. Given these different experiences, as well as the diversity of Africa's geographical, historical, and cultural background, it is difficult to come up with a single set of findings or solutions for the whole continent. However, common issues and constraints do emerge. The identification of these issues can help in shaping a new agenda for the development of agricultural markets in Sub-Saharan Africa.

In general, the results of the market reforms in Sub-Saharan Africa have been less than expected, but some progress is evident in most cases. In the following subsections, we summarize the findings regarding what was expected from liberalization, the implementation experience of the reforms, and their impact on several indicators of crop market performance, agricultural production, input use and productivity, and income growth and poverty alleviation. We then discuss the remaining constraints, and we conclude the chapter with a new agenda for the development of agricultural markets in Sub-Saharan Africa.

Summary of Findings

What Was Expected from Market Liberalization?

An important characteristic of the market reforms in the 1980s is that they focused on reducing government intervention in agricultural markets and increasing the producer price of tradable agricultural commodities. The expectation from aid donors and African policymakers at that time was that improving farmers' price incentive and liberalizing markets would be enough to generate a supply response and lead quickly to the emergence of well-functioning markets. It was believed that the structural and institutional functions previously performed by the state could be easily provided by the private sector. As the response of the private sector failed to live up to expectations, there was increasing realization in the 1990s that, at least in countries where market liberaliza-

151

tion had occurred, the private sector's ability to expand its production and marketing activities was severely limited by institutional deficiencies and the inadequate provision of public good services that are essential for markets to develop. It is now recognized that price reform alone is not enough to increase Africa's economic performance significantly and that more expensive long-term investments will be needed to help Africa out of its dire straits. Price deregulation and adjustment of the exchange rate can often be done through ministerial decrees. However, privatization, institution building, and infrastructure development are complex tasks that need long-term investment and commitment. These types of reforms are not easy to implement given the short-term nature of policymaking. In addition, these changes are more difficult to incorporate in the policy-adjustment lending programs of international donor organizations. This means that the steps ahead for further reform in Africa will be more difficult to achieve and will require readjustment in government and donor behavior.

Has Market Reform Actually Occurred?

Implementation has been a difficult and contentious part of the reform process. The pace and extent of reforms have varied widely across countries, but reforms were rarely fully implemented. Many governments liberalized internal domestic trade but kept their monopoly over external trade (for example, the continued state control over cotton exports in Benin and the processing of unshelled groundnuts for export in Senegal). In southern and eastern Africa, given the thin world market for white maize, the overriding concern over food security has meant that state control over food crop marketing remained more pervasive than elsewhere in Africa. In Malawi, Zimbabwe, and Kenya, a large share of cereal crop marketing is still conducted by marketing boards and price bands are still in effect. In other countries, by contrast, the role of cereal marketing boards has been reduced to noncommercial activities such as food price stabilization, the distribution of food aid, and the provision of market information.

Historically, fertilizers, seeds, and agrochemicals were more heavily controlled by government parastatals than were cereal trading and distribution. In most countries, small-scale cereal trading always coexisted with official marketing activities, while inputs were heavily subsidized and distributed solely by the state. Although private traders have penetrated the fertilizer and seed markets in many countries, input marketing activities are usually dominated by state-owned enterprises or multinational firms. For example, in Benin, the cotton marketing board still allocates and prices fertilizer destined for cotton production. In Malawi, the government is the leading importer of fertilizer.

The implementation of liberalization measures has been fraught with policy reversals. In many instances, owing to various external shocks or changing economic circumstances (such as droughts, wars, or a change in political regime), countries reversed their reform policies and reimposed controls on previously liberalized sectors. For example, although Malawi had adopted a plan to phase out its fertilizer subsidies over 1985–88, the subsidy was reinstated by 1987 because of the escalating costs of imported fertilizers resulting from the devaluation of the local currency and the cutting off of transport routes through war-stricken Mozambique. It was not until 1995 that the fertilizer subsidy was eliminated in Malawi. However, this was followed in the 1998–99 and 1999–2000 seasons by the distribution of free fertilizer packages to all smallholder farmers. Other countries, such as Ethiopia and Zambia, have reintroduced fertilizer subsidies, albeit indirectly by subsidizing input credit or state enterprises that distribute fertilizer. In general, a careful look at the chronology of the reforms in the agricultural sector of most of Sub-Saharan Africa suggests that many countries did not follow a linear path towards liberalization and that reforms were often not seriously implemented until the early to mid-1990s.

Although countries rarely had a clear vision of how to time and sequence the liberalization measures, the question of the appropriate timing and sequencing of policies has been debated at length since the reforms were initiated. Countries that simultaneously eliminated fertilizer subsidies, scrapped state-sponsored input credit, and devalued, witnessed a significant decline in fertilizer use (for example, Malawi and Nigeria). In export crop markets, on the other hand, liberalizing purchases but not processing created bottlenecks initially (such as in the cotton ginning sector of Tanzania), and devaluation without liberalization of the main export crop has led to resource shifts to other free sectors (for example, away from the cotton sector in Mali). Furthermore, rapid liberalization accompanied by macroeconomic instability has led to chaotic markets (for example, in the cocoa market of Nigeria, where cocoa suddenly became one of the few unregulated sources of foreign exchange).

POLITICAL ECONOMIC CONSIDERATIONS. The mounting budget deficits and foreign exchange shortages caused by declining export revenues in Africa have forced its countries to accept reform programs imposed by donor organizations in return for financial bail-outs and balance-of-payments support. However, the commitment of many African governments to reform has been weak, tied mainly to the disbursement of donor funds. Since many reforms would have eliminated significant privileges received by public enterprise employees or civil servants and their patrons, these groups resisted the reforms and slowed the pace of their implementation. Bates (1989) goes further, arguing that the objectives of the reforms, which include reducing the role of the public sector, are inherently in conflict with the interests of the public agencies that are supposed to carry them out. Because the structural adjustment programs are negotiated and implemented by governments, they are, according to Bates (1989), merely a continuation of the old ways of doing business, which could no longer be sustained without outside donor support.

To the extent that the reforms were implemented, the lack of political independence of many African states with regard to their own civil services often led to a reversal of reform policies that ran counter to the interests of the bureaucracy. Governments rarely tried to garner internal support for the reforms or to explain the benefits of the reforms to their broader constituents. Reforms were for the most part implemented in a top–down fashion without public understanding of their objectives or rationale and without the participation of key groups such as private entrepreneurs, nongovernmental organizations, and civil servants in the lower echelons. This created a climate of uncertainty and suspicion about the government's motives and the likely implications of the reforms and rendered their implementation less sustainable. The private sector is usually less willing to invest in an environment in which it cannot trust the actions of the government or there is a lack of belief that the government will sustain its policy measures.

Donor organizations had a major role to play in the implementation process. Most reforms in the agricultural sector were part of conditionalities that accompanied structural adjustment program financing. These were helpful in accelerating implementation but, because they were part of other economy-wide and sectoral reforms and because donors were loath to delay disbursement, compliance with agricultural market reforms was monitored less strictly than if they had been independent of other reform measures.

A major hindrance to effective design and implementation of reform was a lack of coordination in the programs of different donors. In some instances, different donors' conditionalities resulted in contradictory policies. For example, in Malawi, while USAID was pushing for the elimination of fertilizer subsidies to smallholder farmers, the European Union and the World Bank were funding an initiative to distribute free packages of fertilizers and hybrid seeds to poor smallholder farmers.

Compounding these political factors is the generally weak institutional capacity of Africa's state agencies. Many of the new states that emerged after independence had a weak central administration, with underpaid and undertrained civil servants, and lacked the analytical and monitoring capacities needed to advise their governments on options or to elaborate plans to implement the reforms. As a result, foreign technical experts often were used to meet these needs, exacerbating problems of continuity and donor collaboration.

Has Market Performance Improved?

One of the key questions about the impact of agricultural market reforms is whether agricultural markets have become more competitive and efficient as a result of the reform process. To measure the performance of markets following the reforms, the empirical literature has centered around measuring the extent of private trader participation in agricultural markets and the nature of changes in marketing margins and levels of market efficiency. Below, we summarize the major findings regarding the impact of the reforms on these market indicators.

- In almost all reforming countries, market entry by private traders has occurred in food and cash crop markets as well as in fertilizer markets. However, whereas entry into small-scale trading has been relatively extensive, vertical or horizontal expansion of private trading beyond the entry level has been rare, except for a few cases. Private trader entry seems to be more extensive in assembly, small-scale milling, and retailing. Wholesaling and more capital-intensive marketing activities such as motorized transport or external trade have been limited to those groups with strong social networks and state connections.
- In general, greater competition and more cost-effective private sector trading have resulted in lower marketing margins and better market integration (for example, maize marketing margins have declined significantly in several countries including Tanzania, Ghana, Mali, Kenya, and Zimbabwe). As a result, farmers are receiving a greater share of the retail or export price (such as grain producers in Ethiopia and cashew nut growers in Tanzania and Mozambique) and, in many instances, real consumer prices have fallen (in Kenya, for example, the price of maize meal has fallen since the liberalization of maize milling).
- The most important component of marketing margins in Sub-Saharan Africa is transport cost. Estimates from various countries and markets suggest that transport costs represent 30–60 percent of private traders' operating costs. There is some evidence that one of the major factors explaining the differences in the performance of agricultural markets in Asia and Africa, apart from the adoption of technology, is the level of infrastructure development and the costs of transport. Because of low population density, investing in infrastructure and transport networks is more expensive on a per capita basis in Africa than in Asia. The resulting isolation of Sub-Saharan Africa from other regional or world markets exacerbates the impact of shocks such as droughts, wars, and other supply disturbances that can often result in famines.
- Owing to limited access to credit and high transaction costs (including the costs of obtaining market information, searching for buyers or sellers, and enforcing contracts), grain markets remain risky, personalized, and cash based, with limited long-term investment by private traders in transport or storage. In addition, because of limited access to storage and to formal financing mechanisms, cereal grain prices in Sub-Saharan Africa remain highly volatile compared with other developing countries.
- Other important infrastructural and institutional constraints that hinder private sector expansion are a general lack of adequate market informa-

tion, poor communications infrastructure, an absence of laws regulating property rights, market conduct, or grades and standards.

- In some countries such as Malawi and Zimbabwe grain marketing boards still play a dominant role in buying and selling grain on a commercial basis in competition with the private sector. The uncertainty of the private sector about public policy and the planned activities of the state in grain trading results in very volatile and unstable markets. This uncertainty also reduces the private sector's willingness to invest or specialize in this sector and dampens its response to liberalization.
- The presence of multinationals in export markets has facilitated the development of a local and well-coordinated private trading sector. For example, following export crop liberalization in Tanzania, multinationals have contracted with private domestic traders to purchase crops from smallholder farmers. As a result, cash crop traders have not had a problem in accessing credit and finding buyers for their products. Smallholder farmers also have better access to export crop markets. In Malawi, smallholder farmers can now sell their tobacco in auction floors to international buyers, an activity that could be conducted only by estate farms before the reforms.
- The private sector is also offering a wider selection of products that were previously not available. However, the breakdown of state monopoly over export crop marketing has resulted in rising quality control problems. This is exemplified in the deteriorating quality of cocoa in Nigeria and of coffee in Madagascar, whereas the quality of cocoa in Ghana has been maintained because it is still handled by a parastatal.

Is There Evidence of a Supply Response?

The basic premise of agricultural market reform is that improving the incentive structure for smallholder farmers through higher prices and better-functioning markets would lead to a positive supply response, thereby raising aggregate agricultural output and overall income. Arguments on the effectiveness of agricultural reform policies have therefore revolved around the responsiveness of African agricultural production to policy incentives, and more particularly to price incentives. The results in this area suggest the following.

- There has been a positive supply response, although stronger for export crops than for food crops, mainly because liberalization has moved relative prices in favor of tradables and the use of imported inputs such as fertilizer has become more profitable for export crops than for food crops. The most responsive sectors have been the cash crop sectors such as cotton in Benin and Mali, cashew nuts in Mozambique, and coffee in Uganda.
- In some instances, because of resource constraints such as land scarcity and seasonal labor shortages, a relative price shift in favor of one crop may

result in a shift of resources into that crop at the expense of another without an increase in overall agricultural production. However, it seems that higher export prices and real exchange rates have had a beneficial effect on food production. In countries such as Benin and Burkina Faso, where cotton inputs are available on credit through the government, input use has increased and has had positive spillover effects on food production. Because of the complementary nature of food and export crop production in many areas, the returns generated from export production can be used to buy inputs for food production.

- Despite positive changes in some sectors and some countries, the overwhelming current consensus is that the overall limited supply price response in Sub-Saharan Africa is due to structural and institutional constraints that have been ignored by market reforms. These constraints include variables such as infrastructure (roads, irrigation, communication networks, and so on); marketing services; the availability of modern inputs; access to rural credit, research, and extension; public expenditures in agriculture; human capital development; government commitment to reforms; the existence of rural organizations; as well as weather and soil quality.
- In most Sub-Saharan Africa countries, reforms in the agricultural sector were not effectively implemented until the early to mid-1990s and therefore it could still be too soon to give a final evaluation on the impact of these reforms on agricultural supply. Overall agricultural production can increase only if more resources are devoted to the sector or with the introduction of technological change, both of which take a long time to generate positive returns. Because some factors of agricultural production are fixed in the short run (such as land and machinery), farmers are limited in their ability to respond fully and immediately to price changes. Therefore, one should expect long lags between changes in incentives and agricultural output.

Is There Evidence of Productivity Gains in Agriculture?

Equally as important as the supply response is the question of whether there have been any productivity gains as a result of market reforms. The general expectation among many advocates of agricultural market reforms in Sub-Saharan Africa is that the transition from an economy with extensive state intervention to a liberalized market economy will raise productivity by increasing the availability of modern inputs and the incentives to use them. The premise is that liberalized markets will increase farm profitability through higher producer prices and lower input costs, thus expanding the use of modern inputs and overall commercialization as part of a structural transformation process. Whether input and output market reforms increase the profitability of modern input use, and thus gains in overall productivity, depends on the final factor-to-output price ratios faced by smallholder farmers. Hence, much of the analysis on the impact of market reforms on the productivity of smallholder agriculture has generally involved assessing the impact of reforms on the profitability of modern input use.

- Fertilizer prices have risen in response to subsidy removal and devaluation and fertilizer-to-crop price ratios have increased, particularly for nontradable crops such as maize. As a result, fertilizer use has declined in many countries, especially for maize (for example, in Malawi, Nigeria, and Zambia, annual fertilizer use declined by 1 to 3 percent between 1981–85 and 1994–96). Fertilizer use seems to have declined most in countries where devaluation and the elimination of input and credit subsidies occurred at the same time and where fertilizer is mostly applied to maize.
- Fertilizer use in Sub-Saharan Africa remains very low compared with other developing countries. The average application rate in Sub-Saharan Africa is 9 kilograms of nutrients per hectare of arable land compared with 107 kilograms in all developing countries.
- Access to credit for input use has declined in countries where state-sponsored credit systems have collapsed (for example in Malawi and Tanzania). The private sector has not been able to provide input credit to farmers owing to their inability to enforce loan payments and the high transaction costs of lending to small-scale dispersed farmers. The absence of well-functioning agricultural credit markets to finance input purchases has exacerbated the decline in input use.
- The general observation of declining trends in modern input use together with high population growth rates has often meant that land area expansion continues to be an important source of output growth. However, both labor and land productivity increased in the post-reform period for countries such as Ethiopia, Mali, and Burkina Faso. The primary contribution to these positive trends was the expanded use of modern inputs such as fertilizer. Countries such as Kenya, Zimbabwe, and Senegal, in contrast, experienced negative trends in land productivity. Much of these differences can be explained by the extent to which smallholder agriculture was undermined prior to reforms. For instance, countries such as Ethiopia and Mali, with past policies that clearly undermined smallholder production, experienced the largest productivity growth rates, whereas countries such as Kenya and Zimbabwe that initially supported smallholder agriculture experienced stagnant productivity growth rates. For Kenya and Zimbabwe, the effective elimination of many public agricultural services in the rural areas (including state buying stations) reduced the ability of the smallholder to obtain modern inputs in terms of both their availability and cost, with the overall result that land productivity declined or stagnated.

- The evidence on yields is mixed but is in general disappointing: many countries have experienced either marginal increases or decreases in yields. For example, between 1981–85 and 1994–96, maize yields in Malawi increased by only 6 percent, while in Zambia and Zimbabwe they declined by more than 6 percent.
- A number of studies have shown that a high intensity in export crop production schemes tends to encourage farmers to invest in modern inputs. This is primarily because such schemes are both profitable and stable, and often vertically coordinated in both input and output markets. The only concern with such schemes is that they have so far depended on government support to ensure stable prices and access to credit and inputs, which raises the question of whether they can be sustainable in the long run.

What Has Been the Impact on Poverty?

Agricultural production constitutes the most important source of income and employment for the majority of households in Sub-Saharan Africa. By stimulating agricultural supply through higher farm prices and more open access to agricultural markets, market reforms were expected to have a positive effect on rural income generation and poverty alleviation. This section summarizes the evidence.

- Surveys indicate that many smallholder farmers in Sub-Saharan Africa (in some cases the majority) are net foodgrain buyers. The implication is that, in the short run, higher food prices could be detrimental to these households unless market reform can contribute to reducing the margin between producer and consumer prices. In fact, increased competition and greater efficiency brought about by liberalization have reduced marketing margins in many African countries, thereby benefiting both food producers and consumers. Consumer maize prices have fallen in many countries following the reforms, including Ethiopia, Ghana, Kenya, Mali, Tanzania, and Zambia.
- In some countries, market reforms have not had negative impacts on poor households or on food security in general mainly because governments were previously ineffective in providing cheap food to the most needy and created many marketing inefficiencies that were reduced with liberalization. Many poor consumers had to rely on parallel markets to meet their food requirements because government-subsidized grain was often rationed or poorly targeted.
- Following the elimination of noncommercial input supply and procurement at pan-territorial prices, farm households in remote areas are often worse off than they were before the reforms. A common finding in the literature is that the net gainers from reform have generally been the producers with a marketable surplus and producers and consumers close to

urban markets. Households in remote areas that received an indirect transport subsidy through pan-territorial pricing may be hurt by the reforms. On the other hand, many of these households operate largely for subsistence and therefore will have little contact with agricultural markets and will be insulated from changes in product prices.

- There is good evidence that devaluation and export market liberalization have had positive effects (of the order of 20 percent) on the income of small export growers, although this varies greatly across countries and crops. This is mainly because many rural households derive their income from export crop production and sales. Evidence suggests that small export crop growers (for example, cotton growers in Benin, cashew nut producers in Mozambique and Tanzania, and tobacco growers in Tanzania) have benefited from higher producer prices owing to declining marketing margins and the depreciation of the real exchange rate. Similarly, following the liberalization of burley tobacco production and marketing in Malawi, increased tobacco production has contributed to increased cash income for smallholder farmers in the country.

- The impact of the elimination of input subsidies on smallholder farmers is also not conclusive. Many smallholder farmers used to obtain subsidized seeds and fertilizer from marketing boards either in return for selling their produce or without any commitment. The elimination of fertilizer subsidies without developing rural credit markets means that many food crop farmers are using less fertilizer during the post-reform era than before. However, similarly to food subsidies, several factors also made fertilizer subsidies ineffective in reaching the rural poor before the reforms. The benefits from fertilizer subsidies are proportional to the quantity used, so they accrued disproportionately to larger farmers. In addition, subsidized fertilizers were often rationed and arrived long after the planting season. Therefore, the negative impact on poor farmers of a reduction in input subsidies may not be significant.

Remaining Constraints

The overwhelming evidence in Sub-Saharan Africa is that improving price incentives for farmers was necessary but not sufficient to boost agricultural production. Long-run aggregate supply elasticities with respect to prices tend to be much higher for the more advanced developing countries than for other developing countries with poor infrastructure, weak public institutions, and low levels of human capital and private sector development. Furthermore, reforms did not improve price incentives for all farmers in all countries. In some eastern and southern African countries (Kenya, Malawi, Zambia, and Zimbabwe), the elimination of price subsidies on inputs and maize output resulted in lower incentives for maize producers. More generally, market reforms in Sub-Saharan

Africa have been accompanied by large cuts in public expenditures, including public investment in irrigation, roads, research, and extension. An essential challenge for most states in Sub-Saharan Africa is how best to provide these agricultural services and infrastructure in an environment of tight restrictions on fiscal spending. The issue, however, is not so much choosing between, for example, a price policy or investments in infrastructure; instead the two have come to be viewed as complementary.

In general, traders in Sub-Saharan African markets face a great deal of risk because of unstable marketing margins, market thinness, uncertainty concerning government policies, the risk of theft and storage spoilage, and risk due to the unenforceability of contracts that forces most traders to engage in business activities within a narrow circle of traders related through kinship or close personal ties. These risks, together with the high transportation and storage costs, often result in large and unstable transaction costs. They also imply that marketing systems in the post-reform period are still not altogether efficient and have a limited capacity to pool risk or to provide market stability through either temporal or spatial arbitrage.

In addition, in many post-reform African countries the use of both modern seeds and fertilizers continues to be limited, primarily because of higher input prices and limited access to credit. The growth of smallholder maize production and the use of hybrid seeds and fertilizers in eastern and southern Africa in the mid-1970s to mid-1980s were due to state support in marketing infrastructure and to the coordinated supply of subsidized credit and modern inputs and the purchase of crop output. However, this type of support could not be sustained financially and the coordinating and institutional mechanism provided by the state had to be abolished. The subsequent vacuum created by the withdrawal of the state was not filled by the private sector because of several institutional and structural deficiencies and the tightening of government investments in the provision of public goods such as rural transport.

In sum, the constraints that Sub-Saharan Africa faces in its efforts to reduce poverty through agricultural market development can be grouped into four categories:

1. *Implementation factors,* which refer to the fact that reforms were, for the most part, only partially implemented and were often accompanied by policy reversals. There is wide evidence that owing to various circumstances —such as domestic political constraints, poor coordination of donor programs and conditionalities, unforeseen external shocks (including droughts or wars), and the general instability and uncertainty caused by economic change—there was often policy backtracking and stalling. In certain West African countries for example, there has been resistance to the privatization of parastatals that generate sizable state revenues. The tendency to think that reforms are a one-shot event rather than a long-term process has

also complicated their implementation. There were great expectations in the early stages of reform that one-time changes in price policies and exchange rates would be enough to redress declining agricultural productivity and to increase economic growth. As a result, it was harder for the proponents of reform in Africa to stick to the path of reform when its expected impact did not materialize. It has only recently become clear that successful reforms in Africa will involve a more protracted and slower process of adjustment, institution and infrastructure building, and long-term commitment to economic and political change.

2. *Structural factors,* defined here as the basic physical infrastructure needed to support market development, such as road and transport infrastructure, electricity and communication networks, storage and markets facilities, research and extension programs, and market information systems. Such services usually require large investments and, because of their public good nature, cannot be adequately supplied by the private sector. The importance of these investments was often overlooked during the early stages of reforms. Furthermore, the cuts in public expenditures dictated by the structural adjustment and stabilization programs often resulted in lower investment in agricultural and rural services following the reforms.

3. *Institutional factors* that facilitate vertical coordination and constitute the basic framework or building-blocks for the development of efficient private markets. These vary from rural farm organizations and traders' associations to the rules and regulations regarding property rights, enforcement of contracts, grades and standards, and good governance. For example, the absence of official property rights over land means that small farmers do not have a collateral that they can use to obtain agricultural loans. This is exacerbated by high transaction costs (resulting from poor information on the default risk of small farmers, the small amount of loans, and the high cost of accessibility to geographically dispersed farmers) and the poor enforcement of contracts, which discourages private traders from extending loans to farmers. These institutional deficiencies explain why private rural credit markets have failed to develop successfully in Sub-Saharan Africa.

4. *Exogenous factors,* which relate to the susceptibility of Africa to severe external shocks such as recurrent droughts or floods, widespread diseases such as HIV/AIDS, malaria, and tuberculosis, and wars and civil strife. Countries in southern and eastern Africa (such as Malawi, Zambia, and Mozambique) are particularly prone to droughts or floods, which often devastate a whole year's agricultural production. Today about 25 million people in Sub-Saharan Africa are infected with HIV/AIDS. The negative impact of this virus on labor productivity in the subcontinent is alarming and begs for further government resources to stem its rapid spread. Furthermore, most countries in Sub-Saharan Africa have been independent only for about 30 to 40 years and are still grappling with democracy and

the rule of law. Unstable political regimes throughout the continent have retarded economic growth in several countries (for example, Rwanda, Sierra Leone, and Congo). All these factors pose a great threat to economic growth in Sub-Saharan Africa and impose a huge financial burden on African governments and their donors.

In the next section, we present an agenda to address these constraints. We also explain how this new agenda can be implemented. We end by proposing a new type of partnership between governments, donors, and the private sector to move the agenda forward and help develop agricultural markets in Sub-Saharan Africa.

A New Agenda for Agricultural Market Development in Sub-Saharan Africa

Policy Changes and Investment Needs

In order to address the four major factors constraining the development of agricultural markets and poverty alleviation in Africa, the following policy changes and investment needs are proposed.

FULL IMPLEMENTATION OF THE REFORMS.   Progress in the full implementation of reforms will not only require more effort to pursue liberalization, but also involve accompanying policy measures to support sectoral reforms. More specifically, the following policy measures are needed.

- *Complete the implementation of market reform.* In places where reforms are still partial and the government is playing an active role in production and marketing, market reforms should be more fully implemented. Experience has shown that market performance has improved and marketing costs have declined once the government has eliminated its monopoly over trade and a competitive private sector has emerged. Given the political and economic difficulties in several African countries, the resistance to fully implementing market reforms is not surprising. However, this resistance is slowly eroding as government officials realize that state intervention in agricultural production and marketing is not sustainable and it will not be supported by donors and investors in the long run.
- *Commit to a broad path of sustainable reforms.* It is usually difficult for governments to predict an appropriate sequence of reform because of limited information about household behavior and its linkages with various sectors of the economy. And even if governments were able to devise a path that is both economically and politically acceptable, it would not be feasible to pick a path of reform and adhere to it regardless of any unexpected shocks that might occur. Governments need to have a broad vision of how they want the reforms to proceed, but they also need to be

flexible enough to accommodate unexpected shocks or unforeseen consequences of their policies. Despite these difficulties, a few sequencing lessons can be applied within the agricultural sector. First, it is more sustainable to eliminate input subsidies last, in order to prevent declines in the use of improved technology and in soil fertility. Second, it is advisable to avoid skewing relative crop prices, which can result in unsustainable substitution between commodities. Third, it is more effective to start liberalization from the bottom of the marketing chain and move up to the more concentrated wholesale and external trade markets.

- *Adopt accompanying measures to alleviate the negative impact of reforms.* In some cases, the government may be committed to liberalization but is not sure how to go about it. For example, governments may not know how to privatize parastatals without causing disruption through lay-offs and declines in state revenues. This means that the more difficult parts of liberalization will require more careful policy changes and complementary measures to offset the negative effects of reforms. If the government fears losing revenues from the privatization of state-owned enterprises, then an important accompanying measure is the adoption of other forms of taxation such as value-added and income taxes. Some countries have already adopted legislation to revamp their taxation system. As these become more developed and widespread, there should be less stalling on privatization of state marketing boards.
- *Maintain credible and stable macroeconomic policies.* Indirect taxation through overvalued exchange rates and protective industrial policies can have a more negative effect on agricultural incentives than direct taxation through lower agricultural prices. In addition, stable and predictable macroeconomic policies encourage savings and investment, focus private sector effort on efficiency rather than anticipating and reacting to macroeconomic shocks, and provide accurate incentives to consumers and producers regarding the scarcity of goods and services. Unless governments are committed to long-term macroeconomic stability, sectoral reforms will not be effective.
- *Develop appropriate safety nets.* In the short run, market reforms may be associated with economic hardships for some segments of society. The government should adopt appropriate safety nets to protect the most vulnerable groups. Targeted interventions that are well implemented are usually more effective and efficient than universal subsidies on food or inputs such as fertilizer. These include programs such as food for work, food for education, school feeding programs, and focused geographic targeting.

STRUCTURAL CHANGES.   Structural changes are needed to support agricultural production and marketing and to improve the access of small farmers and traders to markets. In this area, the following changes are proposed.

• *Increase investments in infrastructure, research and extension, and market information systems.* Transport infrastructure (roads, railways, and ports) is essential to reduce the costs of export crop marketing, agricultural input delivery, and regional grain trade. Returns to investment in agricultural research are known to be very high worldwide, and research is crucial to develop crop varieties that are suitable for the continent and to improve lagging productivity. Extension services are necessary for the diffusion of technology and the improvement of farmers' management practices. The problem associated with extension services is usually a lack of financial commitment and organizational efficiency to ensure high-quality delivery services. The continued need for the state to provide effective and efficient extension services requires not only increased efficiency in the management of these services but adequate and sustained funding of the services. Finally, the availability of timely public market information is crucial to help stabilize market shocks and provide equal opportunities to all types of market participants.

• *Set investment priorities and partnerships.* Investments in infrastructure, research and extension, and market information systems are expensive and require a long-term commitment. Therefore, priorities have to be set as regards the types of investment that will bring the highest returns in terms of broad-based economic growth. In countries such as Mozambique and Malawi, for example, rehabilitating road infrastructure should be a priority. In countries where transport infrastructure is more developed, such as Kenya and Zimbabwe, investment in agricultural research is perhaps more pressing. Market information systems have also been slowly developing in several African countries through the Famine Early Warning Systems (FEWS) and other donor-supported networks. However, governments have to take ownership of these market information systems or transfer their management to private companies that can deliver information in a more timely and relevant fashion to different stakeholders. Investment in agricultural research can also involve partnerships between private seed companies, governments, and regional or international research centers (see the next section on private/state partnerships).

• *Promote cash crop production.* Another structural issue that should be looked into is the emphasis that some governments place on food versus cash production, on the premise that there is a trade-off between the two. In fact, the observed fall in food production in some export cropping areas may be more the result of a decline in purchased input use than of a shift in resources from food to export crop production, although this remains to be investigated. In many areas, however, food and export crop production are highly complementary and export crop production has positive spillover effects on input use and food crop productivity. In addition, export crop production facilitates access to markets in general. Therefore, promoting smallholder production of cash crops should have beneficial impacts on agricultural production in general and on the food security and incomes of smallholder farmers in particular.

INSTITUTIONAL INNOVATION.   Many institutional changes will be needed to support the development of competitive and efficient agricultural markets and to increase small farmers' access to these markets. These changes include but are not limited to the following.

- *Support contract farming.* Institutional innovation is needed to provide input credit to farmers. Although land titling would help, it will not be enough to solve the problem of market failure in the provision of rural credit; the transaction cost of supplying credit to small farmers is too high even if farmers had land as a collateral. Furthermore, the seasonality and covariate risks of agricultural production have so far limited the replication of micro-finance schemes to small farmers and agricultural traders. There has, however, been renewed interest recently in contract farming schemes that successfully link input and output markets and provide farmers with access to agricultural markets. Under contract farming, traders provide some inputs on credit to farmers at the beginning of the season and deduct input costs from the value of purchased output at the end of the season. Production contracts are widespread for fresh and processed vegetables in Kenya, dairy in Ethiopia, and cotton in Mozambique. Contract farming, however, faces some problems, such as the difficulty of enforcing contracts with farmers, unequal bargaining power between producers and traders, and monopsonistic trader behavior. Governments could help by monitoring anticompetitive behavior and encouraging farmers to organize into groups to increase their bargaining power.
- *Encourage cooperatives and farmers' organizations.* Cooperatives and farmers' associations are another institutional arrangement that can reduce the transaction costs of accessing input and output markets, as well as improving the negotiating power of smaller farmers vis-à-vis large buyers or sellers. Farmers' associations can foster the development of group lending schemes that facilitate small farmers' access to credit. The importance of cooperatives has reemerged in Africa in the wake of agricultural market liberalization. Historically, however, the cooperatives established in the socialist era were not successful at serving the needs of their members owing to various organizational problems and opportunistic behavior. There is interest now in a new type of cooperative that addresses the weaknesses of the traditional cooperatives by strengthening the assignment of property rights to its individual members and reducing the incentives for opportunistic behavior.

- *Support traders' associations.* In most of Sub-Saharan Africa, laws regarding market contracts and property rights are either nonexistent or poorly enforced. Because of the high transaction costs of screening for trustworthy partners, obtaining information about prices or quality, and enforcing contracts, traders have resorted to dealing with a tight network of traders and farmers linked through either ethnic group or other social and family relationships. Small traders also have limited ability to obtain external finance. Traders' associations can play an important role in facilitating the exchange of information between traders and expanding their trading network beyond their limited personal ties. They can be involved in the development of financing mechanisms for their members, thereby increasing the access of small traders to external loans. They can also be useful to identify and eliminate rogue traders who buy from farmers with whom they have no contract or to alert other traders about defaulting farmers. Therefore, they can help make contract farming more successful and they can facilitate market exchange.
- *Develop an official system of grades and standards.* Because of the absence of an official grades and standards system, many traders in Africa spend a lot of time and money to inspect merchandise before buying or selling. This contributes to higher marketing costs and reduces the efficiency of the markets. The development of a well-enforced grades and standards system, especially for major grains such as maize and rice, would go a long way to reducing the costs of obtaining information about quality and should help reduce marketing costs and retail prices to consumers.
- *Institute dispute settlement mechanisms and legal reform.* In the short run, while the judicial and court systems gain credibility and effectiveness in Sub-Saharan Africa, there is a need to develop a simple and effective dispute settlement mechanism (such as small claims courts) to reduce exchange risk and settle commercial disputes for both farmers and traders. Such mechanisms could be established at the local district level, where elected rural representatives could act as arbitrators of disputes between farmers and traders or other market participants. In the long run, however, more effort will have to be made throughout the region to develop and effectively implement a legal infrastructure to support commercial activities. This includes laws regulating property rights, contracts, investment, banking, market conduct, and consumer protection. Although laws and regulations may exist in some countries, they are rarely effectively implemented.
- *Promote effective governance and capacity building of state agencies.* Without proper governance, investments can be channeled to rent-seeking groups rather than distributed to more productive activities. Also, it is very important to improve the capacity of public agencies to collect and analyze market data and monitor the development of markets. This would al-

low governments to anticipate undesirable market developments and devise appropriate responses to eventual short-term difficulties in a timely and effective manner.

ADDRESSING EXOGENOUS SHOCKS.   The policy changes needed to address exogenous shocks vary significantly between countries because some countries may be more susceptible to certain types of shock than others. Countries in southern Africa, for example, will have to devise policies to curb the spread of HIV/AIDS and to better manage the impact of climatic change such as droughts and floods. In West or Central Africa, reducing the incidence of civil war and cross-border conflicts is essential. Further details about how to address these types of shock are beyond the focus of this book, but it is clear that, without such changes in policies and investment, efforts to help Sub-Saharan Africa will be severely jeopardized.

New Roles and Partnerships for the Different Stakeholders

The dominant framework for implementing reforms in the 1980s and 1990s was based on aid conditionalities imposed by donor organizations. This approach to policy reform, however, did not provide a sense of ownership of the reforms by recipient governments and was often seen as window-dressing by policy analysts. Furthermore, the types of policies addressed in the past, such as price liberalization and deregulation, could be easily changed and observed through the promulgation of government decrees. The institutional and structural changes now required from Africa are not conducive to this type of lending policy. They will require more long-term commitment by government and donors, and changes will take time to be felt and measured. It will therefore be hard to link these changes with aid disbursement.

Further progress in market development will require not only further liberalization, but a more concerted effort to go beyond the withdrawal of the public sector from agricultural marketing. Whereas previous reform efforts led to government savings and a reduction in the budgetary burden of the state, progress in the development of markets in Sub-Saharan Africa will require more costly investment. It is clear that African governments cannot embark on the road of recovery alone and that forging partnerships and alliances with donors, international lenders, and the private sector will be critical. For lending in this new environment to be successful, however, there should first be a buildup of trust and a redesign of the policy dialogue between the different partners. In this regard, the roles and responsibilities of the various players will have to change.

Most importantly, an environment of political and economic stability is crucial to attract domestic and foreign investment. Governments have to increase the credibility of their commitment to economic and political change and show their will to devise appropriate policies such as the rule of law, protection of property, and freedom of movement. African governments should disengage from being active market participants and move towards more supportive roles as market facilitators. There should also be more effort to decentralize authority and devolve the provision and cost recovery of rural services to the local level. This would increase accountability and improve the efficiency of public expenditures because local authorities are better able to determine which investments would be most beneficial in their area.

The state should also continue investing in public goods such as the main transport infrastructure, communication and electricity networks, research and extension, and market information. However, given the high costs of these investments, governments should look for new ways to recover the costs of their investment and partner their efforts with the private sector and international lenders. One way to recover the costs of road infrastructure is through toll roads, where small tariffs are imposed on road users. Crop research could be supported through alliances between national or regional research institutes, Consultative Group on International Agricultural Research (CGIAR) centers, and the private sector. The costs of supporting a crop research center at the individual country level are usually high, and regional research centers could be more cost-effective because of economies of scale in research and development. Economies of scale also apply in fertilizer and grain marketing—larger volumes traded are associated with lower per unit marketing costs. Therefore, African governments should collectively commit to liberalize and expand regional and international agricultural trade. This should benefit both producers, who would have access to larger crop markets and lower-priced fertilizer, and consumers, who would face lower food prices.

Donors and private international lenders will have to renew their policy dialogue with African governments to focus more on supporting the long-term goals and visions of their leaders rather than tying aid to narrow and specific policy changes, which are often either reversed or not properly implemented. Developed countries, on the other hand, could help by opening their markets to African products and reducing domestic agricultural subsidies that unfairly harm exports from developing countries. The private sector will have the largest role to play in terms of investment and the generation of wealth. Given the right incentives and the proper institutional environment, the private sector can effectively respond with increased participation in production and marketing activities. Finally, civil society and nongovernmental organizations will be very important in empowering the rural poor and making sure that they can take advantage of the new opportunities for economic growth.

References

Abdulai, A. 2000. "Spatial price transmission and asymmetry in the Ghanaian maize market. *Journal of Development Economics* 63: 327–349.

Abdulai, A., and C. L. Delgado. 1995. Re-establishing agriculture as a priority for development policy in sub-Saharan Africa. Conference proceedings. Washington, D.C.: International Food Policy Research Institute (IFPRI).

Addison, T., and L. Demery. 1989. The economics of rural poverty alleviation. In *Structural adjustment and agriculture: Theory and practice in Africa & Latin America,* ed. S. Commander. London: James Currey, for the Overseas Development Institute (ODI).

Adekanye, T. O. 1982. Marketing margins for food: Some methodical issues and empirical findings for Nigeria. *Journal of Agricultural Economics,* November.

Adugna, T. 1997. Factors influencing the adoption and intensity of use of fertilizer: The case of Lume District, Central Ethiopia. *Quarterly Journal of International Agriculture* 36: 173–187.

Agbodan, M. T. 1989. Prix officiels et prix d'equilibre des denrées alimentaires: Le cas du maïs et du mil à Lomé. *Africa Development* 14: 83–93.

Ahmed, R., and N. Rustagi. 1987. Marketing and price incentives in African and Asian countries: A comparison. In *Agricultural marketing strategy and pricing policy,* ed. D. Elz. Washington, D.C.: World Bank.

Akiyama, T. 2001. Coffee market liberalization since 1990. In *Commodity market reforms: Lessons of two decades* (pp. 83–120), ed. T. Akiyama et al. Washington, D.C.: World Bank.

Akiyama, T., J. Baffes, D. Larson, and P. Varangis, eds. 2001. *Commodity market reforms: Lessons of two decades.* Washington, D.C.: World Bank.

Alderman, H. 1993. Intercommodity price transmittal: Analysis of food markets in Ghana. *Oxford Bulletin of Economics and Statistics* 55: 43–64.

Alderman, H., and G. Shively. 1996. Economic reform and food prices: Evidence from markets in Ghana. *World Development* 24: 521–534.

Alexander, C., and J. Wyeth. 1994. Cointegration and market integration: An application to the Indonesian rice market. *American Journal of Agricultural Economics* 73(3): 303–328.

Alwang, J., and P. B. Siegel. 1999. Labor shortages on small landholdings in Malawi: Implications for policy reform. *World Development* 27: 1461–1475.

171

Amani, H. K. R., and S. M. Kapunda. 1990. Agricultural market reform in Tanzania: The restriction of private traders and its impact on food security. In *Food security policies in the SADCC region,* ed. M. Rukuni, G. Mudimu, and T. S. Jayne. Proceedings of the Fifth Annual Conference on Food Security Research in Southern Africa, October 16–18, 1989. Harare, Zimbabwe: UZ/MSU Food Security Research in Southern Africa, University of Zimbabwe (UZ).

Amha, W. 1994. Food grain marketing development in Ethiopia after the market reform 1990: A case study of Alabo Siraro District. Ph.D. dissertation, Berlin.

Anthony, K., B. F. Johnston, W. O. Jones, and V. C. Uchendu. 1979. *Agricultural change in tropical Africa.* Ithaca, N.Y.: Cornell University Press.

Antle, J. M. 1983. Infrastructure and aggregate agricultural productivity: International evidence. *Economic Development and Cultural Change* 31: 609–619.

Argwings-Kodhek, G., M. Mukumbu, and E. Monke. 1993. The impacts of maize market liberalization in Kenya. *Food Research Institute Studies* 22: 331–348.

Askari, H., and J. Cummings. 1977. *Agricultural supply response: A survey of econometric evidence.* New York, N.Y.: Praeger.

Asuming-Brempong, S. 1994. Effects of exchange-rate liberalization and input-subsidy removal on the competitiveness of cereals in Ghana. In *Issues in African rural development,* vol. 2, ed. S. A. Breth. Arlington, Va.: Winrock International Institute for Agricultural Development.

Atchou, Y. K. 1990. Problèmes relatifs à l'utilisation des engrais au Togo. In *Fertilizer policy in tropical Africa. Workshop proceedings, Lomé, Togo, April 1988,* ed. T. Tshibaka and C. Baanante. Muscle Shoals, Ala.: International Fertilizer Development Center (IFDC) and International Food Policy Research Institute (IFPRI).

Atwood, D. 1990. Land registration in Africa: The impact on agricultural production. *World Development* 18: 659–671.

Azam, J. P., and T. Besley. 1989. General equilibrium with parallel markets for goods and foreign exchange: Theory and application to Ghana. *World Development* 17: 1921–1930.

Badiane, O. 1994. Domestic market liberalization: Challenges for agricultural policy and research. In *Food policy in sub-Saharan Africa: A new agenda for research and donor assistance,* ed. NRI. Chatham, U.K.: Natural Resources Institute (NRI), p. 49.

Badiane, O., and M. Gaye. 1999. Liberalization of groundnut markets in Senegal: Impact on the marketing and processing sectors. International Food Policy Research Institute, Washington, D.C. Mimeo.

Badiane, O., and M. Kherallah. 1999. Market liberalization and the poor. *Quarterly Journal of International Agriculture* 38: 341–358.

Badiane, O., and G. E. Shively. 1998. Spatial integration, transport costs, and the response of local prices to policy changes in Ghana. *Journal of Development Economics* 56: 411–431.

Badiane, O., F. Goletti, M. Kherallah, P. Berry, K. Govindan, P. Gruhn, and M. Mendoza. 1997. *Agricultural input and output marketing reforms in African countries. Final donor report.* Washington, D.C.: International Food Policy Research Institute (IFPRI).

Badiane, O., F. Goletti, C. Lapenu, M. Mendoza, B. Minten, E. Ralison, C. Randrianarisoa, K. Rich, and M. Zeller. 1998. *Structure and conduct of major agricultural input and output markets and response to reforms by rural households in Mada-gascar. Final donor report.* Washington, D.C.: International Food Policy Research Institute (IFPRI) and Centre Nationale de Recherche Appliquée au Développement Rural (FOFIMA).

Baffes, J. 2001. Policy reform experience in cotton markets. In *Commodity market reforms: Lessons of two decades* (pp. 165–190), ed. T. Akiyama et al. Washington, D.C.: World Bank.

Barrett, C. 1996. Market analysis methods: Are our enriched toolkits well suited to enliven markets? *American Journal of Agricultural Economics* 78: 825–829.

Barrett, C. B. 1994. Understanding uneven agricultural liberalisation in Madagascar. *Journal of Modern African Studies* 32: 449–476.

―――. 1997. Food marketing liberalization and trader entry: Evidence from Madagascar. *World Development* 25: 763–777.

Barrett, C. B., and M. R. Carter. 1994. *Does it take more than liberalization? The economics of sustainable agrarian growth and transformation.* Global Studies Research Program Working Paper No. 4, Development at a Crossroads Series. Madison, Wis.: University of Wisconsin-Madison.

Barrett, C. B., and P. A. Dorosh. 1996. Farmers' welfare and changing food prices: Nonparametric evidence from rice in Madagascar. *American Journal of Agricultural Economics* 78: 656–669.

Bassolet, B., and C. Lutz. 1999. Information services and integration of cereal markets in Burkina Faso. *Journal of African Economies* 8: 31–51.

Bates, R. H. 1981. *Markets and states in tropical Africa: The political basis of agricultural policies.* Berkeley, Calif.: University of California Press.

―――. 1989. The reality of structural adjustment: A skeptical appraisal. In *Structural adjustment and agriculture: Theory and practice in Africa & Latin America,* ed. S. Commander. London, U.K.: James Currey for the Overseas Development Institute (ODI).

Baulch, B. 1997. Transfer costs, spatial arbitrage, and testing for food market integration. *American Journal of Agricultural Economics* 79: 477–487.

Bell, C. L. G., and P. B. R. Hazell. 1980. Measuring the indirect effects of an agricultural investment project on its surrounding region. *American Journal of Agriculture Economics* 62: 75–86.

Berg, E. 1989. The liberalization of rice marketing in Madagascar. *World Development* 17: 719–728.

Berry, S. 1993. *No condition is permanent: The social dynamics of agrarian change in sub-Saharan Africa.* Madison, Wis.: University of Wisconsin Press.

Berthelemy, J. C., J. P. Azam, and J. J. Faucher. 1988. *The supply of manufactured goods and agricultural development: The case of Madagascar: The case of Mozambique.* Paris, France: OECD Development Centre.

Bevan, D., P. Collier, and J. W. Gunning. 1989. *Peasants and government: An economic analysis.* Oxford, U.K.: Clarendon Press.

Beynon, J., S. Jones, and S. Yao. 1992. Market reform and private trade in Eastern and Southern Africa. *Food Policy* 17: 399–408.

Bidaux, A., G. Raymond, and B. G. Soulé. 1997. *Evaluation du système d'approvisionnement et de distribution des intrants agricoles du Bénin.* Cotonou, Benin: République du Bénin, Ministère du développement rural.

Binswanger, H. P. 1990. The policy response of agriculture. In *Proceedings of the World Bank annual conference on development economics,* ed. World Bank. Supplement to the World Bank Economic Review. Washington, D.C.: World Bank.

Block, S. A. 1995. The recovery of agricultural productivity in Sub-Saharan Africa. *Food Policy* 20: 385–406.

Bloom, D. E., and J. D. Sachs. 1998. *Geography, demography, and economic growth in Africa.* Brookings Papers on Economic Activity No. 2. Washington, D.C.: Brookings Institution.

Blyn, G. 1973. Price series correlation as a measure of market integration. *Indian Journal of Agricultural Economics* 28: 56–59.

Bond, M. E. 1983. Agricultural responses to prices in sub-Saharan African countries. *International Monetary Fund Staff Papers* 20: 703–736.

Booth, D. 1991. Timing and sequencing in agricultural policy reform: Tanzania. *Development Policy Review* 9: 353–379.

————. 1994. Economic liberalization, real markets and the (un)reality of structural adjustment in rural Tanzania. *Sociologia Ruralis* 34: 45–62.

Boussard, J. M. 1999. The impact of prices and macroeconomic policies on agricultural supply: A synthesis of available results—A comment. *Agricultural Economics* 21: 19–20.

Braverman, A., and J. S. Hammer. 1986. Multimarket Analysis of Agricultural Pricing Policies in Senegal. In *Agricultural household models: Extensions, applications and policy,* ed. I. Singh, L. Squire, and J. Strauss. Baltimore, Md.: Johns Hopkins University Press.

Bromley, D. W. 1995. Development reconsidered: The African challenge. *Food Policy* 20: 425–438.

Browne, R. S., and R. J. Cummings. 1984. *The Lagos plan of action vs. the Berg report: Contemporary issues in African economic development.* Monographs in African Studies. Washington, D.C.: Howard University.

Bryceson, D. F. 1992. Urban bias revisited: Staple food pricing in Tanzania. *European Journal of Development Research* 4: 82–106.

————. 1993. *Liberalizing Tanzania's food trade: Public and private faces of urban marketing policy 1939–88.* Geneva, Switzerland: United Nations Research Institute for Social Development.

Budd, J. W. 1993. Changing food prices and rural welfare: A nonparametric examination of the Côte d'Ivoire. *Economic Development and Cultural Change* 41: 587–603.

Bumb, B. L. 1990. Fertilizer supply in Sub-Saharan Africa—An analysis. In *Fertilizer policy in tropical Africa. Workshop proceedings, Lomé, Togo, April 1988,* ed. T. Tshibaka and C. Baanante. Muscle Shoals, Ala.: International Fertilizer Development Center (IFDC) and International Food Policy Research Institute (IFPRI).

Bumb, B. L., J. F. Teboh, J. K. Atta, and W. K. Asenso-Okyere. 1994. *Ghana policy environment and fertilizer sector development.* Technical Bulletin-T-41. Muscle Shoals, Ala.: International Fertilizer Development Center.

Byerlee, D., and C. K. Eicher. 1997. *Africa's emerging maize revolution.* Boulder, Colo.: Lynne Rienner Publishers.

Chembezi, D. M. 1990. Estimating fertilizer demand and output supply for Malawi's smallholder agriculture. *Agricultural Systems* 33: 293–314.

Chhibber, A. 1989. The aggregate supply response: A survey. In *Structural adjustment and agriculture: Theory and practice in Africa & Latin America,* ed. S. Commander. London: James Currey for the Overseas Development Institute (ODI) and Heinemann.

Chilowa, W. 1998. The impact of agricultural liberalization on food security in Malawi. *Food Policy* 23: 553–569.

Choksi, A. M., and D. Papageorgiou. 1986. *Economic liberalization in developing countries.* New York, N.Y.: Basil Blackwell for the World Bank.

Cleaver, K. M. 1985. *The impact of price and exchange rate policies on agriculture in Sub-Saharan Africa.* World Bank Staff Working Paper No. 728. Washington, D.C.: World Bank.

———. 1997. *Rural development strategies for poverty reduction and environmental protection in sub-Saharan Africa.* Washington, D.C.: World Bank.

Commander, S. 1989. *Structural Adjustment and Agriculture: Theory and Practice in Africa & Latin America.* London, U.K.: James Currey, for the Overseas Development Institute (ODI).

Cornia, G. A., and G. K. Helleiner. 1994. *From adjustment to development in Africa: Conflict, controversy, convergence, consensus?* New York: St. Martin's Press.

Cornia, R., R. Jolly, and F. Stewart, eds. 1987. *Adjustment with a human face.* Vol. 1, *Protecting the vulnerable and promoting growth.* Oxford: Clarendon Press.

Coulter, J. 1994. *Liberalization of cereals marketing in sub-Saharan Africa: Lessons from experience.* Marketing Series No. 9. Catham, U.K.: Natural Resources Institute (NRI).

Coulter, J., and J. A. F. Compton. 1991. *Liberalization of cereals marketing in sub-Saharan Africa: Implementation issues.* Marketing Series 1. Chatham, U.K.: Natural Resources Institute (NRI).

Coulter, J., and P. Golob. 1992. Cereal marketing liberalization in Tanzania. *Food Policy* 17: 420–430.

Coulter, J., and C. Poulton. 2001. Cereal market liberalization in Africa. In *Commodity market reforms: Lessons of two decades,* ed. T. Akiyama et al. Washington, D.C.: World Bank.

Coulter, J., and A. W. Shepherd. 1995. *Inventory credit: An approach to developing markets.* FAO Agricultural Services Bulletin No. 120. Rome, Italy: Food and Agriculture Organization of the United Nations (FAO).

Croppenstedt, A., and M. Demeke. 1996. *Determinants of adoption and levels of demand for fertilizer for cereal growing farmers in Ethiopia.* Working Paper Series/96-3. Oxford, U.K.: Centre for the Study of African Economies, University of Oxford.

Crowder, M. 1968. *West Africa under colonial rule.* Evanston, Ill.: Northwestern University Press.

Dadi, L., A. Negassa, and S. Franzel. 1992. Marketing maize and tef in western Ethiopia: Implications for policy following market liberalization. *Food Policy* 17: 201–213.

Delgado, C. L. 1991. Cereals protection and agricultural development strategy in the Sahel. *Food Policy* 16: 105–111.

———. 1992. Why domestic food prices matter to growth strategy in semi-open West African agriculture. *Journal of African Economies* 1: 446–471.

————. 1995. Agricultural diversification and export promotion in Sub-Saharan Africa. *Food Policy* 20: 225–243.

————. 1996. Agricultural transformation: The key to broad-based growth and poverty alleviation in Africa. In *Agenda for Africa's economic renewal,* ed. B. Ndulu and N. van de Walle. New Brunswick, N.J.: Transaction.

————. 1998. Africa's changing agricultural development strategies: Past and present paradigms as a guide to the future. *The Brown Journal of World Affairs* 5: 175–214.

————. 1999. Sources of growth in smallholder agriculture in Sub-Saharan Africa: The role of vertical integration of smallholders with processors and marketers of high value-added items. *Agrekon* 38: 165–189.

Delgado, C. L., and S. Jammeh, eds. 1991. *The political economy of Senegal under structural adjustment.* New York, N.Y.: Praeger.

Delgado, C. L., and J. W. Mellor. 1984. A structural view of policy issues in African agricultural development. *American Journal of Agricultural Economics* 66: 665–670.

Delgado, C. L., and N. W. Minot. 2000. *Agriculture in Tanzania since 1986: Follower or leader of growth? A World Bank Country Study.* Washington, D.C. Government of the United Republic of Tanzania, World Bank, and International Food Policy Research Institute (IFPRI).

Delgado, C. L., and C. Ranade. 1987. Technological change and agricultural labor use. In *Accelerating food production in Sub-Saharan Africa,* ed. J. W. Mellor, C. Delgado, and M. Blackie. Baltimore, Md.: Johns Hopkins University Press for the International Food Policy Research Institute.

Delgado, C. L., J. Hopkins, V. A. Kelly, P. Hazell, A. A. McKenna, P. Gruhn, B. Hojjati, J. Sil, and C. Courbois. 1998. *Agricultural growth linkages in Sub-Saharan Africa.* IFPRI Research Report No. 107. Washington, D.C.: International Food Policy Research Institute.

Dembele, N. N. 1994. Economic analysis of traders' response to cereals market reforms in Mali. Ph.D. thesis, Michigan State University, East Lansing, Mich.

Demeke, M., A. Said, and T. S. Jayne. 1996. Relationships between grain market performance and fertilizer markets and profitability. Paper presented at the Grain Market Research Project Discussion Forum, sponsored by the Ministry of Economic Development and Cooperation, Government of Ethiopia, Sodere, Ethiopia, November 8–9.

Dercon, S. 1995. On market integration and liberalization: Method and application to Ethiopia. *Journal of Development Studies* 32: 112–143.

Desai, G. M., and V. Ghandi. 1990. Fertilizer consumption in Sub-Saharan Africa: An analysis of growth and profile of use. In *Fertilizer policy in tropical Africa. Workshop proceedings, Lomé, Togo, April 1988,* ed. T. Tshibaka and C. Baanante. Muscle Shoals, Ala.: International Fertilizer Development Center (IFDC) and International Food Policy Research Institute (IFPRI).

Dioné, J. 1989. Informing food security policy in Mali: Interactions between technology, institutions, and market reforms. Ph.D. thesis, Michigan State University, East Lansing, Mich.

Donovan, W. G. 1996. The role of inputs and marketing systems in the modernization of agriculture. In *Achieving greater impact from research investments in Africa,* ed. S. A. Breth. Proceedings of a workshop held in Addis Ababa, Ethiopia, 26–30 September. Mexico City: Sasakawa Africa Association c/o CIMMYT.

Dorosh, P. A., and S. Haggblade. 1993. Agricultural-led growth: Food grains versus export crops in Madagascar. *Agricultural Economics* 9: 165–180.

Dorward, A., J. Kydd, and C. Poulton. 1998. *Smallholder cash crop production under market liberalisation: A new institutional economics perspective.* Wallingford, U.K.: CAB International.

———. 1999. The baby and the bathwater: Agricultural parastatals revisited. Paper presented at a symposium on the African Rural Crisis Revisited at the Annual Conference of the Agricultural Economics Society, Stranmillis University College, Queen's University of Belfast, 28 March 1999. London, U.K.: Agrarian Development Unit, Wye College, University of London.

Duncan, A., and S. Jones. 1993. Agricultural marketing and pricing reform: A review of experience. *World Development* 21: 1495–1514.

Edwards, S. 1992. *The sequencing of structural adjustment and stabilization.* Occasional Paper No. 34. San Francisco, Calif.: International Center for Economic Growth, ICS Press.

Egg, J. 1999. *Etude de l'impact de la libéralisation sur le fonctionnement des filières cerealières au Mali. Rapport de synthèse.* Bamako, Mali: Office des Produits Agricoles du Mali (OPAM).

Eicher, C. K. 1999. Institutions and the African farmer. Third Distinguished Economist Lecture. Mexico City: CIMMYT Economics Program, January 22.

Eicher, C., and B. Kupfuma. 1997. Zimbabwe's emerging maize revolution. In *Africa's emerging maize revolution,* ed. D. Byerlee and C. K. Eicher. Boulder, Colo.: Lynne Rienner.

Ellis, F., B. Trotter, and P. Magrath. 1992. *Rice marketing in Indonesia: Methodology, results and implications of a research study.* Marketing Series Vol. 4. Chatham, U.K.: Natural Resources Institute.

Engle, R. F., and C. W. J. Granger. 1987. Co-integration and error correction: Representation, estimation, and testing. *Econometrica* 35: 251–276.

Fafchamps, M. 1996. Market emergence, trust and reputation. Stanford University, San Francisco, Calif. Mimeo.

———. 1999. Trust and reputation. Mimeo.

Fafchamps, M., and S. Gavian. 1996. The spatial integration of livestock markets in Niger. *Journal of African Economies* 5: 366–405.

Fafchamps, M. and B. Minten. 1998. *Relationships and traders in Madagascar.* MSSD Discussion Paper No. 24. Washington, D.C.: International Food Policy Research Institute (IFPRI).

———. 2001. Property rights in a flea market economy. *Economic Development and Cultural Change* 49: 229–267.

Faini, R. 1992. Infrastructure, relative prices and agricultural adjustment. In *Open economies: Structural adjustment and agriculture,* ed. I. Goldin and L.A. Winters. Cambridge, U.K.: Cambridge University Press.

FAO (Food and Agriculture Organization of the United Nations). 1986. *African agriculture: The next 25 years. Annex V. Inputs supply and incentive policies.* Rome.

———. 1994. *Structural adjustment and the provision of agricultural services in Sub-Saharan Africa.* Rome.

————. 1998a . *FAO fertilizer yearbook.* Rome.

————. 1998b. *Statistical database.* Rome.

————. 1999. *Fertilizer use by crop.* Rome.

FAOStat. *Food and Agriculture Organization database.* Accessed at http:\\apps.fao.org.

Ferreira, L. 1994. *Poverty and inequality during structural adjustment in rural Tanzania.* Research Paper Series 8. Washington, D.C.: World Bank.

Fisseha, T. 1994. Grain markets: Government intervention and liberalisation. Presentation to the Fourth Annual Conference on the Ethiopian Economy, November 28–29, Debre Zeit, Mimeo.

Fontaine, J. 1991. *Macro-micro linkages: Structural adjustment and fertilizer policy in sub-Saharan Africa.* Technical Papers No. 49. Paris, France: Organisation for Economic Co-operation and Development (OECD).

Frisvold, G., and K. Ingram. 1995. Sources of agricultural productivity growth and stagnation in sub-Saharan Africa. *Agricultural Economics* 13: 51–61.

Gabre-Madhin, E. 1991. Transfer costs of cereals marketing in Mali: Implications for Mali's regional trade in West Africa. M.S. thesis. Michigan State University, East Lansing, Mich.

————. 1998. Understanding how markets work: Transaction costs and institutions in the Ethiopian grain market. IFPRI Research Report Draft Manuscript, Washington, D.C.

————. 1999. Of markets and middlemen: An institutional analysis of brokers in Ethiopia. International Food Policy Research Institute, Washington, D.C. Mimeo.

Gbetibouo, M., and C. L. Delgado. 1984. Lessons and constraints of export crop-led growth: Cocoa in Ivory Coast. In *The political economy of Ivory Coast,* ed. I. W. Zarman and C. Delgado. New York, N.Y.: Praeger.

Gebre-Meskel, D. 1996. Structure and conduct of grain markets. MSU/MOPED Grain Market Research Project, Addis Ababa. Mimeo.

Gisselquist, D. 1998. Pro-growth regulatory reforms for agricultural inputs in Malawi, Zambia, and Zimbabwe. Memo-World Bank, Washington, D.C.

Gisselquist, D., and J. Rusike. 1998. Zimbabwe's agricultural input industries 1990–1996: Regulations, reforms, and impacts. Memo-World Bank, Washington, D.C.

Goletti, F., and S. Babu. 1994. Market liberalization and integration of maize markets in Malawi. *Agricultural Economics* 11: 311–324.

Goodland, A., and A. Gordon. 1999. Production credit for small-holders growing cotton: Zimbabwe case study. In *The use of purchased inputs by communal farmers in Zimbabwe,* ed. A. Gordon and A. Goodland. Proceedings of a workshop organized by the Natural Resources Institute (U.K.), Harare, Zimbabawe, March 1–2. Chatham, U.K.: Natural Resources Institute.

Goodwin, B. K., and T. C. Schroeder. 1991. Cointegration tests and spatial price linkages in regional cattle markets. *American Journal of Agricultural Economics* 2: 452–464.

Govereh, J., and T. J. Jayne. 1999. *Effects of cash crop production on food crop productivity in Zimbabwe. Synergies or trade offs?* MSU International Development Working Paper No. 74. East Lansing, Mich.: Michigan State University.

Government of Malawi, Ministry of Agriculture and Irrigation. 1997. *Malawi agricultural statistical bulletin, 1996/1997.* Lilongwe, Malawi.

Govindan, K., and S. C. Babu. 2001. Supply response under market liberalization: A case study of Malawi agriculture. *Southern Africa Development* 18(1): 93–106.

Green, D. A. G., and D. H. Ng'ong'ola. 1993. Factors affecting fertilizer adoption in less developed countries: An application of multivariate logistic analysis in Malawi. *Journal of Agricultural Economics* 44: 99–109.

Guillaumont, P. 1994. Adjustment policy and agricultural development. *Journal of International Development* 6: 141–155.

Gyimah-Boadi, E., and N. van de Walle. 1996. The politics of economic reform in Africa. In *Agenda for Africa's economic renewal,* ed. B. Ndulu and N. van de Walle. New Brunswick, N.J.: Transaction.

Haddad, L., L. Brown, A. Richter, and L. Smith. 1995. The gender dimensions of economic adjustment policies: Potential interactions and evidence to date. *World Development* 23: 881–896.

Harrigan, J. 1988. Malawi: The impact of pricing policy on smallholder agriculture 1971–88. *Development Policy Review* 6: 415–433.

———. 1997. Modelling the impact of World Bank policy-based lending: The case of Malawi's agricultural sector. *Journal of Development Studies* 33: 848–873.

Harriss, B. 1979. There is method in my madness / Or is it vice versa? Measuring agricultural market performance. *Food Research Institute Studies* 17: 197–218.

Harriss-White, B., ed. 1999. *Agricultural markets: From theory to practice.* London: Macmillan.

Hassan, R. M., and D. D. Karanja. 1997. Increasing maize production in Kenya: Technology, institutions, and policy. In *Africa's emerging maize revolution,* ed. D. Byerlee and C. K. Eicher. Boulder, Colo.: Lynne Rienner.

Hawassi, F. G. H., N. S. Y. Mdoe, F. M. Turuka, and G. C. Ashimogo. 1998. Efficient fertilizer use in the Southern Highlands of Tanzania and implications for development policy. *Quarterly Journal of International Agriculture* 3(37): 222–237.

Hayami, Y., and Ruttan, V. 1971. *Agricultural development: An international perspective.* Baltimore, Md.: Johns Hopkins University Press.

Heisey, P. W., and W. Mwangi. 1997. Fertilizer use and maize production. In *Africa's emerging maize revolution,* ed. D. Byerlee and C.K. Eicher. Boulder, Colo.: Lynne Rienner.

Helleiner, G. K. 1994. From adjustment to development in Sub-Saharan Africa: Consensus and continuing conflicts. In *From adjustment to development in Africa: Conflict, controversy, convergence, consensus?,* ed. G. A. Cornia and G. K. Helleiner. New York, N.Y.: St. Martin's Press.

Heyer, J., J. K. Maitha, and W. M. Senga, eds. 1975. *Agricultural development in Kenya: An economic assessment.* Nairobi, Kenya: Oxford University Press.

Howard, J., and C. Mungoma. 1997. Zambia's stop-and-go maize revolution. In *Africa's emerging maize revolution,* ed. D. Byerlee and C. K. Eicher. Boulder, Colo.: Lynne Rienner.

Husain, I. 1994. *The evolving role of the World Bank: The challenge of Africa.* Fiftieth Anniversary Paper Series. Washington, D.C.: World Bank.

Husain, I., and R. Faruqee. 1994. *Adjustment in Africa: Lessons from country case studies.* World Bank Regional and Sectoral Studies. Washington, D.C.: World Bank.

Idachaba, F. 2000. Desirable and workable agricultural policies for Nigeria in the first decade of the 21st century. Lecture on Topical Issues in Nigerian Agriculture, Department of Agricultural Economics, University of Ibadan, Nigeria, January 25.

IFPRI (International Food Policy Research Institute). 1998. *Analysis of input distribution and seed markets.* Prepared by the International Food Policy Research Institute and the Centre National de Recherche Appliquée au Développement Rural (FOFIFA) for the U.S. Agency for International Development.

Jaeger, W. K. 1992. *The effects of economic policies on African agriculture.* World Bank Discussion Paper No. 147, Africa Technical Department Series. Washington, D.C.: World Bank.

Jaffee, S., and J. Morton. 1995. *Marketing Africa's high-value foods: Comparative experiences of an emerging private sector.* Washington, D.C.: World Bank.

Jayne, T. S., and M. Chisvo. 1991. Unraveling Zimbabwe's food insecurity paradox: Implications for grain market reform in Southern Africa. *Food Policy* 16: 319–329.

Jayne, T. S., and S. Jones. 1997. Food marketing and pricing policy in eastern and southern Africa: A survey. *World Development* 25: 1505–1527.

Jayne, T. S., and N. Minot. 1989. *Food security policy and the competitiveness of agriculture in the Sahel: A summary of the "Beyond Mindelo" conference.* MSU International Development Working Paper No. 32. East Lansing, Mich.: Michigan State University.

Jayne, T. S., and L. Rubey. 1993. Maize milling, market reform and urban food security: The case of Zimbabwe. *World Development* 21: 975–988.

Jayne, T. S., A. Negassa, and R. J. Myers. 1998. *The effect of liberalization on grain prices and marketing margins in Ethiopia.* MSU International Development Working Paper No. 68. East Lansing, Mich.: Department of Agricultural Economics, Michigan State University.

Jayne, T. S., L. Rubey, D. Tschirley, M. Mukumba, M. Chisvo, A. P. Santos, M. T. Weber, and P. Diskin. 1995. *Effects of market reform on access to food by low-income households: Evidence from four countries in Eastern and Southern Africa.* USAID Policy Synthesis for Cooperating USAID Offices and Country Missions No. 5. Washington, D.C.: United States Agency for International Development.

Jayne, T. S., M. Mukumbu, J. Duncan, J. M. Staatz, J. A. Howard, and M. Lundberg. 1996. *Trends in real food prices in six Sub-Saharan African countries.* Technical Paper No. 39, SD Publication Series, Office of Sustainable Development, Bureau for Africa. Washington, D.C.: United States Agency for International Development.

Jayne, T. S., J. D. Shaffer, J. M. Staatz, and T. Reardon. 1997a. *Improving the impact of market reform on agricultural productivity in Africa: How institutional design makes a difference.* MSU International Development Working Paper No. 66. Lansing, Mich.: Michigan State University.

Jayne, T. S., J. M Staatz, M. T. Weber, S. Jones, and E. W. Crawford. 1997b. Agricultural policy reform and productivity change in Africa. Paper presented at the XXIII International Conference of Agricultural Economists, Sacramento, Calif., August 10–16.

Jayne, T. S., M. Mukumbu, M. Chisvo, D. Tschirley, M. T. Weber, B. Zulu, L. Johansson, P. Santos, and D. Soroko. 1999. *Successes and challenges of food market reform: Experiences from Kenya, Mozambique, Zambia, and Zimbabwe.* MSU International Development Working Paper No. 72. Lansing, Mich.: Department of Agricultural Economics, Michigan State University.

Jayne, T. S., A. Chapoto, J. Nyoro, A. Mwanaumo, and J. Govereh. Forthcoming. False promise or false premise? The experience of food and input market reform in eastern and southern Africa. In *Perspectives on agricultural transformation: A view from Africa,* ed. T. S. Jayne, G. Argwings-Kodhek, and I. Minde. Huntington, NY: Nova Science Publishers.

Jebuni, C. D., and W. Seini. 1992. *Agricultural input policies under structural adjustment: Their distributional implications.* Cornell Food and Nutrition Policy Program Working Paper No. 31. Ithaca, N.Y.: Cornell University.

Jha, D., and B. Hojjati. 1993. *Fertilizer use on smallholder farms in Eastern Province, Zambia.* IFPRI Research Report 94. Washington, D.C.: International Food Policy Research Institute.

Johansson, R. 1999. National and household food security: Effects of Zambian economic reform. USAID Staff Report. United States Agency for International Development, Lusaka, Zambia.

Jones, S. 1995. Food market reform: The changing role of the state. *Food Policy* 20: 551–560.

———. 1996. *Food markets in developing countries: What do we know?* Working Paper No. 8. Oxford, U.K.: Food Studies Group, University of Oxford.

———. 1998. *Liberalized food marketing in developing countries: Key policy problems.* Oxford, U.K.: Oxford Policy Management.

Jones, S., and S. Wickrema. 1998. *The use of conditionality in reform: Food markets in Africa.* Policy Briefing Note 1. Oxford, U.K.: Oxford Policy Management.

Jones, W. O. 1972. *Marketing staple crops in tropical Africa.* Ithaca, N.Y.: Cornell University Press.

———. 1984. Economic tasks for food marketing boards in tropical Africa. *Food Research Institute Studies* 19: 113–138.

Kahkonen, S., and H. Leathers. 1999. *Transaction costs analysis of maize and cotton marketing in Zambia and Tanzania.* Technical Paper No. 105, SD Publication Series, Office of Sustainable Development, Bureau for Africa. Washington, D.C.: United States Agency for International Development.

Kalinda, T. H., J. C. Shute, and G. C. Filson. 1998. Access to agricultural extension, credit and markets among small-scale farmers in southern Zambia. *Development Southern Africa* 15: 589–608.

Kamara, A. B., and M. von Oppen. 1999. Efficiency and equity effects of market access on agricultural productivity: The case of small farmers in Machakos District, Kenya. *Quarterly Journal of International Agriculture* 38: 65–77.

Kandoole, B., B. Kaluwa, and S. T. Buccola. 1988. Market liberalization and food security in Malawi. In *Southern Africa: Food security policy options,* ed. M. Rukuni and R. H. Bernsten. Proceedings of the Third Annual Conference on Food Security in Southern Africa, November 1–5, 1987, University of Zimbabwe/Michigan State University Food Security Research Project, Harare, Zimbabwe.

Karanja, A. M., T. S. Jayne, and P. Strasberg. 1998. Maize productivity and impact of market liberalization in Kenya. Paper presented at a conference on Strategies for Raising Smallholder Agricultural Productivity and Welfare, Egerton University and Tegemeo Institute of Agricultural Policy and Development, November 28, Kenya, Nairobi.

Kayizzi-Mugerwa, S., and J. Levin. 1994. Adjustment and poverty: A review of the African experience. *African Development Review/Revue Africaine de Développement* 6: 1–39.

Kelly, V., B. Diagana, T. Reardon, M. Gaye, and E. Crawford. 1996. *Cash crop and foodgrain productivity in Senegal: Historical view, new survey evidence, and policy implications.* USAID Policy Synthesis for Cooperating USAID Offices and Country Missions No. 7. Washington, D.C.: United States Agency for International Development.

Kherallah, M., and K. Govindan. 1999. The sequencing of agricultural market reforms in Malawi. *Journal of African Economies* 8: 125–151.

Killick, T. 1993. *The adaptive economy: Adjustment policies in small, low-income countries.* Washington, D.C.: World Bank.

———. 1994. Africa's postindependence development experiences. In *Economic development,* ed. E. Grilli and D. Salvatore. Handbook of Comparative Economic Policies, Vol. 4. Westport, Conn.: Greenwood Press.

Kinsey, B. H. 1991. A regional study of demand, supply and distribution and the potential for intraregional trade in fertilizer: Malawi, Zambia, and Zimbabwe. International Food Policy Research Institute, Washington, D.C. Draft.

Knudsen, O., and J. Nash. 1991. Agricultural policy. In *Restructuring economies in distress: Policy reform and the World Bank,* ed. V. Thomas, A. Chhibber, M. Dailami, and J. DeMelo. Oxford, U.K.: Oxford University Press.

Koffi, K. 1990. Abstract—The fertilizer sector in Côte D'Ivoire. In *Fertilizer policy in tropical Africa. Workshop Proceedings, Lomé, Togo, April 1988,* ed. T. Tshibaka and C. Baanante. Muscle Shoals, Ala.: International Fertilizer Development Center and International Food Policy Research Institute.

Krueger, A. O., M. Schiff, and A. Valdes. 1991. *The political economy of agricultural pricing policy.* Vol. 3, *Africa and the Mediterranean.* Baltimore, Md. and London, U.K.: Johns Hopkins University Press for the World Bank.

Kydd, J. and R. Christiansen. 1982. Structural change in Malawi since independence: Consequences of a development strategy based on large-scale agriculture. *World Development* 10: 355–375.

Kydd, J., and N. J. Spooner. 1990. Agricultural marketing liberalization and structural adjustment in Sub-Saharan Africa. *Oxford Agrarian Studies* 18: 65–79.

Lamb, R. L. 2000. Food crops, exports, and the short-run policy response of agriculture in Africa. *Agricultural Economics* 22: 271–298.

Lele, U. 1971. *Food grain marketing in India.* Ithaca, N.Y.: Cornell University Press.

———. 1990. *Agricultural growth and assistance to Africa: Lessons of a quarter century.* International Center for Economic Growth Sector Studies No. 2. San Francisco, Calif.: ICS Press.

———. 1991. *Aid to African agriculture: Lessons from two decades of donors' experience.* Baltimore, Md. and London, U.K.: Johns Hopkins University Press for the World Bank.

Lele, U., and R. E. Christiansen. 1989. *Markets, marketing boards, and cooperatives in Africa: Issues in adjustment policy.* MADIA Discussion Papers No. 11. Washington, D.C.: World Bank.

Lele, U., R. Christiansen, and K. Kadiresan. 1989. *Fertilizer policy in Africa: Lessons from development programs and adjustment lending, 1970–87.* MADIA Discussion Papers No. 5. Washington, D.C.: World Bank.

Lewis, P., and H. Stein. 1997. Shifting fortunes: The political economy of financial liberalization in Nigeria. *World Development* 25: 5–22.

Lewis, W. A. 1980. The slowing down of the engine of growth. *American Economic Review* 70: 555–564.

Lipton, M. 1987. Limits of price policy for agriculture: Which way for the World Bank? *Development Policy Review* 5: 197–215.

Lirenso, A. 1993. Grain marketing reform in Ethiopia. Ph.D. thesis, School of Development Studies, University of East Anglia, U.K.

Lusigi, A., and C. Thirtle. 1997. Total factor productivity and the effects of R&D in African agriculture. *Journal of International Development* 9: 529–538.

Lutz, C., A. van Tilburg, and B. J. van der Kamp. 1995. The process of short- and long-term price integration in the Benin maize market. *European Review of Agricultural Economics* 22: 191–212.

Mabeza-Chimedza, R. 1998. Zimbabwe's smallholder agriculture miracle. *Food Policy* 23: 529–537.

MAC (Ministry of Agriculture and Cooperatives). 1997. *Agricultural inputs study. Final report.* Dar es Salaam, United Republic of Tanzania.

McCalla, A. F. 1999. Prospects for food security in the 21st century: With special emphasis on Africa. *Agricultural Economics* 20: 95–103.

McPherson, M. F. 1995. *The sequencing of economic reforms: Lessons from Zambia.* Development Discussion Paper No. 516. Cambridge, Mass.: Harvard Institute for International Development.

Mamingi, N. 1997. The impact of prices and macroeconomic policies on agricultural supply: A synthesis of available results. *Agricultural Economics* 16: 17–34.

Maro, W. A. 1999. Agricultural marketing and transportation in Tanzania. Collaborator study prepared for this report. International Food Policy Research Institute, Washington, D.C.

Masters, W. A. 1994. *Government and agriculture in Zimbabwe.* Westport, Conn. and London, U.K.: Greenwood and Praeger.

Masters, W. A., and E. A. Nuppenau. 1993. Panterritorial versus regional pricing for maize in Zimbabwe. *World Development* 21: 1647–1658.

Maxwell, S. 1998. Agricultural development and poverty in Africa. Paper abridged from a presentation made at the Workshop on Agricultural Sector Strategies for Poverty Reduction in Eastern and Southern Africa, Wagenin, the Netherlands, November 23–25. Overseas Development Institute, London, U.K., November 24.

Mbata, J. N. 1997. Factors influencing fertilizer adoption and rates of use among small-scale food crop farmers in the Rift Valley area of Kenya. *Quarterly Journal of International Agriculture* 36: 285–302.

Meerman, J. P. 1997. *Reforming agriculture: The World Bank goes to market.* Operations Evaluation Study. Washington, D.C.: World Bank.

Mellor, J. W., C. L. Delgado, and M. J. Blackie. 1987. *Accelerating food production in sub-Saharan Africa.* Baltimore, Md.: Johns Hopkins University Press.

Michaely, M. 1986. The timing and sequencing of a trade liberalization policy. In *Economic liberalization in developing countries,* ed. A. M. Choksi and D. Papageorgiou. Oxford, U.K.: Basil Blackwell.

Minot, N. 1991. Impact of the fertilizer sub-sector reform program on farmers: The results of three farm-level surveys 1991. Prepared for the Technical Supervisory Committee Government of Cameroon and U.S. Agency for International Development under the Agricultural Marketing Improvement Strategies Project with Abt Associates and the University of Idaho, Post Harvest Institute.

Minot, N., M. Kherallah, and P. Berry. 2000. Fertilizer market liberalization in Benin and Malawi: A household-level view. International Food Policy Research Institute, Washington, D.C. Mimeo.

Minten, B., and S. Kyle. 1995. *Asymmetry in food price transmission in African retail markets: The case of Kinshasa.* Staff Paper No. 95-06. Ithaca, N.Y.: Department of Agricultural Resource and Managerial Economics, Cornell University.

———. 2000. Retail margins, price transmission and price asymmetry in urban food markets: The case of Kinshasa (Zaire). *Journal of African Economics* 9(1): 1–23.

Mkandawire, T., and C. C. Soludo. 1999. *Our continent, our future: An African perspective to structural adjustment.* Trenton, N.J.: Africa World Press for the Council on the Development of Social Science Research in Africa.

Mole, O., and M. Weber. 1999. The cashew debate in Mozambique: Are there alternative strategies? Flash—Research Findings from the Food Security Project in Mozambique, April 14, http://www.aec.msu.edu/agecon/fs2/Mozambique/index.htm.

Morris, M. L. 1988. Parallel rice markets: Policy lessons from northern Senegal. *Food Policy* 13: 283–292.

Mose, L. O. 1998. Factors affecting the distribution and use of fertilizer in Kenya: Preliminary assessment. Prepared for the U.S. Agency for International Development under the Kenya Agricultural Marketing and Policy Analysis Project with Michigan State University, the Kenya Agricultural Research Institute, and Egerton University.

Moser, G., S. Rogers, and R. van Til. 1997. *Nigeria: Experience with structural adjustment.* Occasional Paper No. 148. Washington, D.C.: International Monetary Fund.

Mosley, P. and L. Smith. 1989. Structural adjustment and agricultural performance in Sub-Saharan Africa 1980–87. *Journal of International Development* 1: 321–355.

Mosley, P., and J. Weeks. 1993. Has the recovery begun? Africa's adjustment in the 1980s revisited. *World Development* 21: 1583–1606.

Mosley, P., J. Harrigan, and J. Toye. 1991. *Aid and power: The World Bank and policy based lending.* Vol. 1, *Analysis and policy proposals.* London, U.K.: Routledge.

Muleya, K. 1990. Fertilizer policy in Zambia. In *Fertilizer policy in tropical Africa. Workshop proceedings, Lomé, Togo, April 1988,* ed. T. Tshibaka and C. Baanante. Muscle Shoals, Ala.: International Fertilizer Development Center and International Food Policy Research Institute.

Mwanaumo, A., W. A.Masters, and P. V. Preckel. 1997. A spatial analysis of maize marketing policy reforms in Zambia. *American Journal of Agricultural Economics* 79: 514–523.

Naseem, A., and V. Kelly. 1999. *Macro trends and determinants of fertilizer use in sub-Saharan Africa.* MSU International Development Working Paper No. 73.

East Lansing, Mich.: Department of Agricultural Economics, Michigan State University.

Negassa, A. 1998. Vertical and spatial integration of grain markets in Ethiopia: Implications for grain market and food security policies. Working Paper No. 9. Ministry of Economic Development and Cooperation, Addis Ababa, Ethiopia.

Negassa, A., and T. S. Jayne. 1997 . The response of Ethiopian grain markets to liberalization. Working Paper No. 6. Grain Market Research Project, Ministry of Economic Development and Cooperation, Addis Ababa, Ethiopia.

Newberry, D. M. G., and J. E. Stiglitz. 1981. *The theory of commodity price stabilisation: A study in the economics of risk.* Oxford, U.K.: Oxford University Press.

Nkonya, E., T. Schroeder, and D. Norman. 1997. Factors affecting adoption of improved maize seed and fertiliser in northern Tanzania. *Journal of Agricultural Economics* 48: 1–12.

Ogbu, O. M., and M. Gbetibouo. 1990. Agricultural supply response in Sub-Saharan Africa: A critical review of the literature. *African Development Review* 2: 83–99.

Olayemi, J. K. 1999. *Food security in Nigeria.* Report No. 2. Ibadan, Nigeria: Development Policy Centre.

Omamo, S. W., and L. O. Mose. 1998. Fertilizer trade under market liberalization: Preliminary evidence from Kenya. Paper prepared for the Kenya Agricultural Marketing and Policy Analysis Project, Nairobi, Kenya.

————. 2001. Fertilizer trade under market liberalization: Preliminary evidence from Kenya. *Food Policy* 26: 1–10.

Oyejide, T. A. 1993. Effects of trade and macroeconomic policies on African agriculture. In *The bias against agriculture: Trade and macroeconomic policies in developing countries,* ed. R. M. Bautista and A. Valdes. San Francisco: ICS Press for the International Center for Economic Growth and the International Food Policy Research Institute.

Palaskas, T. B., and B. Harriss-White. 1993. Testing market integration: New approaches with case material from the West Bengal food economy. *Journal of Development Studies* 20: 1–57.

Peters, P. E. 1996. *Failed magic or social context? Market liberalization and the rural poor in Malawi.* Development Discussion Paper No. 562. Cambridge, Mass.: Harvard Institute of International Development.

Pinckney, T. C. 1993. Is market liberalization compatible with food security? Storage, trade and price policies for maize in southern Africa. *Food Policy* 18: 325–333.

Pinstrup-Andersen, P. 1985. Food prices and the poor in developing countries. *European Review of Agricultural Economics* 12: 69–85.

————. 1993. Fertilizer subsidies: Balancing short-term responses with long-term imperatives. In *Policy options for agricultural development in Sub-Saharan Africa,* ed. N. C. Russell and C. R. Dowswell. Mexico City, Mexico: Centre for Applied Studies in International Negotiations, Sasakawa Africa Association, and Global 2000.

Platteau, J. P. 1990. The food crisis in Africa: A comparative structural analysis. In *The political economy of hunger,* Vol. 2, ed. J. Dreze and A. Sen. Oxford, U.K.: Clarendon Press.

————. 1996. Physical infrastructure as a constraint on agricultural growth: The case of sub-Saharan Africa. *Oxford Development Studies* 24: 189–219.

Poulton, C. 1998. Cotton production and marketing in northern Ghana: The dynamics of competition in a system of interlocking transactions. In *Smallholder cash crop production under market liberalisation: A new institutional economics perspective,* ed. A. Dorward, J. Kydd, and C. Poulton. Wallingford, U.K.: CAB International.

Poulton, C., A. Dorward, J. Kydd, N. Poole, and L. Smith. 1998. A new institutional economics perspective on current policy debates. In *Smallholder cash crop production under market liberalisation: A new institutional economics perspective,* ed. A. Dorward, J. Kydd, and C. Poulton. Wallingford, U.K.: CAB International.

Puetz, D., and J. von Braun. 1991. Parallel markets and the rural poor in a West African setting. In *Markets in developing countries: Parallel, fragmented and black,* ed. M. Roemer and C. Jones. San Francisco, Calif.: ICS Press Institute for Contemporary Studies.

Rana, P. B. 1995. Reform strategies in transitional economies: Lessons from Asia. *World Development* 23: 1157–1169.

Reardon, T., C. Delgado, and P. Matlon. 1992. Determinants and effects of income diversification amongst farm households in Burkina Faso. *Journal of Development Studies* 28: 264–296.

Reardon, T., V. Kelly, D. Yanggen, and E. Crawford. 1999. *Determinants of fertilizer adoption by Africa farmers: Policy analysis framework, illustrative evidence, and implications.* Staff Paper No. 99-18. East Lansing, Mich.: Department of Agricultural Economics, Michigan State University.

Reardon, T., V. Kelly, E. Crawford, B. Diagana, J. Dioné, K. Savadogo, and D. Boughton. 1997. Promoting sustainable intensification and productivity growth in Sahel agriculture after macroeconomic policy reform. *Food Policy* 22: 317–327.

Reusse, E. 1987. Liberalization and agricultural marketing. *Food Policy* 12: 299–317.

Robison, L. J., and M. E. Siles. 1997. *Social capital and household income distributions in the United States: 1980–1990.* Julian Samora Research Institute Report No. 18. East Lansing, Mich.: Michigan State University.

Roemer, M., and C. Jones. 1991. *Markets in developing countries: Parallel, fragmented, and black.* San Francisco, Calif.: ICS Press.

Rugambisa, J. 1994. Effect of government agricultural market interventions in Tanzania. In *Issues in African rural development,* Vol. 2, ed. S.A. Breth. Arlington, Va.: Winrock International Institute for Agricultural Development.

Sachs, J. D., and W. T. Woo. 1994. Structural factors in the economic reforms of China, Eastern Europe, and the former Soviet Union. *Economic Policy* April: 104–145.

Sahn, D. E. 1992. Implications of structural adjustment for household food security in Africa. *Food, Nutrition and Agriculture* 2: 18–24.

———. 1994. Economic crisis and policy reform in Africa: Lessons learned and implications for policy. In *Adjusting to policy failure in African economies,* ed. D. E. Sahn. Food Systems and Agrarian Change Series. Ithaca, N.Y.: Cornell University Press.

———. 1999. Economic liberalization and food security in sub-Saharan Africa. In *Food security and nutrition: The global challenge,* ed. U. Kracht and M. Schulz. Munster, Germany: Lit Verlag.

Sahn, D. E., and J. Arulpragasam. 1994. Adjustment without structural change: The case of Malawi. In *Adjusting to policy failure in African economies,* ed. D. E. Sahn. Ithaca, N.Y.: Cornell University Press.

Sahn, D. E., and A. Sarris. 1992. *The political economy of economic decline and reform in Africa: The role of the state, markets, and civil institutions.* Working Paper No. 25. Washington, D.C.: Cornell Food and Nutrition Policy Program.

Sahn, D. E., P. A. Dorosh, and S. D. Younger. 1997. *Structural adjustment reconsidered: Economic policy and poverty in Africa.* Cambridge, U.K.: Cambridge University Press.

Sakala, E. 1990. Fertilizer use in Zimbabwe: Supply, demand, policy, and related problems. In *Fertilizer policy in tropical Africa. Workshop proceedings, Lomé, Togo, April 1988,* ed. T. Tshibaka and C. Baanante. Muscle Shoals, Ala.: International Fertilizer Development Center and International Food Policy Research Institute.

Sanders, J. H., B. I. Shapiro, and S. Ramaswamy. 1996. *The economics of agricultural technology in semiarid sub-Saharan Africa.* Johns Hopkins Studies in Development. Baltimore, Md.: Johns Hopkins University Press.

Santorum, A., and A. Tibaijuka. 1992. Trading responses to food market liberalization in Tanzania. *Food Policy* 17: 431–442.

Sarris, A. H. 1994. *Agricultural taxation under structural adjustment.* Economic and Social Development Paper No. 128. Rome: Food and Agriculture Organization of the United Nations.

Schiff, M., and C. E. Montenegro. 1997. Aggregate agricultural supply response in developing countries: A survey of selected issues. *Economic Development and Cultural Change* 45: 393–410.

Schiff, M., and A. Valdes. 1995. The plundering of agriculture in developing countries. *Finance and Development* 32: 44–47.

Seppälä, P. 1997. *Food marketing reconsidered: An assessment of the liberalization of food marketing in Sub-Saharan Africa.* Research for Action No. 34. Helsinki, Finland: United Nations University, World Institute for Development Economics Research (UNU/WIDER).

———. 1998. *Liberalized and neglected? Food marketing policies in eastern Africa.* World Development Studies No. 12. Helsinki, Finland: United Nations University, World Institute for Development Economics Research (UNU/WIDER).

Sexton, R., C. Kling, and H. Carman. 1991. Market integration, efficiency of arbitrage, and imperfect competition: Methodology and application to U.S. celery. *American Journal of Agricultural Economics* 73(3): 568–580.

Shaffer, J. D., M. R. Weber, H. Riley, and J. M. Staatz. 1985. *Designing marketing systems to promote development in third world countries. Proceedings of an International Workshop on Agricultural Markets in the Semi Arid Tropics held at the ICRISAT Center, Pantacheru, India, 1983.* Pantacheru, India: International Research Institute for the Semi Arid Tropics.

Shapouri, S., and S. Rosen. 1999. *Food security assessment: Why countries are at risk.* Agricultural Services Bulletin No. 754. Washington, D.C.: Economic Research Service, United States Department of Agriculture.

Shepherd, A., and R. Coster. 1987. Fertilizer marketing costs and margins in developing countries. Food and Agriculture Organization of the United Nations and Fertilizer Industry Advisory Council, Rome. Memo.

Shepherd, A. W., and S. Farolfi. 1999. *Export crop liberalization in Africa: A review.* FAO Agricultural Services Bulletin 135. Rome: Food and Agriculture Organization of the United Nations.

Shepherd, A., and G. Onumah. 1997. *Liberalized agricultural markets in Ghana. The role of government in adjusting economies.* Birmingham, U.K.: University of Birmingham Press.

Shively, G. E. 1996. Food price variability and economic reform: An ARCH approach for Ghana. *American Journal of Agricultural Economics* 78: 126–136.

Sijm, J. 1997. *Food security and policy interventions in Sub-Saharan Africa: Lessons from the past two decades.* Amsterdam: Thesis Publishers.

Simler, K. R. 1994. Household expenditure behavior and farm-nonfarm linkages in rural Malawi. In *Malawi agricultural sector memorandum: Strategy options in the 1990s.* Washington, D.C.: World Bank.

Smale, M., and P. Heisey. 1997. Maize technology and productivity in Malawi. In *Africa's emerging maize revolution,* ed. D. Byerlee and C. K. Eicher. Boulder, Colo.: Lynne Rienner.

Smith, J., G. Weber, M. V. Manyong, and M. A. B. Fakorede. 1997. Fostering sustainable increases in maize productivity in Nigeria. In *Africa's emerging maize revolution,* ed. D. Byerlee and C. K. Eicher. Boulder, Colo.: Lynne Rienner.

Soulé, B. G. 1999. *L'Impact des réformes de politiques agricoles sur les petits producteurs au Bénin. Rapport provisoire.* Cotonou, Benin: Laboratoire d'Analyse Régionale et d'Expertise Sociale.

Spencer, D. S. C., and O. Badiane. 1995. Agriculture and economic recovery in African countries. In *Agricultural competitiveness: Market forces and policy choice,* ed. G. H. Peters and D. D. Hedley. Proceedings of the Twenty-Second International Conference of Agricultural Economists, Harare, Zimbabwe, August 22–29, 1994. Aldershot, U.K.: Dartmouth.

Spooner, N. J., and L. D. Smith. 1991. *Structural adjustment policy sequencing in subSaharan Africa.* Economic and Social Development Paper No. 104. Rome: Food and Agriculture Organization of the United Nations.

Staatz, J. M., J. Dioné, and N. N. Dembele. 1989. Cereals market liberalization in Mali. *World Development* 17: 703–718.

Stepanek, J., T. S. Jayne, and V. Kelly. 1999a. Fertilizer marketing costs and farm-level profitability: Policy implications from Ethiopia. Michigan State University, East Lansing, Mich. Unpublished paper.

Stepanek, J., V. Kelly, and J. Howard. 1999b. From a Sasakawa Global 2000 pilot program to sustained increases in agricultural productivity: The critical role of government policy in fostering the Ethiopian transition. Paper presented at the American Agricultural Economics Association Annual Meeting, August 8–11, Nashville, Tenn., U.S.A.

Stewart, F. 1994. Are short-term policies consistent with long-term development needs in Africa? In *From adjustment to development in Africa: Conflict, controversy, convergence and consensus?,* ed. G. A. Cornia and G. K. Helleiner. New York, N.Y.: St. Martin's Press.

Strasberg, P. J. 1999. *Effects of agricultural commercialization on food crop input use and productivity in Kenya.* MSU International Development Working Paper No. 71. East Lansing, Mich.: Michigan State University.

Suret-Canale, J. 1977. *Afrique noire.* Vol. 3, *De la colonisation aux indépendences, 1945-1960.* Paris: Editions Sociales.

Takavarasha, T. 1993. Trade, price and market reform in Zimbabwe: Current status, proposals and constraints. *Food Policy* 18: 286–293.

Thirtle, C., D. Hadley, and R. Townsend. 1995. Policy-induced innovation in sub-Saharan African agriculture. *Development Policy Review* 13: 323–348.

Thirtle, C., J. Atkins, P. Bottomley, N. Gonese, J. Govereh, and Y. Khatri. 1993. Agriculture productivity in Zimbabwe 1970–90. *Economic Journal* 103: 474–480.

Thompson, A. M. 1991. *Institutional changes in agricultural product and input markets and their impact on agricultural performance.* Economic and Social Development Paper No. 98. Rome: Food and Agriculture Organization of the United Nations.

Timmer, C. P. 1988. The agricultural transformation. In *Handbook of development economics,* Vol. I, ed. H. Chenery and T. N. Srinivasan. Amsterdam, the Netherlands: Elsevier Science Publishers.

Tower, E., and R. Christiansen. 1988. Effect of a fertilizer subsidy on income distribution and efficiency in Malawi. *Eastern Africa Economic Review* 4: 49–58.

Townsend, R. F. 1999. *Agricultural incentives in Sub-Saharan Africa: Policy challenges.* World Bank Technical Paper No. 444. Washington, D.C.: World Bank.

Turuka, F. M. 1995. *Price reforms and fertilizer use in smallholder agriculture in Tanzania.* Studien zur Landlichen Entwicklung 51. Munster-Hamber, Germany: Lit Verlag.

Tyler, P. S., and C. J. Bennett. 1993. *Grain market liberalization in southern Africa: Opportunities for support to the small-scale sector.* NRI Report R. Chatham, U.K.: Natural Resources Institute.

USAID (United States Agency for International Development). 1990. *The Malawi fertilizer subsidy reduction program: The impact of the African economic policy reform program.* CDIE Working Paper Report No. 143. Washington, D.C.

van der Laan, H. L. 1975. *The Lebanese traders in Sierra Leone.* The Hague: Mouton.

van der Laan, H. L., and W. T. M. Haaren. 1990. *African marketing boards under structural adjustment: The experience of Sub-Saharan Africa during the 1980s.* Working Paper No. 13/1990. Leiden, the Netherlands: African Studies Centre.

Varangis, P., and G. Schreiber. 2001. Market reforms: Lessons from country and commodity experiences. In *Commodity market reforms: Lessons of two decades* (pp. 5–34), ed. T. Akiyama et al. Washington, D.C.: World Bank.

Vaze, P., S. Kudhlande, J. Wright, and S. Gundry. 1996. A spatial analysis of household grain purchases in Zimbabwe's liberalized marketing system. *Outlook on Agriculture* 25: 37–42.

von Braun, J., and E. T. Kennedy. 1987. Cash crops versus subsistence crops: Income and nutritional effects in developing countries. In *Food policy: Integrating supply, distribution and consumption,* ed. J. P. Gittinger, J. Leslie, and C. Hoisington. Baltimore, Md.: Johns Hopkins University Press.

————. 1994. *Agricultural commercialization, economic development, and nutrition.* Baltimore, Md.: Johns Hopkins University Press.

von Oppen, M., B. K. Njehia, and A. Ijaimi. 1997. The impact of market access on agricultural productivity: Lessons from India, Kenya and the Sudan. *Journal of International Development* 9: 117–131.

Walker, S. T. 1994. *Crafting a market: A case study of USAID's fertilizer sub-sector reform program.* Workshop in Political Theory and Policy Analysis Working Paper No. 94-13. Bloomington, Ind.: Indiana University.

Weber, M. T., J. M. Staatz, J. S. Holtzman, E. W. Crawford, R. H. Bernstein. 1988. Informing food security decisions in Africa: Empirical analysis and policy dialogue. *American Journal of Agricultural Economics* 70: 1044–1052.

World Bank. 1981. *Accelerated development in sub-Saharan Africa: An agenda for action.* Washington, D.C.

————. 1992. *African development indicators.* Washington, D.C.

————. 1994. *Adjustment in Africa: Reforms, results, and the road ahead.* A World Bank Policy Research Report. Washington, D.C.

————. 1995. *Developing the regulatory environment for competitive agricultural markets.* World Bank Technical Paper No. 266. Washington, D.C.

————. 1996. *Uganda: The challenge of growth and poverty reduction. A World Bank country study.* Washington, D.C.

————. 1999. *World development indicators.* Washington, D.C.

————. 2000. *African development indicators.* Washington, D.C.

Yanggen, D., V. Kelly, T. Reardon, and A. Naseem. 1998. *Incentives for fertilizer use in Sub-Saharan Africa: A review of empirical evidence on fertilizer response and profitability.* MSU International Development Working Paper No. 70. East Lansing, Mich.: Michigan State University.

Young, C. 1986. Africa's colonial legacy. In *Strategies for African development,* ed. R. J. Berg and J. S. Whitaker. Berkeley, Calif.: University of California Press.

Zartman, I. W., and C. L. Delgado. 1984. Introduction: Stability, growth, and challenge. In *The political economy of Ivory Coast* (pp. 1–20), ed. I. W. Zartman and C. L. Delgado. New York: Praeger.

Zeller, M., A. Diagne, and C. Mataya. 1997. *Market access by smallholder farmers in Malawi: Implications for technology adoption, agricultural productivity, and crop income.* FCND Discussion Paper No. 35. Washington, D.C.: International Food Policy Research Institute.

Index

Page numbers for entries occurring in figures are followed by an *f;* those for entries occurring in notes, by an *n;* and those for entries occurring in tables, by a *t.*

191

About the Authors

Christopher Delgado is a senior research fellow at the International Food Policy Research Institute.

Eleni Gabre-Madhin is a research fellow at the International Food Policy Research Institute.

Michael Johnson is a fellow of the American Association for the Advancement of Science at the U.S. Agency for International Development.

Mylène Kherallah is the regional economist for the Near East and North Africa at the International Fund for Agricultural Development.

Nicholas Minot is a research fellow at the International Food Policy Research Institute.